An Introduction to Poetic Forms

An Introduction to Poetic Forms offers specimen discussions of poems through the lens of form. While each of its chapters does provide a standard definition of the form in question in its opening paragraphs, their main objective is to provide readings of specific examples to illustrate how individual poets have deviated from or subverted those expectations usually associated with the form under discussion. While providing the most vital information on the most widely taught forms of poetry, then, this collection will very quickly demonstrate that counting syllables and naming rhyme schemes is not the be-all and end-all of poetic form. Instead, each chapter will contain cross-references to other literary forms and periods as well as make clear the importance of the respective form to the culture at large: be it the democratising communicative power of the ballad or the objectifying male gaze of the blazon and resistance to same in the contreblazon – the efficacy of form is explored in the fullness of its cultural dimensions.

In using standard definitions only as a starting point and instead focusing on lively debates around the cultural impact of poetic form, the textbook helps students and instructors to see poetic forms not as a static and lifeless affair but as living, breathing testament to the ongoing evolution of cultural debates. In the final analysis, the book is interested in showing the complexities and contradictions inherent in the very nature of literary form itself: how each concrete example deviates from the standard template while at the same time employing it as a foil to generate meaning.

Patrick Gill is a Senior Lecturer in English Literature and Culture at Johannes Gutenberg University Mainz, Germany, where he also received his PhD. The co-editor of *Constructing Coherence in the British Short Story Cycle* (2018) and *Translating Renaissance Experience* (2021), his ongoing interest is in the efficacy of literary form.

An Introduction to Poetic Forms

Edited by Patrick Gill

NEW YORK AND LONDON

Cover image: Getty

First published 2023
by Routledge
605 Third Avenue, New York, NY 10158

and by Routledge
4 Park Square, Milton Park, Abingdon, Oxon, OX14 4RN

Routledge is an imprint of the Taylor & Francis Group, an informa business

© 2023 selection and editorial matter, Patrick Gill; individual
chapters, the contributors

The right of Patrick Gill to be identified as the author of
the editorial material, and of the authors for their individual
chapters, has been asserted in accordance with sections 77 and 78
of the Copyright, Designs and Patents Act 1988.

All rights reserved. No part of this book may be reprinted
or reproduced or utilised in any form or by any electronic,
mechanical, or other means, now known or hereafter invented,
including photocopying and recording, or in any information
storage or retrieval system, without permission in writing from
the publishers.

Lines from Stephen James Smith's "My Ireland", as published
in *Fear Not* (Arlen House 2018), are reproduced by kind
permission. Lines from Elaine Feeney's "Rise", as published in
her eponymous collection (Salmon Poetry 2017), are reproduced
by kind permission.

Trademark notice: Product or corporate names may be trademarks
or registered trademarks, and are used only for identification and
explanation without intent to infringe.

ISBN: 978-1-032-15404-6 (hbk)
ISBN: 978-1-032-15401-5 (pbk)
ISBN: 978-1-003-24400-4 (ebk)

DOI: 10.4324/9781003244004

Typeset in Bembo
by codeMantra

Contents

List of Figures	viii
Notes on Contributors	ix

1 Introduction: Repetition and Variation
PATRICK GILL

1

SECTION 1
Elements of Form

7

2 Rhyme
STEFAN BLOHM AND CHRISTINE A. KNOOP

9

3 Metre
JESPER KRUSE

23

4 Toeing and Breaking the Line: On Enjambment and Caesura
HEATHER H. YEUNG

38

5 Persona: Its Meaning and Significance
JAMES DOWTHWAITE

51

6 Poetry in Performance
JESSICA BUNDSCHUH

61

SECTION 2
Poetic Forms

73

7 The Ballad
CATHERINE CHARLWOOD

75

vi *Contents*

8 Blank Verse   85
CALISTA McRAE

9 The Blazon   94
JORDAN KISTLER

10 Concrete Poetry   103
TYMON ADAMCZEWSKI

11 The Dramatic Monologue   114
GABRIELLA HARTVIG

12 Ekphrastic Poetry   123
ANJA MÜLLER-WOOD

13 The Elegy   132
PATRICK GILL

14 The Epic   142
RACHAEL SUMNER

15 Free Verse   150
ANDREW ROWCROFT

16 The Heroic Couplet   158
ALEX STREIM

17 The Long Poem   166
PATRICK GILL AND MIGUEL JUAN GRONOW SMITH

18 Mock-Heroic Poetry   175
PURIFICACIÓN RIBES TRAVER

19 The Ode   184
FLORIAN KLAEGER

20 The Prospect Poem   194
ROSLYN IRVING

21 The Sestina   203
MATTHEW KILBANE

Contents vii

22 The Sonnet 213
PATRICK GILL

23 The Villanelle 223
PATRICK GILL

Index 233

Figures

10.1 "Bebe Coca Cola" (1957) D. Pignatari, file
authored by Vinicius Nacif, licensed under the CC
4.0 International, available at https://commons.
wikimedia.org/wiki/File:Bebococapoema.gif   107
10.2 A wall poem in Leiden, the Netherlands, in Japanese,
by Seiichi Niikuni. Photograph by David Eppstein,
licensed under CC 3.0, available at https://commons.
wikimedia.org/wiki/File:NiikuniSeiichiShuKawaLeide
nWallPoem.jpg   109
10.3 Sculptures/objects in the sculpture park *Little Sparta* by
Ian Hamilton Finlay in Scotland/UK. Photograph by
yellow book ltd, licensed under the CC 2.0 Generic,
available at https://commons.wikimedia.org/wiki/
File:Little_Sparta_-_The_present_order_is_the_
disorder_of_the_future_(St_Just).jpg   111

Contributors

Tymon Adamczewski is Assistant Professor in the Department of Anglophone Literatures of Kazimierz Wielki University, Bydgoszcz, Poland, where he teaches literary and cultural studies. His academic interests include critical discourses of contemporary humanities, music, and ecocriticism. He has edited *All Along Bob Dylan: America and the World* (2020) and is the author of *Following the Textual Revolution: The Standardization of Radical Critical Theories of the 1960s* (2016).

Stefan Blohm studied General Linguistics and British Studies and holds a PhD in General Linguistics from Johannes Gutenberg University, Mainz (Germany). His empirical research into poetry and rhyme was funded by the Max Planck Society, the German Academic Exchange Service, and the Radboud Excellence Initiative. He currently works at the Centre for Language Studies at Radboud University.

Jessica Bundschuh is a Lecturer in English Literature & Cultures at the University of Stuttgart. She has a PhD in English Literature and Creative Writing from the University of Houston and an MFA in Creative Writing from the University of Maryland. Her current research project is the Irish prose poem.

Catherine Charlwood (BA, MPhil, Cambridge; PhD, Warwick) wrote her thesis on memory in the poetry of Thomas Hardy and Robert Frost. She has published several articles on poetry (and occasionally prose), spoken at the Hay Festival, and is a Fulbright scholar. Catherine now works in dementia research.

James Dowthwaite teaches English literature at the University of Jena. He is currently working on a project on the relationship between nineteenth-century aestheticism and the concept of fate. His first book, *Ezra Pound and Twentieth-Century Theories of Language: Faith with the Word*, came out with Routledge in 2019.

Patrick Gill is a Senior Lecturer in English Literature and Culture at Johannes Gutenberg University Mainz, where he also received his PhD. The co-editor of *Constructing Coherence in the British Short Story Cycle* x *Contributors*

(2018) and *Translating Renaissance Experience* (2021), his ongoing interest is in the efficacy of literary form.

Miguel Juan Gronow Smith is Professor of English at the University of Seville, Spain. He is the author of *Cultura Postmoderna y Poesía Amorosa* (1998) and *The Poetry of Douglas Dunn: Introductory Remarks* (1997), as well as essays on twentieth-century and contemporary poetry, and other genres in their modernist and postmodern contexts.

Gabriella Hartvig teaches at the University of Pécs. She is the author of two books and her papers have appeared in journals including *The Shandean*, *The AnaChronist*, and *Translation and Literature.* She has contributed chapters on the reception of Sterne, Ossian, and Swift to the series "The Reception of British and Irish Authors in Europe".

Roslyn Irving is pursuing a PhD with the University of Liverpool and Xi'an Jiaotong-Liverpool University. Her thesis uses archival texts to explore how Ann Radcliffe's *The Romance of the Forest* (1791) resonates with eighteenth-century politics and current affairs.

Matthew Kilbane is an Assistant Professor of English at the University of Notre Dame, where he works across the fields of poetry and poetics, media history, and the digital humanities.

Jordan Kistler is a lecturer at the University of Strathclyde. She specialises in Victorian poetry and the exchanges between Victorian literature and scientific discourses.

Florian Klaeger is Professor of English at the University of Bayreuth, Germany. His publications include *Forgone Nations* (2006, on Elizabethan representations of history), and *Reading into the Stars* (2018, on cosmology in the contemporary novel), as well as various articles, book chapters, and edited/co-edited volumes on literary form.

Christine A. Knoop studied German, French, and Theatre Studies in Munich and Paris. After obtaining her PhD in Comparative Literature from UCL, she turned empirical, studying emotional responses to literature at FU Berlin. Drawn to (while often sceptical of) a new formalism, she now researches effects of literary style as a researcher at the Max Planck Institute for Empirical Aesthetics.

Jesper Kruse is Associate Professor of English at the Technical University of Denmark. His research interests include poetic metre in a diachronic perspective, global accents of English, sociolinguistics, spelling systems, and typography.

Calista McRae is an assistant professor at the New Jersey Institute of Technology in Newark, NJ. She is the author of *Lyric as Comedy: The Poetics of Abjection in Postwar America* (2020) and co-editor of *The Selected Letters of John Berryman* (2020).

Anja Müller-Wood is Professor of English Literature and Culture at Johannes Gutenberg University Mainz (Germany). She has published extensively on early modern and twentieth-century British literature and culture and edited and co-edited several essay collections and journal issues, most recently "When Dialogue Fails" for the journal *Language and Dialogue* (2022).

Purificación Ribes Traver is Full Professor of English at the University of Valencia, Spain. She has been head of several research projects on the edition, translation, and European reception of Early Modern English literary texts, and has published extensively on Shakespeare, Ben Jonson, John Donne, W. Wycherley, and Richard B. Sheridan.

Andrew Rowcroft has interests in contemporary literature, criticism, and theory, with additional interests in the philosophy of literature and art, literary theory and literary criticism, and the political economy of culture. He has published essays on British and American authors. His books include *Karl Marx* (2021) and *Criticism, Crisis, and the Contemporary Novel*, which is forthcoming with Reaktion.

Alex Streim is a PhD candidate in English at Johns Hopkins University. His dissertation, "The Pedagogic Muse: Teaching and Learning in American Poetry", discusses the relationship between twentieth-century poetry and progressive education.

Rachael Sumner (BA, Essex; MA, York) worked in higher education in Poland and completed her PhD at the University of Opole. She now lectures in the Department of English and Linguistics at Johannes Gutenberg University in Mainz, Germany. Her current research interests include postcolonial literature and theory, and contemporary literary approaches to myth.

Heather H. Yeung 楊希蒂 teaches poetry and poetics at the University of Dundee. An archive of her artists books and poetic works is held in the Scottish Poetry Library. Her academic publications include *Spatial Engagement with Poetry* (2015) and *On Literary Plasticity* (2020).

1 Introduction

Repetition and Variation

Patrick Gill

If you take a look at your everyday environment – your bathroom fittings, the train you take on your way to college, your lecture hall – everything you see is the product of a mixture of repetition and variation. These are the building blocks of human invention. In the case of the physical features we surround ourselves with, repetition and variation have helped to improve them. The bridge you walk across will seem unremarkable to you, but if you think about it, its design copies previous bridges dating back to Roman times and beyond, but has been varied slightly to avoid flaws and structural weaknesses. An ambulance you see in the street today would be recognisable as an ambulance to a time traveller from 1930, but its engine and medical equipment will have been significantly upgraded since then. The bread you eat for breakfast will be based on decades, centuries, or even millennia, of repetition and variation: of combining the available ingredients but varying their proportions in order to produce a better result. Every single thing that humanity has invented behaves in exactly this way. It doesn't matter what example you pick. Mobile phones, vacuum cleaners, microwave ovens, toothpaste, satellites: all of these practical inventions whose impact on your life is tangible follow the basic path of repetition and variation. And they follow it in pursuit of perfection: every change is designed to make them demonstrably better.

When it comes to cultural artefacts, i.e. statues, sitcoms, plays, songs, hairstyles, poems, and comic books, we can also see the twin factors of repetition and variation at work. After all, no play or sitcom or comic book is ever completely original. They all take aspects of earlier examples and either copy or change them. Repetition and variation. But when we compare them to our physical environment, to the appliances, building materials, and transport systems that surround us, one major difference is that while the latter have all used repetition and variation as stepping stones to bring about a measurable improvement, the former cannot really be said to have benefitted in their development in the same way. After all, how could we even begin to argue that a more recent opera is by definition better than a more traditional work? Is that really a meaningful comparison to make? But if repetition and variation in cultural artefacts do not work in aid of constant improvement, then what is their function?

DOI: 10.4324/9781003244004-1

In fact, in art, a realm of the imagination, repetition and variation are even more important than in the physical domain because they are not aids to something else – they *are* the purpose in and of themselves.

As human beings evolved to shape their environment, to erect dwellings, plant crops, and domesticate animals, they also became aware of their temporal and geographical limitations: they discovered the fact of their mortality, and they found out that the world was quite a big place, especially when contrasted with their limited ability to travel. It is almost too obvious to spell out, but try to remember the COVID-19 lockdowns. Now try to imagine living through those with no means of telecommunication and a significantly shorter lifespan. You would be stuck in one place, knowing that your life was dripping away while you had no chance to communicate with anyone beyond your immediate family. Culture has the power to change that equation. By participating in culture, by coming up with stories and paintings and poems, people create things just as they create bridges and ambulances, but what they create in culture exists in the collective imagination rather than in their physical environment. To survive in this shared imaginary, this common consciousness, our forms of expression have to be based on two central building blocks, viz. the familiar and the new: repetition and variation.

We can consider the significance of repetition and variation on different levels. In terms of basic communication, it marks you out as a competent human being if you respond to your neighbour's remark "Lovely weather we're having!" neither by repeating the exact same thing nor by changing the subject and talking about something else entirely, but by confirming what has been said and adding a little note of your own: "Yes, so lovely, but I hear it's going to rain on Tuesday". So even in everyday conversation that basic recipe is present, but it does of course become somewhat more complex when considered as a way of communicating across multiple generations rather than with your next-door neighbour. In psychological terms, Harold Bloom's *The Anxiety of Influence* (1973) argues that as a reader first and a writer later, every poet always wants to imitate the poets they grew up reading – and at the same time wants to be different from them and feels a need to rebel against them. His book outlines six forms of "revisionary" recipes (14), six different ways for a poet to rebel against and free themselves from their precursors. That revisionism, too, is always based on a pattern of repetition and variation. The most thorough discussion of repetition and variation as the fundamental building blocks of human culture is to be found in Jan Assmann's *Cultural Memory and Early Civilization* (2011) though. Assmann points out that oral cultures have tended to champion repetition: if you retell a story over multiple generations relying on memory alone, your primary aim is not to introduce new ideas and make changes to the story – your primary ambition is to relay the story *as it was handed down to you*. The introduction of writing frees the teller of tales from these strictures but at the same time presents an existential threat to cultural memory, the sense of continuity within human culture: if what we write down can have its own existence without copying anything that has gone before it, everyone can now go off and write down their own ideas in isolation from one another, thus defeating culture's entire purpose of establishing connections between people across time and space. This "break inherent in writing" is "cancel[led] out" by a "framework of references" (Assmann 85), meaning that these quasi-autonomous texts that can now be produced in isolation from one another are still framed in a common cultural space to ensure that they communicate with one another, to ensure that they continue to have meaning. The twin elements of constraint and freedom are still present: repetition and variation.

Since this is a book on poetic forms, these considerations of admittedly fundamental aspects of culture may seem fairly irrelevant to its immediate purpose. After all, no knowledge of oral cultures is required to count the lines of a villanelle, no *Anxiety of Influence* needed to scan a sonnet. But if culture's foundational impulse is the continued communication of ideas and imagined concepts across space and time, we can see why poetic form would take up a particularly privileged position in the study of poetry: it's because, as Caroline Levine says, "forms travel" (5). They represent a matrix against which we can read a poem from a given period and written in a given form, thus adding an entire dimension of meaning to our experience of the poem. Let's imagine an example in which you proceed thematically and decide to write a comparison between two poems featuring dogs. The one is a twentieth-century limerick, the other a passage taken from an Anglo-Saxon poem about a warrior (and his dog). These two portions of words and phrases that happen to be concerned with the topic of dogs share no other points of reference. The one is a humorous ditty, the other a piece of heroic poetry. We have to ask ourselves what role dogs played in the two cultures separated by 1,200 years but are not really given enough contextual information in the texts themselves. Our comparison is meaningless because the main conclusion we will come to will be the less than astonishing insight that there are many differences in the ways these two different writers from different ages treat the subject of dogs. Let's take another example, not imagined but contained within this book: a sixteenth-century poem about a courtier's hopeless love for a lady promised to another, and a twentieth-century poem about a series of lynchings and other hate crimes committed in the southern United States. On the face of it, you would think that these poems had nothing in common, could not possibly engage in a conversation with one another. Turn to the chapter on the sonnet and you will see that, in fact, these poems are having a very fruitful conversation across time and space based on the fact that they are both fourteen-line poems with an interest in their speaker's dilemmas and the question of their agency.

4   *Patrick Gill*

That is the efficacy of form: that it can provide the "framework of references" necessary to put works by different writers, works from different periods, works on different topics, into fruitful dialogue with one another, thus activating an additional level of meaning. Since, within that framework, we still proceed based on the core principles of repetition and variation, the story of many poetic forms is one of gradual separation: relying on inherited structures less and less, and writing *against* the tradition they originate from more and more. You will be able to trace this development in the chapters on the sonnet, the blazon, the elegy, the ode, the heroic couplet, and others besides: that a form ends up being employed to express a counterpoint or a rebuke to its own tradition. That I can read (or write) an elegy that says that there is no consolation for the loss of a loved one; or a poem in heroic couplets that argues that the order this form represents is a sham; or a blazon criticising the objectification of women implicit in the form, means that rather than a set of calcified rules to be heeded by writers past and present, form is a going concern, a live tool employed by writers to reflect their current concerns in response to a tradition they both acknowledge and repudiate. Form, then, is an integral part of poetry, as it is of any genre of art or literature: it simultaneously provides a recipe to follow *and* a tradition against which to rebel. Paradoxically, form gives writers the freedom to express themselves more fully as every sonnet, elegy, or ode written in the present day carries with it the weight and meaning of a centuries-old tradition. By referring back to said traditions, even the shortest of poems can bring multiple expectations, associations, and allusions to bear on the topic of their choice. Poetry is not alone in activating this fount of potential meaning. As we have seen, the same basic ideas hold true for any form, from painting to film-making, from music to sculpture. But perhaps form is particularly relevant to poetry as it is particularly noticeable in such an established genre that frequently relies on brevity.

Introductions to genres such as this also constitute cultural artefacts. They constitute a secondary culture, a commentary on primary works. As such, they are subject to the same rules of repetition and variation. That means that the chapters in this book – while regulated to some extent – will also reflect individual takes on a given topic: the ideas represented here are not wholly new, nor are they an exact copy of what other introductions have done before. Contributors to this volume were invited to select their specimen poems and to make their own arguments with regard to the respective form in which these poems are written. The poems they chose are a mixture of classics and more recent works, depending on the respective argumentative direction of each chapter. That argument may not always constitute the one and only way of approaching the form in question. So while we tend to provide standard definitions at the beginning of our chapters, the direction taken in the further course of each chapter is first and foremost *arguable*, meaning that it will be possible to find poems contradicting the points made. That is because rather than taking an encyclopaedic approach encompassing every twist and turn in the history of their respective form, our contributors are interested in abstracting general insights into how a form shapes the topics that are treated in it. Should you be able to identify a poem that goes against what is claimed in a chapter, that does not invalidate that chapter – it simply extends an invitation to you to read the poem in the light of the chapter's claims and construct your own argument in response to them. Rather than pretending that our chapters contain all the knowledge about a given form and thus constitute the end of a conversation, they are designed as conversation starters providing you with examples of how form, meaning, and cultural developments interact in poetry.

This book is divided into two main sections, "Elements of Form" and "Poetic Forms". The first of these consists of five chapters on various ideas that should inform any reading of poetry. These chapters – slightly longer than the ones in the second section – are equally applicable to virtually any form. They tend to make authoritative points on certain phenomena as well as introducing important terminology. As such, they are subdivided into numbered sections with their own headers, and important terms are given in bold type. The second section alphabetically lists the most important forms of poetry in the English language. No distinction is made between prescriptive forms (i.e. poetic forms that can be identified by counting, like "alternating iambic tetrameters and trimeters" in the case of the ballad) and non-prescriptive forms (i.e. forms that are not governed by external rules but rather by an internal argumentative structure, as in the ode or elegy, for instance, where it is the sequence of ideas that determines a poem's relation to its respective form). The reason no such distinction is made is that this book makes the argument that both types of form are equally important, equally capable of generating meaning. Chapters in the "Poetic Forms" section usually begin with a standard definition of a form before complicating the story and illustrating how shifts in culture or individual artists have changed the form under discussion

To help you develop your own thinking on poetic forms, this book features multiple systems of reference. First of all, chapters within the "Poetic Forms" section feature cross-references (⬀) to refer you to other chapters in the same section whenever a chapter on one form refers to another form. Secondly, each of the chapters in the "Poetic Forms" section features a "Now Read On…" box making suggestions for further reading within the book itself or referring to additional resources outside of it. Thirdly, each chapter features its own list of references, pointing readers in the direction of the most important sources. And, finally, the book's extensive index lists the poets, poems, periods, and technical terms mentioned in the book for easy reference.

6 *Patrick Gill*

References

Assmann, Jan. *Cultural Memory and Early Civilization: Writing, Remembrance, and Political Imagination*. Cambridge UP, 2011.
Bloom, Harold. *The Anxiety of Influence: A Theory of Poetry*. Oxford UP, 1973.
Levine, Caroline. *Forms: Whole, Rhythm, Hierarchy, Network*. Princeton UP, 2015.

Section 1

Elements of Form

2 Rhyme

Stefan Blohm and Christine A. Knoop

1 Introduction

This chapter deals with rhyme as an element of poetic form. It is intended as a general background for the following chapters of this volume, but it provides neither a sketch of the history of rhyme nor a typology of rhyme types or a systematic list of rhyme terms. It contains just as much poetry as Charles Darwin could endure to read: not a single line (Darwin 113). Instead, it aims to shed light on the role that rhyme plays when we read (or hear) a poem. The view of poetry and rhyme that we present necessarily emphasises the temporal dimension of the act of reading and the dynamic and incremental nature of text comprehension. In a sense, it is a view of poetry as a machine, say, a music box that will play a little tune if you open its lid – or better yet: a view of poetry as the cylinder that plays a tune on the music box that is your mind.

Since this is an introductory book, we aim to keep the number of bibliographical references at a minimum. This means that we strive to provide references to starting points for further reading but will sometimes summarise information without reference to the underlying sources, often from literature on the psychology of language and discourse comprehension. We will begin by re-interpreting a standard definition of rhyme in cognitive terms, before we turn to how readers comprehend texts in general and poetry in particular. We will then discuss four commonly assumed functions of rhyme: the euphonic, the mnemonic, the structural and the semantic function. The chapter concludes with guidelines of applying the presented view of rhyme to your own readings and analyses of poetry.

2 What Is Rhyme?

The *Oxford Dictionary of Literary Terms* (ODLT) defines 'rhyme' as "the identity of sound between syllables or paired groups of syllables, usually at the ends of verse lines … . Normally the last stressed vowel in the line and all sounds following it make up the rhyming element" (Baldick).

Note first that rhyme is defined in terms of syllables and not words (as in the definition of 'rhyme' in the *OED*). Although it is quite common to

DOI: 10.4324/9781003244004-3

view rhyme as sound identity between words, there are some properties of rhyming that favour a characterisation in terms of syllables, and phenomena which demonstrate that rhyme is, in principle, independent of the word. However, we will explain below in what sense rhyme can indeed be characterised as a relation between words.

Syllables are speech units that consist of individual speech sounds (i.e., consonants and vowels) and that form basic formal building blocks of words. Syllables have an internal structure: vowels (V) typically form the core of a syllable (technically: the nucleus) which may be preceded and/or followed by a limited number of consonants (C). For instance, the English word *sprints* consists of a single syllable that has the structure CCCVCCC; it is transcribed as /sprɪnts/ in the international phonetic alphabet (IPA) which, contrary to the writing system of English, faithfully represents the sequence of individual speech sounds. The initial consonants of a syllable form its so-called 'onset' (/spr/ in *sprints*) while the vowel nucleus and the following consonants form its 'rhyme' (/ɪnts/ in *sprints*). Thus, "identity of sounds between syllables" means that syllables share the same speech sounds in corresponding positions: while 'alliteration' typically refers to the identity of sounds in syllable onsets, rhyming syllables are identical from the vowel onwards (e.g., *sprints − hints*).

Rhyming creates "paired groups of syllables" if the identity of sound holds between syllable sequences rather than individual syllables, for instance, if rhyming words are longer (e.g., *sprinting − hinting*) or if rhymes span more than one word as in so-called 'mosaic rhyme' (e.g., *famous − shame us*). As the examples illustrate, "the rhyming element" in such cases typically comprises the "stressed vowel … and all sounds following it". In this sense, rhyme is sensitive to and dependent on speech rhythm, i.e., on the relative prominence of syllables.

It is important to understand that speech sounds, syllables and words are not merely abstract theoretical units used to describe the structure of language. They are representational units in our minds that are physically encoded in neural populations of our brains: **mental representations** on which **mental operations** can be performed during cognitive tasks like reading. Part of what it means to 'know a language' is having acquired an inventory of words of that language. This inventory of words in our minds is called the **mental lexicon**. We can think of the mental lexicon as a network of words: each word connects a concept (i.e., its meaning) to a certain form (i.e., a sequence of sounds or letters), and words are connected to each other if they share conceptual aspects (e.g., *apple − pear, over − above*) or formal constituents (e.g., *crime − crisis, rhyme − chime*). Rhyming words in our mental lexicons are connected to each other via the speech sound sequences that they share. In this sense, rhyme is not only mere sound identity but a lexical relation between cohorts of words in our minds.

Words in the mental lexicon are in standby mode most of the time, and we need to select the words that are required for the mental operations

Rhyme 11

we perform. This works via **activation** of the appropriate mental representation. If we think of the mental lexicon as a library and of words as books, then activation is like taking a book from the shelf. All those books are there all the time – properly labelled (form) and thematically arranged (meaning) – but you only take one from the shelf when you actually need it. Books that are used frequently are stored in easily accessible areas of the library and can be retrieved fast, while rarely used books are stuffed away in the vault or in obscure special collections and take a little longer to retrieve.

Luckily, word recognition is a highly automated and very fast process that we experience as effortless most of the time. One of the reasons for this is that the activation of mental representation spreads automatically along the connections in the mental lexicon. The concept connected to a word in the mental lexicon is activated when an acoustic percept matches the associated sound sequence – and an appropriate word form usually comes to our mind when we think of a concept. When we read a word, the visual impression activates letter- and word-form representations which, in turn, activate mental representations of concepts (for comprehension processes) and sounds (for inner speech). Thus, every word that we read activates the representations of its constituent speech sounds which, in turn, briefly activate similar-sounding words as well. In this sense, each word that we hear or read makes an entire cohort of rhyme words accessible to the mental operations we perform, an effect called 'rhyme priming'. Some cognitive processes benefit from such pre-activation (facilitative priming) while others may be impaired by the sound similarity (inhibitory priming). For instance, it is cognitively *less* demanding to recognise an isolated word if it is preceded by a rhyming word (*toys – boys*) than if it is preceded by a non-rhyming word (*cars – boys*). But it is cognitively *more* demanding to integrate a word into an unfolding sentence if we encountered a rhyming word earlier in the sentence (*the girls hid the **toys** while the **boys** were at school*). Be careful, however, not to overestimate the role of rhyme priming, which certainly affects how we read rhymed verse but otherwise typically plays only a minor role in literary text comprehension. As far as we know it is a relatively short-lived effect which – due to the rapid decay of activation in the mental lexicon – is not detectable any more at distances of seven (or more) intervening words. Note that this limit has consequences for the role of rhyme priming in poetry comprehension: while the distance of pair rhymes *aabb* typically falls within the limit of automatic rhyme priming, cross rhymes *abab* frequently exceed it. Moreover, there are other, more potent kinds of priming. In particular, semantic priming, i.e., the (pre-)activation of words with overlapping conceptual representations, more effectively pre-activates cohorts of words in the mental lexicon than sound-based priming. Not least, the sound-based priming effect caused by overlapping word onsets (e.g., in alliteration) appears to be more effective than rhyme priming as well.

We have paid little attention to the observation expressed in the *ODLT* definition that rhyming syllables and syllable groups occur "usually at the ends of verse lines". We will return to this point later. For now, we merely note that, in verse, the position of rhymes is typically determined in terms of metre and its constituents (e.g., metrical feet) so that "rhyme, as a basic component of verse form, is a correspondence between rhythmic measures rather than syllables" (Leech 91). This is equally true for line-internal rhyme and line-final **end rhyme**, which has been the dominant form of rhyming in English verse and which makes entire lines of verse rhyme.

So far, we have sketched how words are represented in our minds and established that the sound identity of rhyming words implies a lexical relation between cohorts of words in our mental lexicon. We have introduced the concept of activation and the idea that activated word (form) representations in turn activate representations of similar-sounding words, which sometimes facilitates ongoing cognitive processes and sometimes interferes with them. Now let us look at what happens when we read an entire text rather than individual words.

3 Text Comprehension

The construction of coherent meaning is usually seen as the ultimate goal of comprehension. In the psychological study of language, the term 'comprehension' usually refers to the entire complex process of converting linguistic symbols into conceptual representations, which comprises non-interpretive, low-level subprocesses like word recognition as well. In this section, we will point out some fundamental properties of text reading and sketch the outcomes of the comprehension process. We base this account among others on Walter Kintsch's *Comprehension*, which is based on an influential theory and on decades of research and which, although no longer fully up to date, still provides an excellent introduction to the topic of text and discourse comprehension. Note though that this is an active field of research and that not all aspects of the view presented here are undisputed. Debates continue, for instance, about the nature and relation of the different levels of mental text representation or about how, when and why readers make inferences.

Let us begin with the uncontroversial observation that comprehension is **incremental**. When we understand a sentence, for instance, we do not wait until we reach its last word before we start making sense of it – instead, we interpret sentences and texts as we go along, i.e., word by word. In literary studies, this view and its implications have for instance been made explicit in Stanley Fish's earlier essays (see, e.g., Fish 27). Incrementality means that readers integrate one piece of information after another but it does not imply that they strictly follow the linear order of words. This becomes apparent in recordings of readers' eye movements during reading, which are closely tied to ongoing cognitive processes and

Rhyme 13

provide a window into text comprehension as it happens in the reader (see, e.g., Rayner, for a classic review). Readers' gaze patterns deviate from the linear order of the text whenever they skip individual words – which they do quite frequently, particularly if words are short, very frequent and/or highly predictable – or when readers jump back (and forth) in the text, for instance, when they have trouble understanding a word, sentence or section of the text. Recordings of readers' eye movements reveal that reading – although most readers typically experience it as a fluent process – is in fact characterised by the succession of so-called 'fixations' and 'saccades'. We gather information during fixations, when our gaze remains focused on a fixed position, say, a word, and our eyes remain relatively still. Saccades are quick eye movements to shift our gaze from one position to the next. We actually perceive very little during saccades although we are unaware of this during reading. In a sense, reading is like jumping although it usually feels like walking.

Text comprehension is **predictive**. In fact, one of the most important insights in the cognitive sciences in the past decades is the idea of **predictive coding**. Essentially, predictive coding means that our brains do not merely register the input from our sensors (eyes, ears, etc.) to passively construct a model of our environment. Instead, brains use (remote and immediate) prior experience to actively *predict* what will happen next and then check the actual sensory input against these predictions. The discrepancy between predicted and actually received sensory input is called 'prediction error'; it requires re-adjustments of our mental model of the environment. In this view, the brain constantly seeks to minimise prediction errors. Generally speaking, predictable information is easy to process while unpredictable information requires additional cognitive effort. With respect to reading, predictive coding means that we anticipate properties of upcoming words and then compare these predictions to the properties of the words we actually encounter. This is true for both form and content. For instance, when we read a sentence like "He likes to work out at …" we anticipate a plausible and grammatically suitable ending like "… the gym". Formally regulated poetry affords more accurate formal predictions than we usually encounter in other types of discourse.

Text comprehension is **genre-specific**, i.e., we read news reports differently than we would read a novel or a poem. This means that we adapt our reading behaviour and our interpretive operations during reading to the text type, and that we attend to and remember different aspects of a text. Readers read literary texts at reduced speed, pay increased attention to their exact wording and mentally represent and retain it more accurately. In the field of literary studies, the idea that literary texts are read differently than non-literary ones has, for instance, been held by Louise Rosenblatt. She distinguishes between an efferent reading stance, which is focused on taking away information and thus is more prominent in non-literary reading, and an aesthetic reading stance, which leads readers to focus on the reading experience itself and is the typical literary reading mode. Note that texts themselves are neither efferent nor aesthetic; instead, the reader's reason for choosing a text of a particular type determines the reading mode they assume (Rosenblatt).

Psychological theories of text comprehension typically assume that we construct at least three kinds or – since one provides the basis of the next – levels of mental text representations (e.g., McNamara and Magliano). Similar ideas of multi-layered text representations in the mind of the reader can also be found in literary theory of the first half of the twentieth century, most notably in Roman Ingarden's *The Literary Work of Art*. The linguistic **surface form** of the text comprises all formal representations, e.g., the sounds, the exact words or the syntactic structures. Our knowledge of the words and the grammar of a language allows us to convert surface forms into semantic representations of the content of the text (= the meaning). Concepts are the basic building blocks of meaning that can be combined into complex meanings. It is widely assumed that complex meanings are represented in the mind as **propositions**, which consist of (at least) a reference to an object, person, idea, etc., and a statement about this referent. This abstract semantic representation is distinct from the surface form expressing it: despite the difference in word order, phrases like *lame lyrics* and sentences like '*Poetry rules!*' have a similar underlying propositional structure *statement* (referent): *lame* (lyrics) and *rule* (poetry). Usually, the meaning of sentences is more complex than that, e.g., the claim that 'lame lyrics rule poetry' corresponds to the complex proposition *rule* (*lame* (lyrics), poetry). The 'meaning of a text' is a whole network of such propositions, which are related to each other by shared referents, e.g., different statements about the same person, and by logical relations like temporality (action A happened before action B) or causality (action A led to state B). In a sense, this is the home of the plot in narratives. Of course, we do not remember every single statement of a text – in fact we often cannot tell whether a statement actually occurred in a text or whether we simply inferred it (e.g., the statement 'the boys played football' typically leads us to assume that the statement 'the boys were outside' is true). When we read a text, we immediately combine and integrate the propositions expressed (and inferred) into representations of the gist of a text. Crucially, though, propositions may be seen as an intermediate step for constructing yet another type of mental text representation, the so-called **situation model**. In a sense this is where much of the magic happens, because this is our mental simulation of the actions and states of affairs referred to, the way we imagine a described event or person based on our world knowledge and our past experiences. Think of this as a scene in a play or a movie that you create yourself from your personal stock of memories, following the instructions of the text. We typically forget the surface forms of texts quite rapidly, once we have extracted the content conveyed. Think of any novel you have read: how many of its sentences do you recall exactly? However, it appears that the surface form of poetry is easier to remember than that of prose, and there have been proposals that readers/listeners recognise and represent the structural regularities of poetic form.

We have so far given an overview of the mental representation of rhyme and of the mental representations that we construct when we read a text. We have highlighted the dynamic nature of comprehension, the role of predictions during reading and the importance of readers' genre-appropriate mindset. Now let us look more specifically at what happens when we read a poem.

4 Poetry Comprehension

Daniel claimed in his *Defence of Ryme* that "all verse is but a frame of wordes confinde within certaine measure" and considered rhyme "an excellencie added to this worke of measure". Daniel's 'measure' refers to the idea that poetry (or more generally: verse) is formally divided into lines which traditionally conformed to metrical constraints on rhythmic patterns and length, e.g., iambic (rhythm) pentameter (length). The metrical line has consequences for how we read a poem, which sets it apart from other literary texts. Of course, we read a poem one word after another as well, but we also read line by line, i.e., lineation divides the text into additional, artificial units that emerge from formal patterns but also correspond to chunks of information.

The end of a verse line is typically associated with a caesura, i.e., a short pause. Both the line structure and the caesura are reinforced if line boundaries coincide with syntactic boundaries, e.g., the end of a sentence. If there is a caesura, the line-final word – not immediately superseded by incoming words – becomes more salient; moreover, the caesura allows for the automatic spreading of activation (associations) and for controlled cognitive processes (reflection).

In so-called regulated verse, the poet controls certain aspects of the verse line such as the number of syllables per line or the distribution of stressed syllables within the line. Such formal regularities of verse are based on equivalence, similarity and contrast. The basic contrast of accentual metre, for instance, is the difference between stressed and unstressed syllables. The pattern of (dis)similarities in end-rhyming is represented in rhyme scheme denotations, e.g., *aabb*, in which identical letters denote identity/similarity and different letters signify contrast/dissimilarity. Crucially, readers develop formal expectations if patterns repeat across lines or stanzas.

The incremental nature and temporal dimension of comprehension give rise to a fundamental distinction in rhyming that is frequently overlooked in theoretical and descriptive work. While it may seem quite trivial that, when we read or hear a poem, one rhyme word necessarily precedes the other, this temporal succession has in fact far-reaching consequences for how we cognitively process rhymes in poetry. There exists a directional asymmetry in rhyming in the sense that the initial rhyme word affects how the second one and following ones are cognitively processed when they are first encountered (*boys* > *toys*), but not vice versa. Hence, we will refer to the initial rhyme word as **pre-rhyme** (*boys* > *toys*) whereas the second and following ones are the actual **rhymes** (*boys* > *toys*). Consider the simple case of a rhyming couplet *aa*. In the temporal flow of the reading experience, the pre-rhyme activates a cohort of rhyming words, one of which will be encountered as rhyme in the second line.

Rhyme in verbal art and song can be of two basic types: **systematic rhyme** occurs consistently in fixed positions of the (metrical) line and thus identical sound sequences recur periodically. This is the most common type of rhyme in English poetry; empirical investigations of rhyme have almost exclusively focused on this kind. By contrast, **sporadic rhyme** occurs occasionally and in varying text positions. Internal rhyme is typically of this kind, even if it occurs in poems with systematic metre and rhyme. The crucial difference lies in the predictability of systematic rhyme, which contrasts with the surprisal induced by sporadic rhyme. Moreover, sporadic rhyme frequently occurs at short distances whereas systematic rhyme may link words that are several lines apart. But in both types the presence of the pre-rhyme highlights the following rhyme word(s). Although we are unaware of a pertinent empirical study, we would expect that sporadic rhyme has detrimental effects on reading fluency, similar to the effect of rhyme in regular sentences. Systematic rhyme, by contrast, is predictable and facilitates processing because the semantic and grammatical constraints of an unfolding sentence combine with the sound constraint of rhyme so that – at the expected end rhyme position – only a small set of possible/plausible continuations remains (Rubin and Wallace); the predictability of the rhyme is further increased if the rhyme word receives activation from the concepts addressed by the words preceding it.

Empirical studies of poetry reading (e.g., Menninghaus and Wallot) have revealed that systematic rhyme reduces the cognitive effort of reading line-final words; unpredictable pre-rhymes are cognitively more demanding than the actual rhymes. However, it appears that in longer poems readers take more time to dwell on the rhyme words that close stanzas or the entire poem.

5 The Functions of Rhyme

5.1 Introduction

Rhyme is a formal element that restricts the poet's options to combine words into sentences – it is a self-imposed constraint on creative freedom and compositional liberty. Why then is rhyme such a widespread and persistent feature of poetic form, shared by myriad epochs and lyrical styles, and by poetic traditions from vastly different linguistic backgrounds? It stands to reason that an element like this must serve certain *functions* that would explain its success and justify the limitations and constraints it imposes. In literary studies, the term 'function' is used in a variety of ways, often without clear definitions (see, e.g., Gymnich and Nünning, 3–27, for a review). Here, we use the term to designate the effects of rhyme on the process and outcome of verse comprehension. We focus on rhyme's assumed euphonic, structural, semantic and mnemonic functions and seek to ground them in the act of reading. Daniel claimed in his *Defence of Ryme* that rhyme gives "to the eare an echo of a delightfull report" (euphonic), that it is "likewise number and harmonie of words" (structural/euphonic) and that it gives "to the Memorie a deeper impression of what is deliuered therein" (mnemonic). Rhyme's semantic function is highlighted in Wimsatt's classic essay "One Relation of Rhyme to Reason: Alexander Pope".

5.2 Euphonic Function

The sound identity of rhyme decisively contributes to the sound *gestalt* of a poem. In the temporal flow of the reading experience, the metrical line provides a recurring pattern of speech rhythm, but lines also instantiate a particular speech melody. The recurring vowels of pre-rhyme and rhymes have similar fundamental frequencies and thus constitute – in analogy to musical melodies – a kind of return to the tonic; when people perform rhymed poetry they also tend to highlight the rhyming words to enhance the effect. Moreover, the periodic recurrence of rhyme highlights the rhythmic pattern of a poem. In this sense, rhyme increases the musical qualities of verse. The euphonic function is certainly more dominant in oral poetry, but readers' inner speech equally re-constructs the sound *gestalt* of a poem.

Empirical research has confirmed that readers perceive rhymed poetry as particularly beautiful, melodious and harmonic, and revealed that rhymed poems are more likely to be set to music. However, the extent to which similarity causes perceived euphony differs between traditions. For instance, the identical repetition of the same word is accepted as rhyme in French poetry (*rime riche*) or in the verses of the Ghazel (a poetic form originating in the Arabic tradition), whereas identical rhymes have mostly been frowned upon in the English and German traditions.

5.3 Mnemonic Function

The mnemonic function of rhyme is the one backed up most extensively by empirical research (see Blohm et al. for a review). To determine rhyme's mnemonic effects, researchers typically present research participants with a text and afterwards ask them to recall sections of it or to identify them in a set of alternatives; the accuracy of responses is used to determine how memorable the tested passages were. A series of experiments on end rhyme has shown that rhyme words are indeed recalled more accurately than non-rhymes. Research on counting-out rhymes further suggests that rhyme improves verbatim memory even in children who otherwise perform below average in standardised memory tasks. But contrary to what Daniel assumed, rhyme does not necessarily result in improved memory of what is delivered therein; in fact, there is some evidence indicating that rhyme improves verbatim memory but reduces memory for content. Similarly, it is unclear in how far end rhymes improve memory for the content of the entire lines they occur in. Although empirical investigations have rarely distinguished rhymes from pre-rhymes, there is initial evidence that the memory effect of rhyme is unidirectional (pre-rhyme > rhyme), which further suggests that pre-rhymes and rhymes are not equal in terms of cognitive salience.

In the temporal flow of the reading experience, rhyme expectations limit the set of possible continuations and sometimes allow for exact predictions of upcoming words. Thus, one possible explanation of rhyme's mnemonic effect is that verbatim memory is improved if readers/listeners encounter what they already anticipated; recall that predictions are representations of expected input which might be consolidated if matched by the actual input. Moreover, rhyme words (re-)activate their pre-rhymes which might resonate with readers' episodic memory of the line the pre-rhyme occurred in and thus lead to improved memory for previously processed sections of the poem.

Memory for surface form is further improved if readers are already familiar with the specific poetic form or rhyme scheme (e.g., the ballad stanza), which favours an account that links rhyme's mnemonic effect to its predictability. Comparable mnemonic effects of local alliteration suggest that sound-based priming may play a role as well. As in the case of euphony, the combination of rhyme with other prosodic parallelisms such as metre or local sound recurrences such as assonance further increases the mnemonic effect. Here the euphonic and mnemonic functions of rhyme are certainly linked, as the structures that aid memory are also analogous to harmonic recurrences in music (Tillmann and Dowling).

5.4 Structural Function

Good poetry is artfully structured by its formal elements; if a poem is rhymed, the phonetic similarity of the rhyming units contributes decisively to its structural make-up. In the temporal flow of the reading experience, rhyme serves as a **boundary signal**. This is most obvious in end rhyme, where rhyme marks the end of verse lines. Of course, this signal is more important in oral poetry than in written verse, where the end of the line is clearly visible and rhyme is redundant as a boundary signal. Moreover, rhyme signals closure of larger poetic units, such as couplets, stanzas or even entire poems. Consider two different quatrain rhyme schemes popular in English poetry: the pair-rhymed *aabb* and the half-cross-rhymed *abcb*. In the *aabb* quatrain, the rhyme relation first becomes evident at the end of line two; line three introduces a contrast in the rhyme position which is immediately resolved in line four. Thus, rhyme signals the boundary that divides the quatrain into two rhyming couplets. In the case of the *abcb* quatrain, the rhyme relation – and thus the internal cross structure of the quatrain and the division into couplets – is only revealed retrospectively when the reader encounters the final word. Prior to the closing syllable(s), the quatrain simply does not rhyme and it seems reasonable to assume that the closure effect is enhanced in this case. Empirical research has revealed that the closure of lines, stanzas and entire poems is conducive to peak emotional experience in poetry reception (Wassiliwizky et al.).

At the same time, end rhyme also structures poetry by **linking** verse lines or even larger poetic units that contain them. In the example of the *abcb* quatrain, rhyme not only marks the two couplets within the stanza (*ab|cb*) but also links their two final lines. 'Linking' here means that the lines in question are equivalent not only in terms of their final sounds but also with respect to their position within the higher-order structure of the couplet. If we assume that poetic structures like couplets and stanzas are associated with a certain processing trajectory (Menninghaus and Wallot), then rhyme-linked lines are functionally equivalent with respect to cognitive processing as well. Consider a poem with the rhyme scheme *abcdabcd*. Again, the rhyme scheme creates a division into two sections *abcd|abcd* and, as in *abcb* quatrains, the first section does not end with a rhyme (no immediate boundary signal). The first rhyme signal of the formal division occurs at the end of the fifth line, but only the following lines establish the actual rhyme pattern: all lines of the second quatrain rhyme with their positional equivalent in the first quatrain. In such cases, the four-line sections often instantiate a processing trajectory that is repeated, typically with variation, in the second section. A possible processing trajectory of this structure might look like this: the first two lines establish a rhythmic, grammatical and/or semantic pattern that is slightly varied in the third line and resolved in the fourth; this basic structure is then repeated with different content and additional formal variations.

5.5 Semantic Function

Literary scholars have argued that the identity of sound in rhyming prompts readers to explore or construct semantic relations between rhyme-linked words (e.g., Nemoianu). The German scholar Schütze even claimed that "rhyme is nothing but the coincidence of two distinct ideas in two unisonous words" (Schütze 16; our translation). Of course, rhyming words convey conceptual information like any other word, but the significance of these concepts, Nemoianu argued, is enhanced due to the salient position of end rhymes (247), which seems plausible considering the cognitive effects of the line-final caesura. Whether the constitution of a rhyme pair per se prompts stable semantic relationships that constrain the interpretation of these verse lines is less clear, although it is certainly true that the creative juxtaposition of certain concepts may be stylistically very effective (e.g., funny). It seems less plausible, though, that – in the temporal flow of the reading experience – readers drastically re-structure their semantic text representations upon encountering a rhyme word; note, though, that observed reading-time increases for rhyme closure in longer poems are consistent with the idea that readers engage in additional interpretive processes at these points. However, rhyming words indeed re-activate their pre-rhymes in our minds and thus resonate with our episodic memory of the line in which the pre-rhyme occurred. If a reader stops to reflect at this point, effects like those assumed by Nemoianu may happen, but more often than not readers simply continue reading. There is an additional, indirect way in which rhyme may affect poetry comprehension. Since rhyme imposes constraints on the selection and combination of words, it may lead poets and performers to use grammatical constructions that require infrequent form-to-meaning mappings (e.g., word-order inversions) and words that allow for some degree of interpretive liberty (e.g., figurative expressions and neologisms).

Finally, there is the notion of **rhyme as reason**, i.e., the idea that the sound identity of rhyme may make counterfactual statements seem more accurate (Wimsatt 336). Empirical research has confirmed that aphorisms and proverbs are perceived as more accurate and persuasive if they rhyme, and the same is true for slogans in commercial advertising. The **misattribution** hypothesis provides a possible explanation for such effects. In this view, readers develop expectations of how easy it will be to process upcoming information. If a word is processed more fluently than expected, this gives rise to "an unconscious inference about the source of processing fluency" (Whittlesea 1235) such that we misattribute the ease of processing to conceptual aspects. This idea can account for the rhyme-as-reason effect as well as for the superficially contradictory empirical evidence that rhyme can make sad poems sadder but humorous poems funnier. Fluency-based misattribution provides a general way in which rhymed poetry may create a deeper impression of what is delivered therein.

6 Concluding Remarks

The traditional work of literary scholars, where it is not primarily theoretical or focused on editorial aspects, is mostly centred around literary-historical questions and interpretation. To what extent, and how, can knowledge of the workings of rhyme inform these areas? We believe that a dual perspective of the poem as both a linguistic stimulus and an emerging mental representation equips literary scholars with a more accurate conception of the literary work of art that enables them to better understand why poetic forms change, how poetic significance emerges or how poetry evokes emotions. Not least, you may deduce some principles from this perspective that may guide your analyses of poetic form.

First and foremost, pay attention to the temporal dimension of the reading experience. Consider, for instance, that the pre-rhyme serves as a stepping stone for the rhymes that follow. Look out for patterns that occur early in the text, as these are likely to create formal expectations that might or might not be fulfilled by the rest of the poem. Poets and performers often establish patterns that they then vary (rules first, exceptions later). Words or text sections that deviate from previously established patterns are thus highlighted and typically worthy of special attention.

Be careful not to overinterpret poetic form and not to infer authorial intentions from the presence of rhyme or other formal features. While poems are usually carefully composed and formal choices are made deliberately, formal features do not represent clear evidence of what the author had in mind. If such arguments are proposed, they should be backed up by the evidence of further examples from the work of the author, which more clearly show that the underlying pattern is not coincidental and better allow to assign a common function to the pattern.

Do not ascribe significance to individual features and generally avoid simplistic conclusions like *formal feature X signifies Y*. With respect to rhyme, be careful not to overemphasise the semantic relations between rhyme words/rhyming units. Instead, analyse the entire form of the poem (do not shy away from counting; the number of (stressed) syllables or certain speech sounds, of words or grammatical units may form part of the pattern), pay attention to the temporal successions of words and concepts and to the mental operations they require you to perform (e.g., reanalysis). Finally, look at the divisions and links that rhyme creates, check whether the sections are otherwise formally identical (e.g., in terms of rhythm or word choice) and analyse where they align with other linguistic divisions (e.g., sentences and clauses). An analysis of poetic form that follows these guidelines is likely to yield a thorough understanding of how the poem works and will provide a solid basis for interpretation.

References

Baldick, Chris. *Oxford Dictionary of Literary Terms*. Oxford UP, 2015.

Blohm, Stefan, et al. "Sound Shape and Sound Effects of Literary Texts". *Handbook of Empirical Literary Studies*, eds. Donald Kuiken and Arthur M. Jacobs. De Gruyter, 2021, pp. 7–38.

Daniel, Samuel. *A Defence of Ryme: Against a Pamphlet Entituled: Observations in the Art of English Poesie*. Edward Blount,1603.

Darwin, Charles. *The Autobiography of Charles Darwin [1958]*, ed. Nora Barlow. Norton, 2005.

Stefan Blohm and Christine A. Knoop

Fish, Stanley Eugene. *Is There a Text in This Class? The Authority of Interpretive Communities*, 6th ed. Harvard UP, 1980.

Gymnich, Marion, and Ansgar Nünning. "Funktionsgeschichtliche Ansätze: Terminologische Grundlagen und Funktionsbestimmungen von Literatur". *Funktionen von Literatur. Theoretische Grundlagen und Modellinterpretationen*. WVT, 2005, pp. 3–27.

Ingarden, Roman. *The Literary Work of Art: An Investigation of the Borderlines of Ontology, Logic, and Theory of Language*, trans. G.G. Grabowicz. Northwestern UP, 1979 [1931].

Kintsch, Walter. *Comprehension: A Paradigm for Cognition*. Cambridge UP, 1998.

Leech, Geoffrey. *A Linguistic Guide to English Poetry*. Longmans, 1969.

McNamara, Danielle S., and Joe Magliano. "Toward a Comprehensive Model of Comprehension". *Psychology of Learning and Motivation*, ed. Brian H. Ross, vol. 51. Academic Press, 2009, pp. 297–384.

Menninghaus, Winfried, and Sebastian Wallot. "What the Eyes Reveal About (Reading) Poetry". *Poetics* 85 (2021), p. 101526.

Nemoianu, Virgil. "Levels of Study in the Semantics of Rhyme". *Style* 5.3 (1971), pp. 246–264.

Rayner, Keith. "Eye Movements in Reading and Information Processing: 20 Years of Research". *Psychological Bulletin* 124.3 (1998), pp. 372–422.

Rosenblatt, Louise M. *The Reader, the Text, the Poem: The Transactional Theory of the Literary Work*. Southern Illinois UP, 1978.

Rubin, David C., and Wanda T. Wallace. "Rhyme and Reason: Analyses of Dual Retrieval Cues". *Journal of Experimental Psychology: Learning Memory and Cognition* 15.4 (1989), pp. 698–709.

Schütze, Johann Stefan. *Versuch einer Theorie des Reims: Nach Inhalt und Form*. G. Ch. Keil, 1802.

Tillmann, Barbara, and W. Jay Dowling. "Memory Decreases for Prose, but Not for Poetry". *Memory & Cognition* 35.4 (2007), pp. 628–639.

Wassiliwizky, Eugen, et al. "The Emotional Power of Poetry: Neural Circuitry, Psychophysiology and Compositional Principles". *Social Cognitive and Affective Neuroscience* 12.8 (2017), pp. 1229–1240.

Wimsatt, William K. "One Relation of Rhyme to Reason: Alexander Pope". *Modern Language Quarterly* 5.3 (1944), pp. 323–338.

3 Metre

Jesper Kruse

1 Introduction

This book provides an introduction to an array of poetic forms, many of which have in common that their basic definition makes explicit reference to metre: blank verse is iambic pentameter without rhyme, ballads typically combine iambic tetrameter and trimeter, and sonnets traditionally contain fourteen lines of iambic pentameter. Metre – the abstract rhythmic patterns that structure individual poems and genres – is, in other words, a central aspect of formal analysis, and still most people find the study of metre boring, yet difficult.

One reason for this has to do with the arcane terminology that is conventionally used in metrical analysis. Almost all of the terms associated with the study of metre have been borrowed from ancient Greek, leaving us with a rag-bag of decidedly awkward words such as *iamb, pentameter, catalexis* and so on to work with. There is no easy way around this, but throughout this chapter we will do our best to keep terminology manageable by rendering need-to-know terms in **bold** the first time they occur in a significant manner.

Another reason has to do with the device of metre itself. Unlike, say, rhyme or alliteration, which are picked up by the ear quite easily, the effects of metre tend to be more elusive and typically require a bit of training to be fully appreciated. This means that many new readers of poetry struggle to understand what metre is, how it works, and – most importantly – how it contributes to poetic meaning.

This chapter aims to provide new readers with the necessary tools and strategies to analyse and understand metre in English poetry. Section 2 outlines the central terms and concepts that are required for metrical analysis, and Section 3 applies them.

2 Metre in Theory

2.1 Syllables and Stress

By far the most common metrical system in English poetry is called **accentual-syllabic metre**, and it is based on the ability of English

DOI: 10.4324/9781003244004-4

speakers to distinguish with ease between **stressed syllables** and **unstressed syllables**. So crucial is stress in English that all words of more than one syllable come with a fixed stress profile: in a word like *zebra*, the first syllable is stressed – in a word like *giraffe*, the second is.

If we annotate unstressed syllables with a dot (.) and stressed syllables with a slash (/), then the difference between our two example words would be annotated like this:

/ .   . /
zebra vs. giraffe

Crude as they may seem, these annotation devices are useful if we want to analyse how stress is assigned to longer stretches of speech. Consider, for instance, the most likely stress profile of a sentence like this:

/ .   . / . . . . /   /   /
Lily was tired after a long day's work.

At first sight, the stress profile of this sentence appears random. This is because assignment of stress in spontaneous speech is motivated, not by deliberate design, but solely by meaning. Thus, stress tends to be assigned to those words that carry most meaning (*Lily, tired, long, day's* and *work*), whereas words that mostly serve a grammatical function (*was, after, a*) rarely attract stress. As a result, the stress patterns of both prose and spontaneous speech are highly complex and may even seem haphazard.

Metrical verse is strikingly different. In metrical verse, stress profiles are extremely regular because metre in English works by alternating between stressed syllables and unstressed syllables in fixed conventionalised patterns. Consider for instance the opening of Andrew Marvell's poem "The Garden":

.   / . /   .   / . /
How vainly men themselves amaze
.   / . /   .   / . /
To win the palm, the oak, or bays

Both lines alternate with complete regularity between unstressed and stressed syllables in a pattern that is clearly discernible when read aloud – in stark contrast to the haphazard stress profile of the sentence that we looked at earlier. This is because Marvell's poem is metrical, whereas prose and spontaneous speech are not.

2.2 Feet and Lines

In the most traditional way of analysing accentual-syllabic metre in English, formalised stress patterns like the one used by Marvell in the excerpt above are broken down into smaller constituents called **feet**. Thus, instead of saying that Marvell's lines contain eight syllables that alternate between unstressed and stressed syllables, we say that Marvell's lines are made up of four feet, each of which consists of an unstressed syllable followed by a stressed syllable – like this:

<blockquote>
   .   /   . /   . /   . /
How vain- ly men   themselves amaze
   . /   . /   . /   . /
To win   the palm,   the oak,   or bays
</blockquote>

The particular foot that Marvell employs in these lines – an unstressed syllable followed by a stressed syllable – is a called an **iamb**. This is not the only foot used in English poetry, but it is by far the most common: Chaucer's *Canterbury Tales,* Shakespeare's plays and sonnets, Milton's *Paradise Lost*, Wordsworth's *Prelude* and countless other poems and hymns are all **iambic**. That is, their basic line structure can be analysed as strings of iambs (with variations, on which see Section 2.3).

In theory any number of iambs can be strung together to make up a metre, but in reality the number of feet per line in English verse is usually at least three and rarely exceeds six. For instance, each line in the passage by Marvell quoted above contains four iambs. Lines with this profile are said to be composed in *iambic tetrameter*: *iambic* because the most prevalent foot is the iamb, and *tetrameter* because *tetra* means four in Greek.

Greek also provides us with terms that specify metres ranging from a single to as many as eight feet, here exemplified with iambs:

1 foot	monometer	. /
2 feet	dimeter	. / . /
3 feet	trimeter	. / . / . /
4 feet	tetrameter	. / . / . / . /
5 feet	pentameter	. / . / . / . / . /
6 feet	hexameter	. / . / . / . / . / . /
7 feet	heptameter	. / . / . / . / . / . / . /
8 feet	octameter	. / . / . / . / . / . / . / . /

Three of these metres are particularly important in the context of English literature: **iambic trimeter**, **iambic tetrameter** and **iambic pentameter**:

<blockquote>
                       . / . / . /
Iambic trimeter   The Only Shows I see—
                       . / . / . /
                       Tomorrow and Today—
                         (Emily Dickinson, "The Only News I Know")
</blockquote>

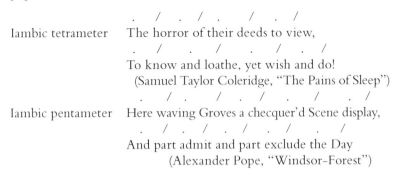

```
                    .   /   .   /    .    /   .   /
Iambic tetrameter   The horror of their deeds to view,
                    .   /    .    /    .     /    .  /
                    To know and loathe, yet wish and do!
                        (Samuel Taylor Coleridge, "The Pains of Sleep")
                      .   /   .    /     .   /     .    /    .    /
Iambic pentameter   Here waving Groves a checquer'd Scene display,
                      .  /   .    /    .   /    .    /   .   /
                    And part admit and part exclude the Day
                        (Alexander Pope, "Windsor-Forest")
```

These metres have been used by a vast number of poets since the time of Chaucer and continue to be used to this day, whereas the other metres – particularly the very short ones and the very long ones – have suffered a more marginal existence in the canon of English poetry. Extremely short iambic lines have been used to great effect by, for instance, Robert Herrick and Ogden Nash, whereas lines longer than the pentameter were used with some frequency in the Elizabethan era. However, with a thorough understanding of how the most common iambic metres work, it is not difficult to analyse less common metres when and if we should encounter them.

Up until this point, the only foot we have made mention of is the iamb. However, to describe English accentual-syllabic verse in all its diversity, an inventory of six feet is needed. These six feet are:

```
            Iamb:       . /
            Anapaest:   . . /
            Trochee:    / .
            Dactyl:     / . .
            Pyrrhic:    . .
            Spondee:    / /
```

In theory, it is possible to combine at least some of these feet with each of the eight line designs outlined above to concoct potential metres like anapaestic pentameters and trochaic hexameters. However, in reality it is quite rare to come across metres in English that are not based on iambs, so for now we will stick with iambic metres and examine conventional means for adding variation to such metres.

2.3 Variation and Regularity

One very common variation in iambic verse is the addition of a single unstressed syllable after a line's final iamb. Consider, for example, this line from Alexander Pope's "On a Certain Lady at Court":

```
                  .   /    .    /    .   /    .   / (.)
              Not grave through pride, nor gay through folly;
```

Such a line is still regarded as an instance of iambic tetrameter (because it contains four feet that are predominantly iambic) – in spite of the 'extra' unstressed syllable at the end. Traditionally, such an added unstressed syllable has been referred to as a feminine ending, but some readers may prefer not to introduce gender into the equation, and they can instead refer to this type of ending as **hypermetrical**. The addition of a hypermetrical final syllable is not rhythmically disruptive – i.e. it does not break the general flow of the line's cadence – but it has a softening effect that is made more palpable when underscored by rhyme (see, for example, Shakespeare's Sonnet 20).

An even more common source of variation in iambic verse is **substitution**. This is a device by which one or more iambs in a line is substituted by another foot. It is important to notice that substituting an iamb or two does not alter the basic metre of a line: an iambic pentameter with a substitution or two is still regarded as being in iambic pentameter.

Trochaic substitution of iambs is very common and is sometimes called **inversion** because a trochee (/ .) has the inverse stress profile of an iamb (. /). Trochaic substitution virtually never occurs in the final foot of iambic lines – but it is very common in the first foot:

/   .   .   /   .   /   .   /   .   /

Aspens must shake their leaves and men may hear
(Edward Thomas, "Aspens")

Trochees can also substitute iambs in mid-line positions. This occurs most commonly immediately after a conspicuous syntactic juncture within the line:

.   /   .   /   .   /   /   .   .   /

What though the sea be calm? Trust to the shore
(Robert Herrick, "Safety on Shore")

In this line, there is a conspicuous syntactic break after the third foot – a so-called **caesura** – which is typically realised as a slight pause in recitation, and that in turn facilitates the inversion of the fourth foot. Line-initial and post-caesural inversions like the ones above should first and foremost be regarded as conventional means for poets to vary their cadence in accordance with line structure and syntax and are not necessarily expressive.

However, when inversions occur without being prompted by a line break or a caesura, they should always trigger our critical attention. Consider, for example, the opening line of John Milton's epic poem *Paradise Lost*:

.   /   /   .   . /   .   /   .   /

Of Man's first disobedience and the fruit

Here, Milton inverts his second foot without any licence from line breaks or caesuras. It gives the line a somewhat abrupt beginning and calls attention to the fact that as Milton introduces his poem's major theme of transgression, he also transgresses against the metre of the poem.

Dactylic substitutions virtually never occur in iambic verse, but anapaestic substitutions are very common and typically have the effect of loosening the rhythm of the line without disrupting it. This is because iambs (. /) and anapaests (. . /) are both 'right-strong', i.e. the stressed syllable comes last, which means that anapaestic substitution in principle can occur anywhere in the line, including in the final foot:

> .   / . . / . / . . /
> To drum <u>on the floor</u> with scur<u>rying hoofs</u>
> > (Robert Frost, "The Need of Being Versed in Country Things")

The addition of extra unstressed syllables into an iambic metre often adds a sense of increased speed or liveliness to a line's cadence. Therefore, it is not uncommon to find anapaestic substitutions in lines that make reference to swiftness or movement – like "scurrying hoofs" in Frost's line above.

If anapaests have the effect of speeding up and loosening iambic verse, spondaic substitutions have the effect of temporarily slowing down the cadence. This effect is put to good use by Marvell in the second line of the final couplet in "To his Coy Mistress", where the phrase "Stand still" may be analysed as a spondee (/ /):

> . / . / . / . /
> Thus, though we cannot make our Sun

> / / . / . / . /
> <u>Stand still</u>, yet we will make him run

At this point, it should be said that not all commentators on metre accept the spondee as a meaningful unit in English verse. After all, even in a sequence like "Stand still", the two words will typically not be pronounced with an equal force – most speakers would probably put more force on "still" than on "Stand" – giving us instead two perfectly regular iambic tetrameters. While there is merit to this observation – and while it is always a good idea to be looking first and foremost for iambs in iambic verse – the notion of spondaic substitutions in iambic verse is useful for critical purposes as it draws our attention to potential cruxes of meaning, such as "Stand still" in the excerpt above.

Pyrrhic substitutions in iambic verse are rarely worth commenting on in their own right. Given that a pyrrhic contains two unstressed syllables (. .), it does not exactly call attention to itself, and furthermore – like we saw with the spondee above – it is doubtful whether it makes sense to speak of two contiguous syllables in English as having an equal degree of stress (or lack thereof). Still, readers should be aware that pyrrhic-like sequences often creep into iambic verse – and virtually always immediately before a spondee-like sequence to create the pattern . . / /, which is occasionally referred to as a 'double iamb':

. . / / . / . / . / (.)
Or to <u>take arms</u> against a sea of troubles
(William Shakespeare, *Hamlet*)

Deviations from the 'expected' pattern of a given metre should first and foremost be viewed as a way for poets to vary their cadence, sometimes for expressive purposes – as we saw with Milton's "first Disobedience", Frost's "scurrying hoofs" and Marvell's "Stand still" – but also for the sake of rhythmic variation in its own right. After all, a poem in which every line had the exact same rhythm would quickly fall into monotony, for which reason painstakingly regular instances of iambic verse lines are more the exception than the rule in English verse. Accordingly, hyper-regular verse lines can in certain contexts be as expressive as any variation, as when Shakespeare at the beginning of Sonnet 12 exploits a metronome-like iambic rhythm to evoke a clock tick-tocking away:

. / . / . / . / . /
When I do count the clock that tells the time

The degree of metrical freedom that we find in English poetry varies greatly across time and across genres: modern iambic poetry tends to be freer than, say, Augustan poetry, and dramatic verse tends to be freer than, say, epic verse. However, to appreciate these differences and begin to enjoy and understand the role that metre plays in individual works and genres of poetry, we must first be able to identify which metre we are dealing with and what types of variation occur. This process of discovery is called **scansion**.

3 Metre in Practice

3.1 Scansion

Scansion is not an exact science. But it is also not an art. Rather, scansion ought to be a skill that critical readers of poetry possess, and whose underlying assumptions they are aware of. Some find it both easy and intuitive to scan a line of verse; others find it difficult and obscure. The following procedure for scansion is intended as a guide for the latter type of reader and a checklist for the former.

30   *Jesper Kruse*

When presented with a poem in English that has the shape on the page of a metrical poem, one's working assumption should be that it is probably iambic. This may turn out not to be the case, but we will not cross that bridge until we get to it.

Although scansion takes place at the level of the single line, it is often a good idea to begin by surveying a couple of lines and counting their syllables. Try it out with these lines from Shelley's poem "Mont Blanc":

> Where woods and winds contend, and a vast river
> Over its rocks ceaselessly bursts and raves.

By my count, the first line has eleven syllables, and the second has ten. Combined with our initial assumption of iambic structure, this leads us to suspect that we are dealing with a poem set in iambic pentameter.

The next step is to assign stress to those syllables that *must* be stressed. At the beginning of this chapter, we noticed that all English words of more than one syllable come with a fixed stress profile. So we look for such words in our poem and find four of them: *contend, river, over* and *ceaselessly*. The latter three are all stressed on the first syllable, whereas *contend* has stress on the second syllable, so we can be certain of the following stretches of rhythm:

>   . /   / .
> Where woods and winds contend, and a vast river

> / .   /   .   .
> Over its rocks ceaselessly bursts and raves.

At this point in the process we are usually reminded of how extremely prevalent words of a single syllable are in English: of the sixteen words in our passage, twelve are monosyllables. But which of them are likely to receive stress? To find that out, we should first and foremost use our ears, but it is also instructive to consider the important linguistic distinction between **content words** and **function words**: content words carry meaning in and of themselves, whereas function words primarily provide syntactic mortar:

Content words		*Function words*	
Nouns	e.g. *cat*	Articles	e.g. *the*
Full verbs	e.g. *catch*	Auxiliary verbs	e.g. *can*
Adjectives	e.g. *crisp*	Conjunctions	e.g. *and*
Adverbs	e.g. *rarely*	Prepositions	e.g. *to*
Numerals	e.g. *five*	Pronouns	e.g. *they*

Generally speaking – as we saw in Section 2.1 when we looked at the sentence about Lily who was tired after a long day's work – we tend to stress content words, and very rarely function words. Accordingly, we now mark as (most likely) stressed the monosyllabic content words in our passage. They are *woods, winds, vast, rocks, bursts* and *raves*. Conversely, we mark the monosyllabic function words as (most likely) unstressed. They are *where, and, and, a, its* and *and*:

. / . / . / . . / / .
Where woods and winds contend, and a vast river

/ . . / / . . / . /
Over its rocks ceaselessly bursts and raves.

The next step is to determine the exact foot structure of each line, and to do that we should first remind ourselves that our working assumption is that we are dealing with iambic pentameter (even though none of our two lines has the structure . / . / . / . / . /). This means that we expect a total of five feet per line, and that we should be looking for iambs.

The first line begins auspiciously with three iambs in a row:

. / . / . / . . / / .
Where woods and winds contend, and a vast river

But then ambiguity sets in: how should the rest of the sequence − . . / / . − be scanned? One possible solution would be anapaest (. . /) + trochee (/ .), but this is a bad idea because trochees virtually never occur in final position in iambic verse. The other option would be pyrrhic (. .) + spondee (/ /) + hypermetrical ending. This is a much better solution because, as we saw in Section 2.3, both pyrrhic-spondee sequences and hypermetrical endings are established features of iambic verse in English.

The second line does not begin with an iamb:

/ . . / / . . / . /
Over its rocks ceaselessly bursts and raves.

But is the first foot a trochee (/ .) or a dactyl (/ . .)? There are several reasons to go with trochee. First, the line has only ten syllables, and given that we think it is in pentameter, this means that all five feet must be disyllabic − and dactyls are trisyllabic. Furthermore, as we saw in Section 2.3, dactyls virtually never occur in iambic verse whereas trochaic substitutions are very common except in final position. So, the first foot must be a trochee, and the second foot must be an iamb. But then, in the next foot, irregularity rears its head again, but as with the first foot (and for the same reasons) our best option is trochee, which leaves us with two final iambs:

32 *Jesper Kruse*

```
      .     /     .    /     .  /      .  .    /   /   .
Where woods   and winds   contend,   and a   vast riv  er
```

```
/   .   .   /     /   .   .  /      .   /
Over   its rocks  ceaseless ly bursts  and raves.
```

By now, our initial assumption of iambic pentameter has been con-firmed: both lines may be analysed as having five feet, and the iamb is the most prevalent foot in both lines. The first line has a pyrrhic-spondee sequence and a hypermetrical ending; the second line has two trochaic substitutions: the first one is licensed by the line break immediately be-fore it, but the second one, in the third foot, is more interesting given that it is not licensed by a caesura. As such it calls attention to itself and invites commentary.

★ ★ ★

The process that led us to this scansion may be formalised in five steps:

Step 1: Assume iambic structure
Step 2: Count syllables and divide by two to gauge line type
Step 3: Assign stress to polysyllables
Step 4: Assign potential stress to lexical monosyllables
Step 5: Determine most likely foot structure

Let's run through a few examples. First, consider these lines from Robert Frost's "Neither Out Far nor In Deep":

> As long as it takes to pass
> A ship keeps raising its hull

Steps 1 + 2: Each line contains seven syllables, so we assume iambic trimeter with variations.

Step 3: The disyllable *raising* must have stress on the first syllable.

Step 4: The lexical monosyllables *long, takes, pass, ship, keeps* and *hull* are likely to be stressed.

This gives us:

```
       .   /    . .   /    .   /
As long as it takes to pass
```

```
      .   /    /   /   .   .   /
A ship keeps raising its hull
```

Step 5: The first line can be scanned like iamb (. /) + anapaest (. . /) + iamb (. /), which is in accordance with our assumption of iambic trimeter

Metre 33

with variations. The second line can be scanned as iamb (. /) + spondee (/ /) + anapaest (. . /) – although I think it is safe to assume that most readers will probably prefer to put less emphasis on "keep" so that a better scansion would be iamb (. /) + iamb (. /) + anapaest (. . /).

Conclusion: This is indeed iambic trimeter.

Another example: consider these lines from Matthew Arnold's "Youth and Calm":

> Because on its hot brow there blows
> A wind of promise and repose

Steps 1 + 2: Each line contains eight syllables, so we assume iambic tetrameter.

Step 3: The disyllables *because* and *repose* must have stress on the second syllable; *promise* on the first.

Step 4: The lexical monosyllables *hot*, *brow*, *blows* and *wind* are likely to be stressed.

This gives us:

> . / . / / . /
> Because on its hot brow there blows
> . / . / . . /
> A wind of promise and repose

Step 5: The first line begins with an iamb (. /) followed by our now familiar sequence of pyrrhic + spondee (. . + / /), and then an iamb (. /). The second line begins with two iambs (. / + . /) followed by what looks like a pyrrhic (. .) and an iamb (. /). However, in this context it makes more sense to analyse all four feet as iambs – after all, in recitation the word 'and' is likely to receive more stress than its neighbouring syllables on both sides, and furthermore we are not fond of pyrrhics in iambic verse unless they are immediately followed by a spondee.

Conclusion: This is iambic tetrameter.

But what about poems that are *not* iambic? Consider as our final example this line from Byron's "The Destruction of Sennacherib":

And his cohorts were gleaming in purple and gold

If we run this line through our five steps, we get this:

Steps 1 + 2: This line contains twelve syllables, so we assume iambic hexameter (but we are wrong!).

Step 3: The disyllables *cohorts*, *gleaming* and *purple* must have stress on the first syllable.

Step 4: The lexical monosyllable *gold* is likely to be stressed.

This gives us:

34 *Jesper Kruse*

. . / . . / . . / . . /
And his cohorts were gleaming in purple and gold

Step 5: If we insist, we could scan this line as consisting of pyrrhic + trochee + iamb + pyrrhic + trochee + iamb. However, this is hardly a satisfactory solution: first of all, the ratio of iambs is quite low, and, second, pyrrhics are usually followed by spondees and not trochees. When we get weird and unexpected results like this, we should go back and revise our initial assumption of iambic verse – could this be something else? In this case, the first foot could also be an anapaest (. . /) – and indeed so could the next one, and the one after that, and the one after that.

Conclusion: Byron's line is not iambic hexameter, but rather anapaestic tetrameter.

The five-step model for metrical scansion outlined in this section is not foolproof. There are lines in English poetry that are so unusual that they defy systematic attempts at pinning down their structure (e.g. Gerard Manley Hopkins' idiosyncratic "sprung rhythm"), and there are types of variation that can interfere with our scansions. Two examples of such potentially confusing types of variation are catalexis and elision.

Catalexis refers to an "incomplete" foot in a line of metrical verse. This occurs very rarely and should only be used as an explanation when all other attempts have failed.

Elision is more common and refers to the omission, or slurring, of an unstressed syllable in recitation, e.g. a word like *glittering* may in some contexts be pronounced *glit'ring*, which will impact how we scan the line. If elision is indicated in the text by means of an apostrophe, our scansion of the line should reflect this; if a possible elision is not indicated typographically, we must use our ears and scan the line accordingly.

Because of such variations, it is always a good idea to scan at least a couple of lines before settling on a metrical analysis: chances are that if a given line proves tricky to pin down, then the next ones will yield insights about the metre that can then be used to explain the trickier ones retroactively.

3.2 Metre in Context

In order to understand why iambic metres are so much more prevalent than other metres in English poetry, it is instructive to read aloud the example of anapaestic tetrameter that we just analysed above:

. . / . . / . . / . . /
And his cohorts were gleaming in purple and gold

Notice how quickly a highly regular – and somewhat artificial – rhythm imposes itself in verse like this. It is a rhythm that is palpable and impossible to ignore. The same can be said of metres based on trochees and dactyls (like the ones used by Henry Wadsworth Longfellow in *The Song of Hiawatha* and *Evangeline*): they foreground rhythm at the expense of sense.

For this reason, non-iambic metres are mostly used for somewhat specialised purposes. Anapaestic metres are a staple of children's verse and humorous forms like the limerick, whereas trochaic and dactylic metres are frequently used to evoke more or less problematic notions of "otherness" – the witches at the beginning of *Macbeth* chant in trochees:

/ . / . / . / .
Double double toil and trouble

Iambic rhythm, on the other hand, is far more subtle and elusive, for which reason it readily accommodates variation and substitutions. This unobtrusiveness of iambic rhythm compared to the rhythms of other metres is what accounts for the great versatility of iambic verse throughout the history of English verse, where iambic metres have been successfully employed across all poetic genres and modes.

Iambic versification in English can be viewed as comprising two distinct traditions: a short-line tradition centred around the tetrameter (sometimes in combination with trimeter) and a long-line tradition centred around the pentameter. Speaking in *very* general terms, the long-line tradition of iambic pentameter has historically been preferred for serious, lofty subject matter, whereas the short-line tradition has been favoured for topics of a more personal and homely quality.

There are also a number of formal differences between the two traditions. The short-line tradition retains a close connection to music and song, and is therefore often used in stanzaic poetry, and almost always employs rhyme. Iambic pentameter, on the other hand, finds its most emblematic use in non-stanzaic poetry, either in fixed forms like the sonnet or in open-ended forms like epics and drama. Furthermore, iambic pentameter is frequently used without rhyme, in which case we refer to it as blank verse.

The association between metrical form and poetic genre is one that goes back to antiquity where dramatic, narrative and lyric genres would usually be distinguished from one another through the use of different metres. The same holds true – albeit to a lesser extent – in English poetry where dramatic and narrative genres are primarily associated with the long-line tradition of the iambic pentameter, whereas lyric genres are primarily associated with the short-line tradition. However, there are very many exceptions to this general pattern: most ballads are narrative in spite of being short-lined, and sonnets are generally intensely lyric in spite of usually being written in iambic pentameter.

Even so, this historical, or conventional, view on certain metres as being particularly suited for certain genres and subjects is one that we should be aware of in our readings. Thus, if we encounter a poem written in

36 *Jesper Kruse*

blank verse, that form's association with tragic and epic genres should inform our understanding of the poem, in much the same way that a poem set in neatly rhymed tetrameter stanzas should instil a different set of expectations in us.

Poets may choose to adhere faithfully to these conventional mappings between metre and genre, as we see in, for instance, Wordsworth's choice of blank verse for his philosophical poem *The Prelude* and short-line stanzas for his Lucy poems. In such cases, poetic convention and poetic meaning reinforce one another in a manner that is fairly straightforward.

At other times, however, poets may choose to work against the traditional connotations of a metrical form, creating instead tension between convention and meaning. Consider, for example, Alexander Pope's choice of the stately iambic pentameter for his burlesque poem *The Rape of the Lock*, which relates a very trivial series of events in a manner that invites comparison with the epic tradition, partly because of the metre. Or, consider Tennyson's choice of rhymed tetrameter quatrains for his lengthy elegy *In Memoriam A.H.H.* Given that this poem is a sustained meditation on mourning in the wake of Tennyson's friend Arthur Henry Hallam's death, one might have expected the poem to be set in iambic pentameter, perhaps even blank verse, which would invite comparison with tragedy, or loosely rhymed, which would evoke Milton's poem "Lycidas", which is also an elegy for a dead friend. However, with his choice of the tetrameter quatrain, Tennyson instead taps into a far more unassuming and even innocent tradition that is profoundly moving as a vehicle for mourning.

Metre is sometimes described as a poem's heartbeat by well-meaning poets and critics. We know what they mean, of course, but at the same time we are also wary of such metaphors because they at once overstate and understate the significance of the phenomenon they seek to explain. A more tenable way to think of metre is to view it as a set of shared conventions between poet and reader that allow us to interact with one another across vast stretches of time, space and genre. Sometimes in ways that are familiar and expected, and sometimes in ways that are surprising and thought-provoking, but never without reward.

References

Arnold, Matthew. *Selected Poems*, ed. Timothy Peltason, Penguin, 1994.
Byron, George Gordon. *The Complete Poetical Works*, ed. Paul E. More. Houghton Mifflin, 1905.
Coleridge, Samuel Taylor. *The Complete Poems*, ed. William Keach. Penguin, 1997.
Dickinson, Emily. *The Complete Poems*, ed. Thomas H. Johnson. Faber and Faber, 2016.
Frost, Robert. *The Collected Poems*, ed. Edward Connery Lathem. Vintage, 2013.
Herrick, Robert. *Works of Robert Herrick*, ed. Alfred Pollard. Lawrence & Bullen, 1891.

Marvell, Andrew. *The Poems of Andrew Marvell*, ed. Nigel Smith. Pearson Education, 2003.

Milton, John. *Paradise Lost*, ed. John Leonard. Penguin, 2000.

Pope, Alexander. *The Poems of Alexander Pope*, ed. John Butt. Routledge, 1992.

Shakespeare, William. *The Arden Shakespeare: Complete Works*, eds. Richard Proudfoot, Ann Thompson and David Scott Kastan. Arden/Methuen, 1998.

Shelley, Percy Bysshe. *The Major Works*, eds. Zachary Leader and Michael O'Neill. Oxford UP, 2003.

Thomas, Edward. *Collected Poems*. Faber and Faber, 1945.

4 Toeing and Breaking the Line
On Enjambment and Caesura

Heather H. Yeung

1 Introduction: Morphology[1]

Let us begin with two common definitions:

1 *Noun: Enjambment; Verb: to Enjamb.* The carrying-over of a poetic unit of sense from the end of one poetic line to the beginning of the next.
2 *Noun: Caesura.* A break of or pause in the unit of sense *within* the poetic line.

Modern Anglophone poetry, i.e. poetry written in English(es) from Chaucer to the present, is distinguished from prose by its use of the 'line'. The poetic line interrupts, breaks, or marks in other ways the progress of grammar and syntax, and thence supports the creation of a specifically *poetic* meaning and argument. Poetic effects are born out of the interrelationship of the rival forces of the spatial line-unit and the temporal lexical, grammatical, or syntactic-unit (sometimes called 'unit of sense') ordered into verses or verse-paragraphs. In accentual syllabic, syllabic, and 'free' or strophically ordered verse alike, the line or lines of a poem are created out of language – enjambment and caesura are the two primary extralinguistic features whose effects demonstrate to us the linguistic and rhythmical possibilities of that line whilst themselves being neither lexical nor related to interpunction, or sharing effects with assonance or apostrophe. Enjambment and caesura exist, instead, significantly *outwith* the marks on the page which constitute the poem, poetic form, and poetic syntax. Enlivening metre and meaning, they are unmarked but 'appear' when we make sensible the poem in the process of reading. Thus the poetic line 'makes' itself not only through its meaning but also in the resonance and rupture of its 'breaks'.

The following five interlinked propositions provide a working definition of the poetic line and its breaks:

1 Modern poetry is language ordered in lines whose primary material of composition is words. The grouping of these lines is not governed by the rules of grammar or syntax, and punctuation can often be

DOI: 10.4324/9781003244004-5

absent or misleading; poetry is in this way distinct from prose. The language with which poetic lines are composed is often heightened, viz. embellished with figurative and rhetorical effects.

2   The lines of a poem have a visible beginning and end which contributes to the overall spatial organisation of the poem. Their beginning is often (but not always) a sentence-beginning. Their end may be terminal (marked by a full-stop), but more often than not is not so. When the end of a poetic line is not grammatically terminal, the poem's unit of sense moves across its end to the beginning of the next line. This is 'enjambment', and can occur multiple times in a single poem, and will always occur at the end of a poetic line until the grammatical unit is concluded. In poetry written from the twentieth century onwards such an effect might even lead to the poem's being enjambed into the white space of the page and thus concluding inconclusively. The opposite of this is an effect sometimes found in contemporary poetry whereby the title of the poem is also its first line and enjambs into the poem's body, creating a heightened sense of a poem's *in medias res* beginning, or questioning the nature of the title as 'capital' or 'frame'.

3   The poet's control of the beginning and end of a poetic line in combination with either metre or rhythm is often not enough to ensure that the line itself is not dull or monotonous. The longer the poetic line, the more important, and more likely, it is that some form of caesura occurs within it. *Within* the poetic line it is often important to create a rhythm of starting and stopping distinctive from that of prose, of placing emphasis on more than one word in the line by pausing either before or after those words. This is commonly understood to be 'caesura'.

4   Whereas in contemporary editions of poetry (in which punctuation has been carefully edited) enjambment is easy to identify, caesura, whose poetic sense the Anglophone line inherited from and developed out of the metrical rules of Latin and ancient Greek poetics, adapting their applications to the quantitative syllabic metre of Latin and Greek to the accentual syllabic metre of Early Modern English, is more difficult to definitively identify. To 'see' enjambment is often as simple as *not* seeing terminal punctuation or noticing that a phrase or sentence does not end with the end of a line; to 'see' caesura, on the other hand, one must read the line and notice its rhythmic and syntactic patterning and where this creates pauses or breaks. On the question of caesural emplacement you will often find that literary critics disagree. The longer the poetic line, the higher the possibility the reader encounters both 'true' and 'false' caesura, the former being the ultimately logical moment of pause or break, the latter, moments of slight (or light) pause ultimately subordinate to the line's 'true' caesura(s).

5   The pace at which the poetic lines appear to move is created out of a combination of the silence of enjambed and caesural effects and the

40   *Heather H. Yeung*

relative ease or difficulty of the reader in speaking (internally or aloud) the sound world of the poem.

The above propositions are necessarily interlinked, and cover the practical or technical means by which we might observe and evaluate the effects of these two major invisible morphological features of poetry: enjambment and caesura.

2 Metapoesis

Complex and nuanced also are the means by which poets themselves address these important extralinguistic poetic effects – the language of poetic form doesn't only serve a scientific, morphological purpose, it also operates on a figurative level of which poets are often preternaturally conscious. Thus are caesura and enjambment 'animated' in some poetry, while they also 'animate' the potential linguistic monotony of the poem. This figurative level is often spatial and embodied, and is a way through which the inscape and 'instress' of poetry (to use Gerard Manley Hopkins' terms (*Collected*, 503–525)) is connected to and made distinct from the 'real', 'phenomenal' world (for the seminal account of the 'phenomenal world' of the poem, see Jonathan Culler's work on lyric ('Reading', and *Theory*)). It may also be metapoetic: a means through which the poem becomes painfully or playfully self-conscious of its construction. Poets play with the sense of 'verse' as 'versus' or 'turning point' and 'strophe' as a 'turn' or movement around the lines. Across the *oeuvre* of Seamus Heaney, the poet borrows from this connection between line and land, likening each of his enjambed line-endings to the 'boustrophedon' of a plough at the end of a field. Each line thus becomes a furrow into which grain is sown, the poet is the person who holds the digging instrument, or pen, the poem the ploughshare (*Preoccupations*, 41–60).[2]

The same sort of metapoetic playful philological and figurative logic can be found in the poetic working not only of enjambment but also of caesura. For the former in addition to the above we can see immediately a link to the idea of the writer's works as a body or 'corpus', in which the limbs (from the French – *jambe*, or leg) reach or stretch over each other and turn, connected by the body (or principal form) of the poem. In Heaney's "Follower" (1966), the movements of the bodies of the horses and plough at the end of each furrow is connected to the effects of enjambment, the phrase 'round and back' enacting itself across the line-break: "the sweating team turned round / And back into the land" (ll. 9–10). This mode of equating enjambment with a body may also compass the movement of a different animal body *along* a space – as in Thom Gunn's "Considering the Snail" (1961): "He / moves in a wood of desire"(ll. 5–6) in which the pronoun designating the poetic subject appears to move so slowly 'he' only achieves a verbal being with the start of the next line – or a movement in concert with the reading direction of a poem on the page *downwards*, as in Wilfred Owen's "Strange Meeting" (1919) whose speaker "escaped / down some profound dull tunnel" (ll. 1–2).

As enjambment 'embodies', it can also populate the poetic topos. Another of its effects of extension is to give a sense of abundance, overflowing, and complexity – a sentence, an argument, a list, or an epic catalogue continues apparently unendingly across a series of lines. This is an effect for which John Milton is notorious, in both his epic world-building and also his shorter lyrics where the running-over of the lines is mimetic of the diegetic superabundance and masculinist empire-building tendencies which characterise his work. We also frequently encounter such an effect of superabundance (albeit with a different politics) in the Romantic poet John Keats. In the ode "To Autumn" the line breaks frequently "o'er-brim" with sensual syntax, "set budding more, / and still more" (ll. 8–9), pushing the work into the realm of aesthetic difficulty; in "Ode to Psyche", "wrung / By sweet enforcement" (ll. 1–2) *wrings out* suspense between pain and pleasure through the manipulation of the line-break (both poems 1819). Taking to an extreme the possibility of fluidly enjambed lines are suites of poems such as Louis MacNeice's "Flowers in the Interval" (1952), where a syntax is suspended and enjambed over so many lines (and indeed across a series of poems) that enjambment, and the anticipation of the conclusion of the grammatical line across so many poetic lines, becomes a habit and thence the dominant mood of the poem over and above the catalogue of descriptions of the beloved who is the poetry's subject matter and addressee. In Carolyn Kizer's odic "A Muse of Water" (1959), where "white streams flow / Artesian" (ll. 8–9), the verb, and the post-partum female body's seemingly unending production of breast milk, moves in both suspended time and fluid abundance across the line-break, in contrast with the caesuras later in the poem which occur often between moments of exclamation as pregnant, breathless, pauses.

These are, of course, scant examples amongst many, demonstrating some of the ways in which the enjambed line combines the metapoetic and the mimetic. Other poets, particularly those who write in accentual syllabic metre, begin differently: with the idea of the metrical 'foot'. They then extend this figurative, formal, idea of the poem's shifting body politic to its limbs, or enjambments, and its overall 'life' and 'death'. We have the 'galloping' of the horses' feet and the metrical feet extending at the end of each line with the narrative pace in Robert Browning's trochaic "How They Brought the Good News from Ghent to Aix" (1845). In the penultimate stanza the linear and limbic extension and swift movement through a landscape halts with a terminal line (l. 54) – the end of the poetic narrative and the start of the final stanza's reflection. In John Milton's sonnet "On the Late Massacre in Piedmont" (1655) the sounds of the just-living are made to extend over the landscape and soundscape, or, the poetic topology:

42   *Heather H. Yeung*

> . . . Their moans
> The vales redoubled to the hills, and they
> To Heaven.   (ll. 8–11)

The unit of sense runs across two line-breaks. The 'moaning' living of the eighth and ninth lines are carried into the space beyond the eighth line, naturally 'redoubling' in an implied echo-effect, then unnaturally extending over the ninth line (unnaturally or 'forced' because here the line-break ruptures the unit of grammatical sense). The forced enjambment draws attention to poetic artifice and also expands the physical world of the eighth and ninth line towards the metaphysical of the tenth; this 'break', too, the poem implies, is a terminal rupture – the 'moaning' bodies populate not hills but Heaven, are therefore by implication beyond life. After this caesura, the poem re-starts.

3 Existence

Caesura extends this idea of the poem as body (or 'corpus'; work); the way in which it works figuratively is perhaps more painful than enjambment, as it is likely that its etymology comes from the Latin 'caedo', to cut open, and which is linked to the apocryphal caesarean incision associated with Julius Caesar's birth (we will note briefly later the difficulty of this metapoetics when gender comes into play). 'Caesura' is thus a 'cut' in the 'body' of the line, linked to the implication of the production of 'new life' after the cut. More often than not, such a 'cut' operates as a pause; in the work of a dexterous poet working with a long line, there may be more than one such pause, and there may also be some 'false' and 'true' pauses. Note again the central (complete) line quoted above from Milton. Here there is a short pause (or false caesura) after the first foot ('The vales'), and again after the next foot ('redoubled'). This is typical, as caesura often acts in concert with the extension of rhythm and grammar. The strongest break in this line is where the comma is marked, which is a *late* position for a caesura, but this late positioning and previous hesitation underlines the meaning of the line, which is to produce (as we have noted above in relation to the effect of the enjambment of the same line) an expansive sense of a long drawn-out movement from physical to metaphysical realms. The 'fatal' cut in the poem occurs after 'Heaven' is reached; there is nowhere further (in this poetic universe) for the bodies to go. Here caesura serves an existential, even metaphysical, function.

In a similar way, in Shakespeare's King Lear's final soliloquy (1606), the caesuras mark repetition, change, and ultimately death, pointing finally towards an extralinguistic absolute: "Do you see this? Look on her! look! her lips! / Look there, look there! [*He dies*]" (A.V Sc.3 ll. 3500–3501). Whereas in Milton's line there is a hesitation with the soft pauses, and something definite about the 'true' caesura, here are too many possible true caesuras; in a sense this is a clear example of the effects of over-breaking a line: after the first foot, the second, the third, until the end. The lines are riddled with as much articulate, exclamatory, space as language. The breaks in the line become the break of reason into mad gesture and in-articulacy, and, as the closing apostrophe loses sense through an excess of repetition, the break of the speaking living body into dumb death. The line, and Lear, are broken and reach a terminus. Such existential 'breaking' of the accentual syllabic line reaches an apotheosis in the hyper-apostrophic poetry of the Victorian poets such as Swinburne, Tennyson, and the Brownings. Around the time of Ezra Pound's infamous statement, "to break the pentameter, that was the first heave" (l. 54), as well as the World Wars, the existential and betimes apostrophic medial 'breaking' of the poetic line becomes an effect so rife as to be commonplace.

However, if this sense of rupture is taken less painfully or fatally, it may also be thought of as an anthropogenic creation of place from poetic space. Indeed, in his *Defense of Poesy* (c.1580), the Elizabethan poet and courtier Sir Philip Sidney remarked on the importance to the English poetic line of "caesura, or breathing place in the midst of the verse" (Sidney, n.p.). It is worth noting how Sidney, so early in the development of modern English verse, softens the meaning of caesura to something more akin to genius (locus) or inspiration ('breathing place') than severance ('caedo', or fatal cutting), and yet that it is related to a sense of the poem itself as body, or as profoundly embodied and phenomenologically indebted. This meaning of 'caesura' haunts other means by which more contemporary poetic lines than Sidney's are controlled without violent rupture, such as the 'opening' of the poem (and 'heart') to the line *as* breath and the 'field' of the page in Charles Olson's highly influential "Projective Verse" (1950). We must always bear in mind, however, how, in theoretical resonance and poetic practicality even to this day 'caesura' can, at times paradoxically, carry with it the sense both of a fatal cut and of a breathing space, and in all cases, the longer the poetic line, the more we might expect frequent use of caesura, as breathing space for or fatal cut in the body of verse.

Caesura can be gestured towards lexically; note the highly formally self-conscious final lines of Gerard Manley Hopkins' sonnet "The Sea and the Skylark" (1877):

> Our make and making break, are breaking, down
> To man's last dust, drain fast towards man's first slime. (ll. 13–14)

These are lines which break articulately (a neat metapoetic shift at the end of this sonnet, which is typical in many ways of the genre), straining against the strictures of the metre. This breaking, however, is effected through a combination of alliterative movement, repetition, and caesura/ enjambment. Lexis that connotes brokenness or multiplicity – "break", "breaking", and "dust" – is followed by pauses in the line, whereas lexis

44 *Heather H. Yeung*

connoting creation or movement is not. Caesural effect moves from mimetic break, to hesitation, to continuation or bridging; a fluid undermining of readerly expectation which is characteristic of Hopkins' line. Indeed, the case of the enjambment here is such that not only is the break mimetic (the verb moving 'down' to the next line), but also the meaning of this clause divided by the line-break changes as we move from the first to the second lines. Such movement is in part influenced by the Welsh poetic line's ordering through 'consonant chime' (*cynghanedd*), and a move towards the rhythm- and sound-indebted line that he is perhaps most famous for (the idea of a 'sprung rhythm' which marked a radical rejection of the strictures of classical Anglophone accentual syllabary on this poet's part).

When the poetic subject is affective rather than an object or concept, enjambment works to make and to underline meaning, and sometimes to complicate apparent meaning. In the first three lines of Audre Lorde's "Who Said It Was Simple" (1973), the dominant affect of anger is also the tenor to the vehicle of the tree; what is first made to seem surprising, then all-consuming and disrupting, and then destructive, underlines the effects of the steady decrease in line length and gradual decomposition of the meaning within the line units (the first line is a full clause enjambing into a secondary clause, the second line enjambs across a clause with the verb – to shatter – also shattering, or breaking, the line), the implication of which is that regardless of how full and apparently complete, or small and apparently incomplete, things may be, that all can be further affected by anger. On formal and metaphorical levels, each stage builds on and complexifies the last; the "tree of anger" (l. 2) is a tree whose very roots break its branches and prevent its flowering and fruiting. There is a complexity here, as the poet's use of enjambment ensures this accretion of anger's force and inarticulacy – across the three lines, even as (and perhaps *because*) the length of each line also diminishes, as too, the poem implies, does the tree's yield. And yet this is the beginning of the poem; a tortuous and self-contradictory start whose line-breaks steadily become 'difficult' (viz. no longer work in concert with syntax), which helps to emphasise the irony set out by the title. The breaking of the line, here, signals both pain and protest, as well as demonstrating a certain deftness on the part of the poet, a will to make it complex rather than easy for their reader.

Poetry makes complicated things out of words. But it is when we attend to what words are not – the breaks and spaces of enjambment and caesura – that we can see the greatest effects of these complexities. It is important for us, in recognising a single moment of 'breaking the line' as a crux, to read this crux alongside the other, perhaps lesser or anticlimactic, breaks. Alice Moore Dunbar-Nelson's short poem "Hope" is part of a sequence, "Impressions" (1895), which engages with and poetically illustrates different affective states; the line length ebbs and flows around the iambic metre, and a cursory glance at punctuation might suggest that there is nothing complex about the way in which the poetic sketch progresses. The first two lines are indeed somewhat mimetic of the image that the poem produces – the medial pause of the first line producing an expected ebb and flow in relation to the "[w]ild seas" (l. 1), the w-based alliteration enjambs softly across the line, a countercurrent to the contained clauses of this poetic list. The second line of the poem (with no 'true' caesura) allows for an extension of the sense of the line which allies itself mimetically with the "gloom" with which the line ends. At first glance the medial caesura of the third line appears to reinforce the mimetic work of the first two lines; the poem really begins to 'writhe' and we are no closer to coming towards the definition of 'hope' the title hints at. The breaks after "desperately", and then after "raves", simple at first, are in fact the moment where the syntax of the poem splits, producing two possible readings of the 'blotting' in the fourth line: in the first possibility, what blots is the desperately clinging man, and in the second it is raving Boreas. Neither quite makes sense; the syntax (and the function of the caesura and linebreak) is murky. Yet the final line of the poem makes it clear that this movement from writhing, through gloom, to total unclarity, is purposive: literally and figurative 'hope' is implied by "light". But after the dramatic "flash of light" comes another caesura which brings another redefinition, this time wholly anticlimactic: the light is not a light which saves, but a "gleam" from "afar". Hope, the poem implies, is to be found in between the sudden illumination and the striving to reach the far shores; it is the caesura central to the poem which produces drama, and the final caesura is salutary, even recuperative.

At its most dramatic, caesura can force a full break of the line in a sort of rugged and disturbing enjambment. We see this force at work in W.B. Yeats' sonnet "Leda and the Swan" (1924), in which the third line of the sestet is divided thus: "And Agamemnon dead. / Being so caught up" (l. 11). The prolepsis of the clause which concludes at the start of this line cannot go any further forward. This caesura is a quite literal climax, which elides capture, rape, orgasm, and conception, and which 'engenders' the children of Leda and Zeus who give rise to epic (Helen of Troy) and tragic (Clytemnestra) literature. The line-breaks after the third iambic foot, and is, literally, broken on the page. The gerund which follows the blank space (is this caesura, or enjambment, or both?) allows for reflection on the dramatic future, but also brings us back to the moment of the rape which is the ongoing subject matter of the sonnet. In this broken line lies possibility, as well as a multiplicity of different violent ruptures. The volta of the sonnet combines with a caesura so dramatic that it also forces enjambment. Although perhaps this is what we ought expect from a poem whose subject matter compasses the mythic rape of a girl by a swan or god, and, by analogy, the violent birth of canonical Western Civilisation, its habits of warmongering and empire-building, as well as its habitual domestic, dynastic violences.

46 Heather H. Yeung

4 Conclusion

Enjambment in accentual syllabic, syllabic, and free verse alike produces three main effects each of which is qualitatively different in each poem you might read. In each case when we read the poem aloud we suspend our breathing across the line-break in order to ensure that we are saving enough breath to complete the clause of the poem with which we, in reading, are currently engaged.

1   Over-running: this is perhaps the most common and identifiable form of enjambment, which exists across all modes of poetic writing equally. Here, the line extends into the next, as if a single line cannot contain everything that the poem wishes to encompass. Rhetorically, this mode is often linked to the poetic catalogue. The poetic effects that this might produce are feelings of abundance, sensory maximalism, or a more diplomatic 'bridging' effect between various components of the poetic syntax.
2   Over-reaching: distinct from the over-running line, the line whose enjambment over-reaches can feel less fluid or 'natural', since even though poetic sense is not entirely disrupted such enjambment creates a sense that the meaning is suspended across the line-break. Often this is because a line will begin with a subject and end on a verb, whose object only appears in the next line. Rhetorical effects related to such splitting might include hendiadys. The poetic effects that this might produce are suspense, attenuation, hesitation, ambivalence.
3   Disrupting: here the breaking of the line does not occur in relation to syntactic progression at all; the effect thus is one more often of rupture rather than of hesitation – however, when used consistently across a poem (as is often the case in Anglophone syllabic verse) an overall effect of extreme tentativeness, or slowness, might be produced.

Caesura, over and above its function to vary the overall rhythm of a poem, preventing monotony and underlining poetic argument, works in three main ways:

1   Hesitation: this effect of caesura, related to its relative strength (or weakness), is also connected to the Sidneyan sense of the caesura as a 'breath' or 'pause' in the line, rather than a break absolute. Thus, the 'soft' medial caesura and its effect of light pause, breath, or hesitation before the sense of the poem continues.
2   Propulsion: a stronger effect of caesura, where the break in the centre of the line also enacts a role as a bridge or tipping point in the syntax. This builds on the light breath, producing either a dramatic pause or prelude to – often – a crescendo in the poem, or a 'volta'-like moment of rhetorical flourish and redefinition.

3   Rupture: at its most dramatic, caesura can force a full break of the line, in terms of sense, mood, and scene, as well as of sound world and rhythm. This can result in a sense of either violence or radical loss. Often this sort of caesura is marked by a full-stop in the centre of the line, with the poem subsequently 're-beginning'; at times (for the most part in poetry written after 1900) such caesura can tip into enjambment, as the line itself is visibly broken.

Between these three modes might also sit the effect of the caesural break after an apostrophe (either non-linguistic (ah!) or deictic linguistic address (oh god!)), and before the 'sense' of the poem begins. The intensity of the affect subsequently explored within the poem resounds *outwith* language: there is a pause, bridge, or break, and subsequently 'reason' – language with grammatical order – kicks in. Dependent on our interpretation of the poem, such caesura might carry with it any of the above three modes, or, as in many of the poems of Emily Dickinson, for instance, more than one of these modes simultaneously.

When we encounter a 'received' genre or a poem which takes on a particular subject matter or argument, we can predict some of the uses to which the extralinguistic features of the line might be put. Since their poetic forms and arguments are predicated on turns and counterturns, the ode and the sonnet are forms in which we can anticipate not only highly wrought uses of enjambment, but also marked terminal stops, within and at the end of the lines. These genres build up the flow of their arguments towards false and true conclusions. The breaking of the line allows for flow, but also for moments of pause when the poetic argument might divide, allowing for a sometimes virtuosic layering of meaning and suspension of syntax within the poem. In the ballad and the dramatic monologue, associated with enunciation and orality rather than argument and textuality, we might expect enjambment and caesura to support the overall 'story' of the poem. The uses of breaks and overflow in the line are more likely in these poetic genres to *support* rather than *complexify* the poetic meaning, and are also more likely to signal moments of pause in performance, viz. to work more readily with a 'story' rather than 'argument' in mind. In an elegy we might expect caesura to function 'existentially' in concert with the speaker's grief, and for enjambment to mirror an overflow of emotion or demonstrate the abundance of remembered attributes of the lost figure.

On a metapoetic level caesura is bound up in the idea of the fatal cut (thus, often, how epic or heroic caesura function), but also how it is related to the idea of the apocryphal birth of (Julius) Caesar by caesarean section. The rupture that caesura creates indicates not one but two bodies: the 'sectioned' maternal (female) body and the infant body thence 'produced'. It bears with it, too, the sense of the *Lex Caesaria* (a Roman law which prevented the burial of a pregnant woman; caesura in this sense was pragmatic, civic, and – for one of the two bodies implied by caesura –

48 *Heather H. Yeung*

post mortem). Hereby the gender politics hidden in the figure of caesura (as mentioned previously) are exposed. By a classical extension of its most famous figuration, what is produced from the surgical rupture of the feminine body is a future emperor, future imperialisms. But how much do we think of the ruptured body if we consider it constituent, rather than remainder? This lets us read caesura differently in many Anglophone poems which incorporate the breaking of the line as an explicit effect to underline moments of rupture and birth. A counterpoint to many of our previous masculinist examples, which write, albeit sometimes problematically, the female body back into this metapoetic discourse, includes Yeats' "Leda and the Swan" and (for the post-natal) Kizer's "Water". A virtuoso engagement with caesura and enjambment's metapoetic potential is Mina Loy's "Parturition" (1914) throughout whose medial and terminal line-breaks arrange the poetic space, and serve different functions variously: of parody of rhythm of speech, hesitant pause, emphasis, and even imply rather than a pause the blank of repression, omission, or censorship.

Caesura and enjambment, the palpable unspoken invisibles of poetry, form two important aspects of the critic's toolkit. As we must attend to their metapoetic dimensions, it behoves us to attend more acutely to the international politics of the line and its breaks, to think more finely about the multiple, nuanced, and different traditions of poetic lineation and what it thus means to 'break' a line. 'Caesura' and 'Enjambment' are certainly important constituent extralinguistic effects within the Western poetic tradition(s), but we must bear in mind in an age where forms are borrowed cross-culturally with some profligacy that we do not mistake these for other modes of controlling the line which bear morphological similarity. For example, the medial break of the Germanic alliterative line, the hemistichich *bait* (or *bayt*) of classical Arabic poetry, the *kirije* of the Japanese haiku, and the flexible bi-partite Russian *dolnik*. If we learn to read critically attuned to traditions of breaking the line which are *not* bound up with 'caesura' and 'enjambment', indeed when 'caesura' and 'enjambment' disappear as the dominant extralinguistic poetic modalities and are replaced by non-Anglophone, non-Western lines, breaks, and silences, we might begin to read international resonance more acutely in modern poetry, and avoid the risk of exerting a Western-centric terminological imperium on works translated and/or taking on formal attributes from different literary traditions.

Returning to the spatial aspects of metapoiesis and thinking again of the poem as body/land/place, we might by extension also begin to attend to the fact that the use of caesura or enjambment in a given poem might produce a qualitatively different poetic sense for a female, queer, or trans-bodied reader and/or for the colonised rather than the colonial body (oeuvre, and language). A poem may or may not toe the line in an expected way, not only in its linguistic, figurative, and formal meaning but also in the presence of its extralinguistic aspects. Going forward, the question then is: first toed, what does it then mean when that line is broken?

Notes

1 Please do note that all poems referred to throughout this chapter are (at the time of writing) available online via *poems.org*, the Academy of American Poets' website, or *poetryfoundation.org*, the UK Poetry Foundation's website.
2 Such images permeate Heaney's poetry, as well as his essays. In the "Glanmore Sonnets" (in *Opened Ground: Selected Poems 1966–1996* (London: Faber and Faber, 1996), the analogy between pen and plough is made explicit, as well as in the infamous "Digging" (in *Death of a Naturalist* (London: Faber and Faber, 1966): 7) the exegesis of which Heaney makes in "Feeling into Words", in *Preoccupations: Selected Prose 1968–78* (London: Faber and Faber, 1980): 41–60.

References

Browning, Robert. "How They Brought the Good News from Ghent to Aix". *The Poetical Works*, vol. 6. Smith and Elder, 1894, pp. 9–12.

Culler, Jonathan. "Reading Lyric". *Yale French Studies* 69 (1985), pp. 98–106.

———. *Theory of the Lyric*. Harvard UP, 2017.

Dunbar-Nelson, Alice Ruth Moore. "Hope", *Violets and Other Tales*. n.p. www.gutenberg.org/files/18713/18713-h/18713-h.htm. Accessed 01 April 2022.

Gunn, Thom. "Considering the Snail". *My Sad Captains*. Faber and Faber, 1961, p. 39.

Heaney, Seamus. "Follower". *Death of a Naturalist*. Faber and Faber, 1966, p. 8.

———. *Preoccupations: Selected Prose 1968–78*. Faber and Faber, 1980.

Hopkins, Gerard Manley. "Collected Works of Gerard Manley Hopkins". *Diaries, Journals, and Notebooks*, ed. Lesley Higgins, vol. 3. Oxford UP, 2015.

———. "The Sea and the Skylark". *The Poems of Gerard Manley Hopkins*, 4th ed. Oxford UP, 1970, p. 68.

Keats, John. "To Autumn" and "Ode to Psyche". *Collected Poems*. Oxford UP, 1908 rpr, 1940, pp. 245, 235.

Kizer, Carolyn. "Water". *Cool, Calm, Collected: Poems 1960–2000*. Copper Canyon P, 2000, pp. 53–55.

Lorde, Audre. "Who Said It Was Simple". *Selected Works of Audre Lorde*, ed. Roxane Gay. Norton, 2020, pp. 228–229.

Loy, Mina. "Parturition". www.poetryfoundation.org/poems/145363/parturition. Accessed 01 April 2022.

MacNeice, Louis. "Flowers in the Interval". *Ten Burnt Offerings*. Faber and Faber, 1952, pp. 92–94.

Milton, John. "On the Late Massacre in Piedmont". *The Poetical Works of John Milton*. George Routledge and Sons, 1853, pp. 491–492.

Olson, Charles. "Projective Verse". nwww.poetryfoundation.org/articles/69406/projective-verse. Accessed 01 April 2022.

Owen, Wifred. *The Poems of Wilfred Owen*, ed. Jon Stallworthy. W.W. Norton, 1986.

Pound, Ezra. "Canto LXXXI". www.poetryfoundation.org/poems/54320/canto-lxxxi. Accessed 01 April 2022.

Shakespeare, William. "King Lear". *The Arden Shakespeare*, ed. Reginald Anthony Foakes, Third series. Thomson Learning, 1997.

Sidney, Sir Philip. "A Defense of Poesy". www.poetryfoundation.org/articles/69375/the-defence-of-poesy. Accessed 01 April 2022.

Yeats, William Butler. "Leda and the Swan". *The Collected Poems of W.B. Yeats.* Macmillan, 1961, p. 241.

5 Persona

Its Meaning and Significance

James Dowthwaite

1 Introduction

It is a common, understandable, perhaps even sensible move to identify the speaker of a poem with the person who wrote it. If not given instruction otherwise (say by a title, or by some other identification), is it not the logical conclusion that the person who says 'I' is the one whose name is attached to the work? This conclusion serves us well in letters, emails, text messages, signed confessions, notes left for spouses, and signed statements read out in parliament, so why should it not apply to poetry? After all, poetry is an art form derived from human communication, so surely we must encounter the human in the person who speaks to us? Of course, we do indeed encounter a person who speaks (sometimes to us, sometimes to others, sometimes to no one), but we might raise the question of whether it is necessary to identify this person with the writer. What we encounter is a 'persona', that is, a figural speaker or writer or observer who serves, normally, as the primary consciousness of the poem – though other figures in the poem may also be personae.

So what do we mean by 'persona'? The term derives from drama. The *dramatis personae* are the characters in a play, and the word *persona* comes from the Latin for the masks worn by actors in ancient drama. As M.H. Abrams pointed out in his 1957 literary glossary, the term is most often applied to the "first-person speaker who tells the story in a narrative poem or novel, or whose voice we hear in a lyric poem" (Abrams 217). In addition to this, however, "we are aware of a voice beyond the fictitious voices that speak in a work, and a persona behind all the dramatic personae, and behind even the first-person narrator" (218–219). Following the critic Wayne C. Booth, Abrams thus also speaks of an 'implied author' who stands behind the persona. This difference between the actual author, the persona of the author, and the use of personae in a text allows for a variety of critical approaches which divorce a text from the personal expression of the author. Summarising their own definition of 'persona', Childs and Fowler conclude that this concept "implies a way out of the ego into an objective vision communicable to others" (Childs and Fowler 171). In recent years, approaches to personae have changed

DOI: 10.4324/9781003244004-6

slightly. In light of structuralist and poststructuralist insights into the role of language in constructing reality, there has been a shift more recently in favour of identifying persona with 'deixis', or general words which derive their meaning from use in context: such a word is 'I' or 'you'. For Keith Green, this means that persona is related to "the encoding in an utterance of the spatio-temporal context and subjective experience of the encoder", meaning that it is contained primarily on the linguistic level (Green 127). In many postmodern interpretations, then, persona is less a matter of encountering a person than it is a matter of encountering certain features of language. The argument runs thus: we identify the primary persona of a work by an 'I', for example, but we should bear in mind that 'I' is a deictic term, a shifting sign, with no singular referent. It is a linguistic sign, given meaning only by social contexts, and not any essential relation to a given speaker. According to such a view, it is the linguistic features of deixis, rather than any notion of selfhood, which is at the centre of the persona concept. Given that most analysis of persona focuses on lyric poetry, partly because of the predominance of personal expression and dramatic situation in the genre, this shift can be felt most strongly there. In his introduction to the lyric, Scott Brewster writes, "the stress on sincerity, feeling and intimate expression also tends to overlook the irreducible problem that the lyric self who speaks is a linguistic construct" (Brewster 33). Thus we see a reduction of the persona to the level of language itself.

In the following, I wish to suggest that what for Brewster seems a problem is in fact part of the creative capacity of persona. Postmodern readings of texts have been immensely fruitful but one pitfall is that the focus on linguistic markers, such as the 'I', tends to obscure the holistic nature of expression in lyric poetry. The persona is present in more than the pronoun. By looking at a few examples, we may find that persona does not reduce to the deictic 'I' but instead comprises a holistic, human element of poetry. First, however, let us look at how we may conceive that crucial separation of author and persona on which the concept depends.

2 Some Versions of Persona

It is best to look at an example. John Donne's "The Sun Rising" (1633) is a famous aubade, in which the speaker derides the sun and the passing of time as meaning nothing to two young lovers, as love is more powerful than time itself. The poem is spoken from the perspective of a male lover, referring to his female counterpart, and is addressed to the sun. The persona of the poem is thus this male lover. He asserts proudly, arrogantly, that their bedroom – the space of their love – is the centre of the universe, and that nothing matters more than their relationship: "She's all states, and all princes, I, / Nothing else is" (ll. 21–22). But who is this 'I'? The immediate, obvious answer is John Donne himself – his name is indeed assigned to the poem. But this is not a necessary connection to make. The

Persona: Its Meaning and Significance   53

poem stands on its own without any reference to Donne's own life. The identity of the woman is unknown, and so the identity of the young man also becomes inconsequential: the poem revolves around the expression of faith in love, regardless of who makes the point. This does not, however, have the effect of making the poem arcane and abstract. What matters is that someone speaks, rather than who it is; the persona is wholly necessary to assert the beauty of their relationship; he is one of its concrete constituent parts. The persona is necessary; his identity with Donne is not.

Now the identification of poet and persona may not only be unnecessary, but perhaps also undesirable. It may reduce the range of interpretation and may cause us to miss the range of meanings the poem expresses. The potential dislocation of persona from author is drawn from the fictional space that the literary work sets up. The independence of the persona has a liberating quality: it allows the author a fictional space and a range of possible expressions; this space is opened up by the distance from the author. The reason for this distance may be manifold: it may be personal, it may serve an artistic purpose, it may be formal, or it may be conventional. Whichever way, it is an essential and constitutive part of poetry's fictionality.

It may even be essential when it is not of immediate importance. In Percy Bysshe Shelley's "To a Skylark" (1820), the speaker addresses a skylark in flight (perhaps a skylark of the imagination, perhaps a real one). The poem thus has two *dramatis personae*: the speaker and the bird. The latter is, of course, the addressee, and so we will focus on the persona adopted by the poet as speaker. This persona is nameless, and identifies him- or herself in the first person only once or twice. The poem shifts between description and meditation, filtered through the voice of the speaker, but the focus is on the bird. The first person singular does not appear until the fourth stanza, in the line "thou art unseen, but still I hear thy shrill delight" (l. 20). We learn nothing of the speaker, other than what we guess by inference: he (if it is a he) is philosophical, prone to speculation, perhaps melancholy. The actual identity of the speaker is by and large left by the wayside, however, and his or her personality is revealed solely in the act of speculation and in the selection of images. One reason for this is the nature of the poem itself: it is an invocation to listen to the skylark, to observe and learn from its ways of existing. The poem ends with the line, spoken again to the bird, "the world should listen then as I am listening now" (l. 105). The focus is thus on the act of listening and the persona of the speaker, though clearly a feature, appears to be relegated to the background.

Critical work on Shelley reflects this ethos – and so here we can see how the treatment of persona influences our readings of a poet's work as a whole. In the popular imagination, the Romantic poet is concerned with self-expression, individual liberty, and self-consciousness. At the same time, there is a notion of the 'sublime', that state of heightened emotion where we transcend our own personal being and our rational states.

Comparing Shelley with his friend Byron, John Beer writes of the former's little "self-regard" (Beer 166). Andrew Welburn similarly claims that the Romantic theme of self-consciousness is slightly different in Shelley, for whom self-consciousness is "the ability to see one's own self as if from outside, and so to that degree enter into the awareness of others" (Welburn 31). While she sees Shelley's lyrical poems as being deeply involved in his existence, Karen Weisman looks at the interactive nature of his writing, claiming that his poems "open to include the dialectical negotiations by which poetry comprehends the world" (Weisman 63). So is the persona in fact unimportant? Quite the opposite. What we see is that Shelley's constructed personae, though their identities and personalities may be pushed to the background, are at the centre of our interpretation. The backgrounding of the personality of the persona becomes the central feature of the work. In many ways this reflects what Thomas Weiskel writes in *The Romantic Sublime* (1976), namely that "the essential claim of the sublime is that man can, in feeling and in speech, transcend the human" (Weiskel 3). The persona remains crucial then, as it is that which the poet tries to transcend. Even in poems where the persona is intentionally pushed from the centre of the poem, it can have a crucial, constitutive role.

From poetry in which the persona is transcended, we may now turn to the opposite: poetry which deals with the persona in and of itself. Robert Browning's poetic reputation rests on the mastery with which he was able to adopt a number of different voices in his development of the ⟳ dramatic monologue. Stefan Hawlin notes this as Browning's particular skill: "the fact that a Browning character speaks for him- or herself *apparently* unmediated by the poet, allows us to be drawn into their world, their mindset, their view of things" (Hawlin 63). Hawlin notes the apparent distance of the poet, as it is of course also clear that Browning uses persona in order to express certain ideas or sentiments, but we shall focus solely on the persona figure. In "My Last Duchess" (1842), for example, the Duke of Ferrara talks through a painting of his recently deceased wife, revealing himself as a jealous murderer through a lax tongue and intemperate speech. In *Sordello* (1840), Browning composes an epic in persona, taking the figure of the Renaissance Italian poet in order to explore the nature of the dramatic monologue itself. In these poems, we see a clear adoption of a mask in order to delineate a particular theme, often treating it with delicate complexity, irony, and indeterminacy. In "Caliban upon Setebos" (1864), however, Browning goes even further. The poem concerns the lowly, servant character from Shakespeare's *Tempest*, initially modelled on a deeply unsettling image of the non-European other, speculating on the nature of the divine through the figure of his mother's god, Setebos. There are a number of complications in this difficult poem, starting with the use of pronouns. Caliban refers to himself often in the third person – indeed, he often refers to himself without any pronoun whatsoever. At times he shifts to the third person, which adds to the confusion. There is thus a distance

Persona: Its Meaning and Significance 55

of personhood. At the same time, the expression of the persona constitutes the entire poem itself.

What I am suggesting here is that in "Caliban upon Setebos", Browning shows us how persona is a totalising effect rather than simply an aspect of the poem: the expression of the poem is entirely filtered through the speaking persona. The poem is notoriously difficult to read but this makes it useful for our purposes. We have three primary pronouns, 'I' referring to Caliban, 'he' also referring to Caliban, and 'He' referring to Setebos. Two examples from the poem should suffice to show the difficulty, first "Thinketh, He dwelleth i' the cold o' the moon", a moving speculation on the resting place of the god (l. 25). But "thinketh" is a strange term; it is third-person singular. Browning omits the pronoun, so we do not know if it is 'he' referring to Caliban, 'He' referring to Setebos, perhaps 'she' referring to his mother (though, she being dead, this would be grammatically odd), or referring to another character, or perhaps even to speculation in general. It is difficult to say. Later we find another moving line, in which Caliban wonders about how he would create the world and himself were he a god: "would not I take clay, pinch my Caliban / Able to fly?" (ll. 77–78) – in other words, he would give himself wings. This is an unproblematic line: we see the speculation and the deixis clearly refers to the persona. Combined with the first line, however, it becomes more difficult. Is Caliban referring to himself both with "thinketh" and with "I would"? If so, why the grammatical confusion?

The poem generally disrupts grammar and one place to begin trying to understand this might be to think through the character of the persona himself. Caliban is presented in the *Tempest* as a 'savage', a disturbing portrayal of a Renaissance vision of otherness. He is also presented as having keen intelligence and a speculative nature. Browning unifies these things. Caliban's use of English is idiosyncratic, it is not his mother tongue, and his theological speculations concern a fictional divinity with which we have only cursory acquaintance. Of course, we are invited to see in Caliban's investigations on the nature of his god reflections of our own difficulties with faith. This is not a matter that, if it is to be fully expressed, can be treated with rational clarity: to do so would deny the contradictions and difficulties of a struggle with belief or unbelief. Not least because any reflection on faith in God is also necessarily a reflection on one's self. Browning, aware of this, fills the whole of the poem with the force of Caliban's personality. The disruption of the grammar is an expression of the persona. Each aspect of the poem is contained within the totality of his self. As E. Warwick Slinn notes, "Browning's poetry illustrates the way the meaning of that world is shaped and patterned by those who perceive it" (Slinn 3). As readers we must therefore engage with the being of the persona, which becomes the absolute centre of the poem. Browning's poetry demands acts of interpretation that begin with the specific speaking subject.

56 *James Dowthwaite*

In modernist literature, the notion of persona is complicated even further. In H.D.'s (Hilda Doolittle's) "Evening" (1916), we have an example of a poem with no clear persona whatsoever. H.D.'s poem displays all the qualities of the imagist technique for which she is famous: the language is hard-clipped and shorn of cliché and superfluous description; the free verse structure allows for an economy of language; the focus is entirely on the concrete – the poem describes the passage of light in a garden at evening, and what meaning we derive from its atmospheric presentation is embodied, wholly, in the images and their connotations. We begin with how "[t]he light passes, / from ridge to ridge" and end with an image of how the flowers, the leaves "and leaf-shadow are lost" (Doolittle ll. 1, 19). There is no explicit subject, no speaker, seemingly no human presence at all. Indeed, one may even speak of this as a poem of objectivity, rather than subjectivity (in contrast to Donne's aubade or Shelley's or Browning's monologues, in which we have an individual expressing emotion). In all senses, this seems to fit a modern drive towards a poetry shorn of the self-conscious Romanticism of previous generations (in contrast to Shelley, H.D. does not even use persona negatively to transcend personality).

This technique H.D. seems to have taken from one of her major influences, the ancient Greek poet Sappho. As Eileen Gregory asks of one of Sappho's fragments: "where is the authority determining what is most beautiful? – the radical I?" Gregory concludes from this that "the emphasis is not merely here on the subjective" (Gregory 23). But is there a way in which this poem can be understood with the idea of a subjective persona in mind? One may perhaps go further: is there a way in which persona is essential? Let us look at the poem again. The first stanza describes how the light "passes" over the ridges, moving from flower to flower (l. 1); we seem to have an image of the behaviour of the light over time and the plantlife's responses to it. Eventually, the light falls, and the flowers and leaves are "lost" (l. 19). It is this lostness that should arrest us. How are the flowers "lost"? They are not lost to the light, for the light itself has disappeared, has been lost, so to speak. They are not lost to the evening, which still contains them; neither are they lost to the garden, nor, surely, lost to themselves. 'Lost' is a human concept; it is a word that asserts a sense of emotional weight, one which is surely alien to the flowers, and alien to the falling light. The flowers are lost to a perceiver, and this perceiver is presumably the speaker of the poem, describing the passage of the light. It is presumably this perceiver who follows the light from flower to flower, leaf to leaf. This poem abounds in specific, imagistic details, but these details are selected out of the whole range of possibilities of evening. The selection of the leaves, for example, of the ridges, or the petals, is done by following the movement (and narrative) of perception: this perception is what implies the persona. Thus what H.D. gives us in the poem is the subtle establishment of an implied persona, one whose conscious observation is embedded in the real world of the evening. H.D.'s subject emerges from the context of the evening and the passing light; this does not reduce to the linguistic level alone, but is instead part of the whole presentation of the poem.

This is further implied in the second stanza, where we learn that the buds are "still" white: this is a moment of temporal pause (l. 11). Though the flowers are "lost" the cornel-buds retain their colour. The still-ness here is another human intervention in this sequence. What is established in this poem is a narrative sequence of the light passing, one which is necessarily also a temporal sequence. The transformation of this temporal sequence into an event, and a selection of the details which provide a narrative of this event, similarly implies the existence of an observer. Once again, this is a subtle implication but one which completes the poem: the poem ends by stating that the leaves and the shadows of the leaves are both "lost" (l. 19). The final word of both stanzas ("lost") asserts the humanity of the experience – or at the very least the conscious subjectivity of it. The atmosphere of the falling light is transformed into a significant emotional experience by an implied persona.

That this persona is implied should not lead us to doubt his or her existence, however. The subtle implication of the observer is a result of the interconnectivity of the subject and the environment. H.D.'s persona in this poem is an embodied subject, no less a part of the evening's context than the leaves, the flowers, and the shadows. They are the point of reference from which the falling light and the 'loss' of the flowers derive their expression, and which confers meaning. What is lacking is the deixis: H.D. refuses the 'I'. But that there is no 'lyrical I' should not lead us to conclude that there is no persona. To do so would be to accept too readily the idea of personhood as cut-off and abstract. Far from impersonal, this poetry is deeply personal: deep, because it is profoundly embedded in the images. A persona need not speak; it is enough that they consciously observe.

We should not conclude, however, that modern poetry is marked by implied personae. Confessional poetry, for example, is abundant in self-referential and self-reflexive markers. Indeed, though I have insisted on a separation between poet and persona, this seems to break down in confessional and identitarian poetry which makes such prominent use of biography and autobiography. Here the poets themselves seem to move beyond the formal bounds of the poem, becoming a persona outside of its textual limits. The broad lines we can draw between Donne and his speaker seem less possible in an age where writers can unify themselves with persona by the power of celebrity.

Let us look at the example of Sylvia Path's "Daddy" (1962). This famous poem has been subject to a vast array of biographical and psychoanalytical readings. The poem concerns a girl who remembers her German father, who died when she was ten. First she recalls how he was god-like to her (l. 8), but as the poem goes on he becomes intolerable, even evil, and she identifies him with a Nazi soldier (l. 29), his language with the atrocities

58   *James Dowthwaite*

of the Nazi period (l. 30), and sees herself – metaphorically – in the role of the Nazis' victims (l. 32). Much of this chimes with Plath's own life: she lost her father when she was eight (though she may have been mis-remembering or exaggerating her own father's political sentiments), and the unhappy situation of her family famously continued in her unhappy marriage to Ted Hughes.

In the first stanza, we come across the first instance of the word 'I', just as the final line ends with the powerful statement "Daddy, daddy, you bastard, I'm through" (l. 85). Much of what we have said about poet and persona applies here: even if we are to think of this 'I' as Sylvia Plath, is it not still a fictionalised Sylvia Plath? Plath as persona, Plath as poet and speaker, and not Plath as one might have known her personally? Do we not instinctively reach for her biography in order to make sense of the poem? Perhaps, but the question is really whether this is necessary. The speaker, whom we will here call Sylvia Plath, outlines enough of their biography and sentiment to stay within the poem. We learn of the father's death (l. 7), of his German background (l. 16), of his authoritarian status (l. 50), of the difficulty the child had in forming a relationship to him (l. 24); we learn of the consequences of this relationship: she struggles to hear the German language (l. 25) and, though he must have died before the war, the mirroring of her relationship with him in the associations of German with the Nazi regime (ll. 41–45); we learn of the structure of her relationship through the disturbing appropriation of Jewish suffering, through the ironically constructed attraction of the boot in the face (l. 49); his association with Hitler (l. 70) and his association with the devil (l. 54), and her association, one presumes, with the villagers who are dancing on his grave at the end of the poem (l. 83). All of this is contained in the poem, and is expressed by the speaker. The poem is in fact addressed to "Daddy" (a term no less deictic than 'I'), meaning that we as listeners or readers are witness to an expression of a relationship.

But still, surely we are witnesses to Sylvia Plath's posthumous attack on her father? Were we to reach for our biographies, we would seem-ingly seek to confirm the accuracy of the poem, and the accuracy of our reading of it, by mapping it on to the realities of her life. A conscientious reader of her work, Jacqueline Rose states that "it is impossible to read Plath independently of the frame, the surrounding discourses, through which her writing is presented" (Rose 69). We note the similarities and affinities between the "Daddy" of the poem and the life of Otto Plath, the author's father. This in turn seems to confirm the reality of the poem, and thus confer on its expression the value that it is a truthful confession. Here, however, we may notice an interesting reversal. It is not, really, that the poem should confirm reality that is of interest to us; we are not really trying to use the persona to understand the real Sylvia Plath; the confes-sion is not made to us as priests or psychiatrists, but as readers and listeners who can pass critical judgement. Rather, in reaching for our biographies, we are attempting to use the real Sylvia Plath to confirm our judgements about the speaker of the poem, the Sylvia Plath persona.

What this means is that we are still thinking through the literary category of persona; it is not necessarily the case that confessional poetry brings the literary under the category of the real and the biographical, but rather that the real and the biographical become extensions of the literary form of the persona. The Sylvia Plath whom we research is, in many ways, the Sylvia Plath persona of the poem, seeing as this is how we encounter her. Here we might think of Irving Howe's critical judgement of Plath's work, that "the personal-confessional element, strident and undisciplined, is simply too obtrusive to suppose the poem no more than a dramatic picture of a certain style of disturbance" (Howe 12). But why "no more"? Is this "style of disturbance" not what the poem achieves? When Sylvia Plath declares "Daddy, daddy, you bastard, I'm through", it is as the speaker of a poem: this is not a private communication on which we are eavesdropping; it is not a confession to a priest in a booth to which we press our ears, but a fictionalised account, and a fictionalisation that moves beyond the limits of the poem itself. In Plath's poem, the persona has a moving and totalising meaning.

3 Conclusion

What I have outlined here is a number of ways in which we can think through the concept of persona, a concept which is essential to poetry as a human action. The persona is less often a mask than it is the human face, as it were, of the poetic text, and a deeper understanding of the way persona works in individual poems, as well as how it works generally, provides an insight into the most human elements of the art form. The postmodern period saw an attempt to reduce the primary persona to the linguistic sign 'I', seeing it as an expression of an abstract, free-floating selfhood or as a self-reflexive linguistic act. I have tried to show that this is not always the case, and that persona can be the most significant concretisation of poetry; it is most often that point of contact between us as readers of or listeners to poetry and a speaker to whom we attend.

References

Abrams, Meyer Howard. *A Glossary of Literary Terms*. Heinle & Heinle, 1999.

Beer, John. *Romantic Consciousness: Blake to Mary Shelley*. Palgrave Macmillan, 2003.

Brewster, Scott. *Lyric*. Routledge, 2009.

Browning, Robert. "Caliban upon Setebos". *The Major Works*, ed. Adam Roberts, Oxford UP, 2009, pp. 328–335.

Childs, Peter, and Roger Fowler. *The Routledge Dictionary of Literary Terms*. Routledge, 2006.

60 *James Dowthwaite*

Donne, John. "The Sun Rising". *Selected Poems*, ed. John Cary, Oxford UP, 2008, p. 85.

Doolittle, Hilda. "Evening". *Selected Poems*, ed. Louis L. Martz. Carcanet, 1997, pp. 4–5.

Green, Keith. "Deixis and the Poetic Persona". *The Language and Literature Reader*, ed. Ronald Carter and Peter Stockwell. Routledge, 2008, pp. 127–136.

Gregory, Eileen. "H.D.'s Heterodoxy: The Lyric as a Site of Resistance". *H.D.'s Poetry: The Meanings that Words Hide*, ed. Marina Camboni. AMS P, 2003, pp. 21–33.

Hawlin, Stefan. *The Complete Critical Guide to Robert Browning*. Routledge, 2002.

Howe, Irving. "The Plath Celebration: A Partial Dissent". *Sylvia Plath: Modern Critical Views*, ed. Harold Bloom. Chelsea House, 1989, pp. 3–16.

Plath, Sylvia. "Daddy". *Collected Poems*, ed. Ted Hughes. Harper Perennial, 2008, pp. 222–224.

Rose, Jacqueline. *The Haunting of Sylvia Plath*. Virago, 1991.

Shelley, Percy Bysshe. "To a Skylark". *The Major Works*, eds. Zachary Leader and Michael O'Neill. Oxford UP, 2003, pp. 463–466.

Slinn, E. Warwick. *Browning and the Fictions of Identity*. Macmillan, 1983.

Weiskel, Thomas. *The Romantic Sublime: Studies in the Structure and Psychology of Transcendence*. Johns Hopkins UP, 1976.

Weisman, Karen. "The Lyricist". *The Cambridge Companion to Shelley*, ed. Timothy Morton. Cambridge UP, 2006, pp. 45–64.

Welburn, Andrew J. *Power and Consciousness in the Poetry of Shelley*. Macmillan, 1986.

6 Poetry in Performance

Jessica Bundschuh

1 The Longevity of the Lyric

Some readers find their relationship with lyrical poetry restricted to its typographic manifestation alone. However, to deepen our encounter with lyrical poetry, it is helpful to recall its generic roots in ancient Greece as a text originally sung to accompany the lyre. In a slightly delayed but similar trajectory, the oral performance of *written* poetic texts also "reaches back through the Renaissance and medieval cultures to the classical world" (Middleton 272). As a result of this dual tradition, the communal listening and reciting of lyrics was *de rigueur* until after World War I, with the influx of competing forms of group leisure activities, as Peter Middleton explains in his history of the contemporary poetry reading. The genre's longevity extends, both in temporality and tenor, far beyond the mild-manner stereotype of the academic poetry reading made languorous by monotone recitations and polite, gentle nods from a docile audience.

When readers celebrate the lyric's performative capacities – baked in from its generic inception – it becomes easier to recognise the genre as a call to action, encouraging listeners to unite in effecting change to the status quo. Herein, we may, likewise, align poems in performance with poetic manifestoes. That is, effective poems in performance, like effective manifestoes, avoid us-versus-them critiques, allowing for collaborations across difference or mistrust. For instance, one ongoing social division that has necessitated a 'poetry in performance intervention' is the current vilification of science and scientists in reaction to the climate crisis and the pandemic. Sam Illingworth and Dan Simpson (both UK-based poets) have tapped into this need as co-producers of a project called *Experimental Words* (2021) in which they harness oral poetry's talent of finding common ground where there had been fissure. To do so, Illingworth and Simpson paired ten scientists and ten poets to jointly write and record a series of poems in performance, with titles like "The Ocean Remembers" and "Mechanisms & Multitudes", thereby expanding the limits of interdisciplinary vocality.[1] This project embodies Charles Bernstein's conviction that "[u]nsounded poetry remains inert marks on a page, waiting to be called into use by saying, or hearing, the words aloud" (7). However, once

DOI: 10.4324/9781003244004-7

62 *Jessica Bundschuh*

called into action, these words may enact the "the maximum inflection of different, possibly dissonant, voices" through the "dialogic dimension of poetry" (7). Indeed, such a fruitful state of a "maximum inflection" is the core of all truly democratic poetry performances.

This investigation into poetry in performance is an appeal both to readers who have savoured lyrical encounters *primarily* between the covers of a book and to readers who have yet to discover poetry's expansive reach. It is my contention that the experience of *listening* to the performance of a poem one has appreciated as a typographic gem offers readers (and now listeners) an enrichment of their earlier encounter(s); this is a result of the revelatory and dynamic energy of performance. As Walter Ong, the well-known champion of orality, asserts, "[s]ight isolates, sound incorporates" (71). That is, hearing a poem and reading a poem constitute very different sensory experiences:

> Whereas sight situates the observer outside … [and] at a distance, sound pours into the hearer … . Vision comes to a human being from one direction at a time … . When I hear, however, I gather sound simultaneously from every direction at once: I am the centre of my auditory world, which envelopes me, establishing me at a kind of core of sensation and existence. (Ong 71)

In this regard, the addition of sound to a poetic interaction opens up the possibility of repositioning the poet and the reader in relation to one another, now enveloped (even if at staggered times) in a three-dimensional, all-around sound experience.

This chapter will explore the generic breadth of poetry in performance through a consideration of a canonical work from W.B. Yeats, "The Lake Isle of Innisfree" (1893), set in dialogue with the performative and typographic iterations of two Irish poems from approximately 120 years later, "Rise" (2017) from Galway poet Elaine Feeney and "My Ireland" (2018) from Dublin poet Stephen James Smith. In so doing, we may investigate how poetry in performance, on the page and the stage (including the recording studio and the video performance), has engaged, and continues to engage, in a long-standing and ongoing democratic commitment to both the physicality of vocalisation and to the thrust of a poetic manifesto.

2 The Singular Incantation of W.B. Yeats' "The Lake Isle of Innisfree"

Poems in performance ground their listeners in a particular historical moment, both those enclosed in the same space and time as the poet and those who listen to a recording at a later date. Further, it is the act of performance itself that brings the recited poem alive as a singular instance of vocalisation. In fact, we might approach the performing poet as "an actual, living medium for the poem" (Pinsky 61). Still, such an evocation is distinctly different from that of hyperbolic spectacle. As Robert Pinsky contends, the lyric's power resides in the "unity and concentration of a solitary voice – such as might be accompanied by the sound of a lyre, a harp small enough to be held in one hand" (18). This vocalised, individual human voice invites listeners into its rhythmic intensity.

An incantatory recitation within the trajectory of Irish poetry immediately calls forth W.B. Yeats and the recordings he made for the BBC in the 1930s (ten in total). Of particular interest is a recording from 4 October 1932 in which Yeats devotes two full minutes to setting up his one-minute poem "The Lake Isle of Innisfree", written in 1888 when Yeats was twenty-three (first published in *The National Observer* in 1890, and then in the 1893 volume *The Rose*). As Yeats explains in his BBC introduction, "if you know anything about me, you will expect me to begin with it". Interestingly, Yeats anticipates a critique of his reading style and thus explains his approach before proceeding: "I am going to read my poems with great emphasis upon their rhythm. And that may seem strange if you are not used to it". Additionally, Yeats justifies his recitation style in response to William Morris, who he once saw departing a lecture hall in a "rage" because of a sloppy recitation of his epic poem *The Story of Sigurd the Volsung and the Fall of the Niblungs* (1876). Like Morris, a poet keenly focused on musicality, Yeats declares that he had "a devil of a lot of trouble to get that thing into verse". Therefore, Yeats emphatically declares that he will *not* perform his poems as "if they were prose", offering his listeners a profound illustration of this generic distinction (Yeats, "On 'The Lake Isle'").

Yeats' reading of "The Lake Isle of Innisfree" is impossible to 'unhear', so haunting and unforgettable is its delivery. To be sure, Yeats' rhythmic patterns contribute to a poetic invocation that is closer to singing and chanting than speaking. The first line, "I will arise and go now, and go to Innisfree", sets up the slowness of the poem's hexameter line that will continue over the course of the three quatrains. Additionally, Yeats' voice wavers at the end of each line through a sliding vowel in diphthongs like "slow" and "glow". Ultimately, Yeats' performance of the "The Lake Isle of Innisfree" sets him up as the poem's "medium" in all three exceedingly similar BBC recordings from 1932, 1936 and 1937.[2] A decision to inhabit the role of disembodied speaker on behalf of a poem would have agreed with Yeats, who firmly believed in the viability of the séance from 1914 onwards (once under the influence of his wife Georgie). And, yet, even a Ouija Board session requires the grounding ritual of a particularised location and engaged participants to take off, just like a poem in performance in the act of bringing a poem to life.

Significantly, all three of the Irish poems in this investigation, from Yeats to Feeney and Smith, rely on the word 'rise', which is also central to a famous Irish blessing of departure (originally written in Irish): "May the road *rise* up to meet you / May the wind be always at your back … ."

64   Jessica Bundschuh

(McBride 110). Thus, through "rise" and "arise", Yeats, Feeney and Smith offer their listeners a similar call-to-action cue to mark the shift from stasis to motion. While grammarians would usually distinguish these two transitive verbs of "rise" and "arise"– with the former suggesting *upward movement* and the latter suggesting *emergence* – Yeats' arch use of "arise" invokes both meanings. That is, as part of a refrain that begins all three stanzas of "The Lake Isle of Innisfree", to "arise" suggests both the act of standing up to ready oneself for departure *and* the sudden transformation of a subject in reverie who takes leave of the "pavements grey" (l. 11) on Fleet Street in London's West End.

In his BBC introduction, Yeats recalls that his twenty-three-year-old self was startled by the sounds of an advertisement for "cooling drinks" in a London shop window: "I heard a little tinkle of water". This sound awoke in him, as Yeats clarifies, the myth-shrouded island in Lough Gill called Innisfree that he had coveted as a child, after his father read aloud Henry David Thoreau's *Walden*. Perhaps this is what motivates Yeats' half-chanting performance, capable of transporting listeners first to the BBC recording studio in 1932 London (and to 1888, in his recalled London memory) and then to his childhood in Sligo, situated even further back in his history and memory. Yeats' listeners mimic the speaker of the poem, called to "arise" from one location to another. In effect, listeners hop from pavement to heather, which Yeats explains in his introduction is a description of the midday's "purple glow", namely, "the reflection of heather in the water" (Yeats, "On 'The Lake Isle'"). Thus, Yeats' dramatic reading of "The Lake Isle of Innisfree" orally enacts collocation, embedding one space in another and converting readers into location-hopping collaborators.

3 The Balance of the Individual and the Social in Elaine Feeney's "Rise"

Whether or not a poem in performance succeeds greatly depends on its ability to find a receptive audience, and this is subject to the individualised conditions of its historical context. From 1932 to 1933, for instance, Edna St. Vincent Millay advocated for radio as a modality capable of broadening poetry's reach on a national scale in the United States. Through recitations of poems like "Recuerdo" (first published in the May 1919 issue of *Poetry* magazine), listeners experience Millay's commitment to orality in a refrain, like Yeats', that she literally sings, punching the rhyming words in an undated recording: "We were very tired, we were very *merry* – / We had gone back and forth all night on the *ferry*" (l. 1–2) [emphasis added]. Performing her work on the airwaves offered Millay a novel opportunity to leverage what was for her innovative technology and overcome the distance inherent to a conventional typographic relationship between poet and reader. Ultimately, Millay's actions utilise – long before the preponderance of poems in performance available today online – the newness of radio to expand poetry's democratic potential during changing times.

One of the greatest rewards a performed lyric can offer its readers is an invigorated exchange between the realms of the social and the individual, like in the example above from Millay. This is a challenge that Elaine Feeney also fully assumes in her poem "Rise" (2017). And she carries out this responsibility in a variety of ways, depending on where, when and in which modality the readers and listeners encounter her poem. For instance, although "Rise" is formally structured as a list, its parallelism is not immediately apparent on the printed page, since Feeney abstains from using upper-case letters and full stops at the end of sentences, preferring to employ line breaks and varied indentions to convey pauses:

rise up in a balloon   be a clown

rise into the station

arouse the nation. (l. 13–15)

Therefore, her decision to forgo conventional punctuation creates a sense of typographic orality. Still, this visual complexity also allows Feeney to grant her readers an aesthetic experience *different* from what she offers listeners who hear her performance in the absence of the poem's typographic accompaniment.

It is likely Feeney's "Rise" began as a(n) (anti-)commemorative work in response to the 1916 Easter Rising, composed in the centennial year; however, it deliberately flouts a number of characteristics common to public commemoration, like the exclusion of profanities, like "fuck" (l. 6), "cunt" (l. 7) and "asshole" (l. 8). It is dissimilar, for instance, from the 2016 project of "A Poet's Rising", commissioned by the Irish Writers Centre, in which well-known Irish and Northern Irish poets, like Paul Muldoon and Nuala Ní Dhomhnaill, composed poems about persons and events surrounding the Rising (even downloadable as an app directing listeners to relevant locations in Dublin). One contribution from Eiléan Ní Chuilleanáin, for instance, kindly honours one of the most beloved of Easter Rising leaders, James Connolly. In contrast, Feeney's speaker is unwilling to relinquish her idiosyncratic position for the sake of communal grieving. In the various online recitations of "Rise", Feeney introduces the poem through the *dual* lens of the public and the private. For instance, prior to a 2019 recitation, Feeney explains that "it is a long list poem of my response to the 1916 Rising and a little personal message just to myself" (Feeney, "'Rise' in the UCD Poetry Reading Archive"). But in an earlier 2017 recitation of the poem, Feeney instead deflects its political import in her opening: "People say it is quite a political poem, but it is actually really

66   *Jessica Bundschuh*

personal. It is all about my own experience" (Feeney, "'Rise' at the UCD Festival 2017"). These comments, from differing oratorial contexts, reflect a hesitancy about the obligations of the public poet. This is a common concern of poems in performance, since orality often prompts the question, for whom the vocalising poet speaks. Identifying a specific addressee, however, is frequently less important than establishing the expansive potentiality of *multiple* addressees. It is the latter that transforms a poem in recitation into an enactment of democracy in action.

The beginning of "Rise" suggests that Feeney does *not* wish to position the poem narrowly as an exclusively personal work. In these opening lines, the speaker aligns the living with the dead, signalling the possibility of a conventional commemoration of 1916:

> rise out of the ground
>
> rise up out of bed
>
> rouse out of your sleep
>
> wake the dead
> arouse the living. (l. 1–3)

Feeney's use of repetition and parallelism throughout the poem is mnemonic; it creates an echo in the mind. Indeed, poems in performance often integrate auditory-driven features, like colloquial language, repetitions and refrains, and mnemonic devices that are emphatic and participatory. In this regard, the vocalised lyric becomes a physical experience aligned with Ong's description of a sound encounter that surrounds listeners on all sides.

Over the course of the poem, Feeney offers her readers a chance to engage with the concept of 'rise' in all its variations, starting with its most common usage: to stand up, to wake up, to mount and to reach a greater height. Feeney enacts these actions both on a physical (if exaggerated) level, "rise to the sunrise and scald yourself" (l. 45), and on a metaphorical level, "rise out of their history books and into your history" (l. 80). The early spondees of "rise up" and "rise out" generate a momentum that propels Feeney's lines forward, aligning it with the Easter Rising's 'rising' of rebellion and revolt, like in the opening lines above. Once the performing poet has the attention of her listeners, though, the next step is to *name* the change, which Feeney accomplishes with the modified preposition of "rise *into*".

Feeney's refrain of 'rise' (+ preposition 'up/out/into') behaves akin to a poetic manifesto, calling for a change of the status quo. This becomes all the more pronounced because she carries out her communal call to action in a second-person address in which listeners become equals to the speaker, who, likewise, addresses herself. Herein, Feeney taps into the historical roots of the lyric, in line with Robert Pinsky's contention that although "poetry's history may link it to hierarchical, pre-democratic societies, the bodily nature of poetry links it to the democratic idea of individual dignity" (17). Poetry's "vocality", in other words, "the mind's energy moving toward speech, and toward incantation" (Pinsky 18), heightens its ability to advocate for democratic exchange, community building and social engagement. As a literary version of a town-hall event, "Rise", as a result, comes to inhabit a public space that nurtures, and is nurtured by, divergent points of view.

In this expansive space, Feeney's list poem also welcomes deeply personal variations of 'rise', like "tell me you didn't rise her, tell me you / kissed her madly on the lips" (l. 10–11). In this instance, Feeney's provocation is intimate in scale, following idioms like *to get a rise out of someone,* or in the Irish usage *to knock a rise out of someone.* This enactment of 'rise' is domestically bound, and potentially violent: "rise another all night" and "rise your screams" (l. 54), which follows from the prior line of "punch it" and "punch him" (l. 53). Feeney's speaker, here, is determined to call attention to a buried and internalised pain by dramatically externalising it: "rise your mother break her / crystal" (l. 19–20). Thereafter, the speaker transforms a breakage into an aesthetic aftermath in which the mother's broken crystal becomes a stand-in for a *Hansel and Gretel* breadcrumb trail. Thus, this variant of 'rise' calls listeners to participate in a revolt alongside those who recognise that the accompaniment of broken glass may inflict pain on those undertaking the journey: "scatter it on the path" and "watch it glisten" (l. 21).

Feeney's embrace of dissonant voices in "Rise" especially highlights the experiences of women: "rise the baby in your belly / rise the bread in the oven and watch it blow" (l. 42–43). In Feeney's vocalisation of these lines, she accelerates her pacing considerably. Thus, her listeners experience a dynamic call to emerge (like a baby), then to transform (like bread, shifting from dough to loaf) and, ultimately, to empower (like a female subject who facilitates nurturing, internally and externally). And while Feeney calls for a forceful response to earlier provocations, it is mitigated by play, since the instruction to "dual with your neighbour" includes the caveat that one use "water guns" (l. 71) to do so.

In Feeney's expansive manifesto, the repetitions become most pronounced in a command to "rise up your hand" and "question", directed especially at those feeling powerless and disenfranchised:

> rise up your hand and answer my *question*
> rise up your hand and *question* my *question*
> > *question* their *question*
> *question* your answers   rise up and laugh
> throw your head back and fuck them. (l. 46–51) [emphasis added]

To raise one's hand is to occupy a classroom setting in which one makes oneself known to a figure of authority. However, Feeney quickly shifts from *answering* questions, to *questioning* questions, thereby freeing her addressees to become their own questioners.

68   *Jessica Bundschuh*

Another important feature of poetry in performance is its flexibility to respond to the varying needs of each oratorial occasion. In four different online recitations, Feeney continually reshapes "Rise", allowing its written transcription to be more like a guide than a prescription. In essence, Feeney leaves out or edits lines that, firstly, might offend: "wake the feminists *jaysus don't* some say let them sleep / *they're only cunts*" (l. 5–6); that, secondly, might limit the scope of possible addressees: "rise the red blush on your breasts to your face" (l. 25); and that, third, might fail to respond to current events, with the addition of a line that does not appear at all in the typographic version: "rise to the racist in his taxi car. Shout" (Feeney, "'Rise' on The Poetry Programme"), potentially included in response to Nigerian taxi drivers receiving abuse for the colour of their skin in 2016 in Galway. Lastly, in multiple performances, Feeney has chosen to dramatically change the poem's ending. The typographic version, referring to history, reads:

> write it down yourself
> bring it with you
> even on the back of your hand to remind you
> it's there, rising. (l. 81–84)

Yet, in a 2019 performance on a feminist podcast, Feeney abbreviates the ending considerably: "write it down for yourself to remind you it's there, rising" (Feeney, "'Rise' on Pantisocracy"). In contrast, in a 2016 performance in honour of the Easter Rising Centennial, Feeney revises the poem's ending to emphasise history's grand plurality: "write it down yourself on the back of your hand to bring it with you, remind you history is yours, *ours*, rising" (Feeney, "'Rise' on The Poetry Programme"). Here, Feeney deliberately aligns the singular with the plural, you *and* we, perhaps to call attention to her earlier reference of calling out racism in Ireland mentioned above. In so doing, she underlines the poem's connection to a ballad in which the individual singer acts a substitute for the community, jointly standing (or rising) up to racism, in addition to sexism in this case.

Memorable poems in performance demonstrate an agility in responding to individualised contexts, thereby heightening their immediate cultural relevance. Such an agility is in line with the history of the ballad, sung and recited across many historical occasions and in the mouths of different balladeers, each reacting to the events at hand. Indeed, Feeney's willingness to 'unhinge' her performances of "Rise" from the typographic version not only heightens her poem's ability to come alive anew with each retelling, like a ballad, it also demonstrates her sincere commitment to finding (and continually re-negotiating) a balance between the realms of the public and the private. In terms of the poem's overarching rhetorical argument, Feeney's speaker ultimately encourages listeners to rise like a phoenix from the ashes, since the list poem begins with the command to "rise out of the ground" (l. 1). Profoundly, this rebirth is doubled at the end in the female addressee who may simultaneously facilitate the birth of others (if she wishes, since she's given the option *not* to do so, as well), while also birthing herself. Here again, Feeney asks her listeners to find a balance between singularity and plurality, self and other.

4 The Physicality of the Direct Address in Performance

As we have seen in Feeney's "Rise", a successful poem in performance begins in embodiment, and ends in dialogue. That is, it upholds Diane Wakoski's famous dictum: "the poem must speak to someone or it is silly. It is like talking to yourself in the kitchen. But if it speaks to one person, then it is a poem. We all hope, of course, that many others will be listening in" (194). To fully appreciate the dialogic quality of poems in performance, it is useful to, likewise, expand our sense of physicality; as poet Donald Hall argues, a poetic work spoken aloud

> exists in the whole body of the person absorbing it, and most particularly in the mouth that holds the intimate sounds touching each other ... . The ear and the eye, listening and reading, are devices for receiving signals that are dispersed throughout the body. The poem happens *out-loud*. (49)

In this way, the poem in performance engineers a path backwards, to morph into old "poetic ways of thinking: Ways of fantasy, ways of magic, transformation, metaphor, metamorphoses" (Hall 49). And in each encounter, then, the poem in performance reaffirms its longevity contingent on corporality, as we can witness in Yeats' "The Lake Isle of Innisfree", hopping from grey London to magical Innisfree.

Within this inclusive and communal space, listeners of poems in performance encounter poets who have long relished in giving poetry readings to rapturous audiences, like William Carlos Williams who – in a 1942 recording of "To a Poor Old Woman" (1935)[3] for the National Council of Teachers of English at Columbia University – invokes the presence of an anonymous woman at the height of the Great Depression "munching a plum on / the street" out of a hand-held "paper bag" (ll. 1–2). Williams' dynamic performance thoroughly enriches his lyric's typographic import by bringing his lines on the page to life; as he reads the second stanza, he sequentially shifts his auditory emphasis from "taste" (the action), to "good" (the evaluation of that sensory experience), to, ultimately, spotlight the word "her" (the encountered subject, engaged in an oral experience all of her own). Thereby, the subject's physicality, like that of the performer's, becomes fully embodied in performance.

To expansively conclude this examination of poetry in performance, I offer a final contemporary Irish example that brings to the fore all of the characteristics discussed herein: Stephen James Smith's poetic manifesto titled "My Ireland" (2018) is a rich enactment of Donald Hall's conviction that recitation revives a lyric's ancient and magical roots, aligning the speaker and the represented subject(s), like in Williams' "To a Poor Old Woman". In Smith's expansive poem of muscular acceleration and multi-vocality, polished into a highly produced 12-minute video with musical accompaniment commissioned by the St. Patrick's Festival 2017,[4] Smith invites his listeners into an open public space in which they may become engaged in a democratic conversation that is dialogic, participatory and socially responsive. Here, Smith asks *his* Ireland to "to move on from: / bacon and cabbage, / potatoes, leprechauns" (ll. 22–24) and set aside the 2016 centennial "celebrations arising from the Proclamation" (l. 32), to welcome, instead, its diaspora, its undocumented, and its "fluid queers" (l. 157).

What distinguishes a poem in performance is its ability to champion a communal impulse, while holding tight to the idiosyncratic centre of the speaking subject, as we have seen in Yeats and Feeney. Similarly, Smith centrally positions his speaker as the vital orator of this oral manifesto, a tale sung to his 'tribe' assembled on St. Patrick's Day and drawn in by the lyrical elements of rhythm, tempo, pitch, intonation, timbre and accent. On this occasion, Smith facilitates for those present a hypnotic and communal exchange. Still, "My Ireland's … more than a list poem!" (ll. 227–228). That is, although the poem's overarching experience is one of breadth and modulated speed – since there is lots of ground to cover in Ireland's long history – Smith recognises the value in slowing the speed down with the circularity of a refrain, in parallel with Yeats and Feeney. Even as Smith shifts to a curtailed metre in the refrain, the earlier grandness persists in his inclusion of the classical apostrophe. That is, Smith's speaker calls forth an Ireland of expansive fluidity, made literally dynamic through its intersecting rivers. Smith's list of rivers – "Corrib, Nore, / Foyle, Suir, Shannon, / Lagan, Liffey, Lee" (ll. 127–130) – acts as a unifying touchstone for the poem as a whole. Immediately thereafter, each repetition of the refrain, five times in total, ends with a declarative request in triplet, "wash over me" (l. 78). In the final instance, the last lines of the poem, the request to be cleansed by Ireland's healing waters, expand beyond the speaker, *me*, to include the addressed nation, *you*, and, most importantly, the communal listeners, *us*. Thus, any gesture of distant apostrophe in this, and most other manifesto-driven poems in performance, becomes merely a transitional step before turning directly to the listeners present and aligned in an oral embrace, such that they may jointly *rise* and join the recitation.

References

Bernstein, Charles. "Introduction". *Close Listening: Poetry and the Performed Word*, ed. Charles Bernstein. Oxford UP, 1998, pp. 3–26.

Feeney, Elaine. "Rise". *Rise*. Salmon Poetry, 2017, pp. 104–107.

———. "Rise". *The Poetry Programme Saturday 1 October 2016, RTÉ Radio 1*. https://www.rte.ie/radio/radio1/the-poetry-programme/programmes/2016/1001/819249-the-poetry-programme-saturday-1-october-2016/.

———. "'Rise', recorded June 10, 2017". *UCD Festival 2017*. https://www.youtube.com/watch?v=Lai_6Glc64s.

———. "'Rise', recorded August 27, 2019". *Pantisocracy, Season 4, Episode 7, RTÉ Radio 1*. http://pantisocracy.ie/s4-e7/.

———. "'Rise', recorded October 10, 2019". *Irish Poetry Reading Archive, UCD Library Special Collections*. https://www.youtube.com/watch?v=nFvZHr7nq_I.

Hall, Donald. "Poets Aloud". 1971. *Goatfoot Milktongue Twinbird: Interviews, Essays and Notes on Poetry 1970–76*. The U of Michigan P, 1978, pp. 49–50.

McBride, Doreen. *The Little Book of Fermanagh*. History P, 2018.

Middleton, Peter. "The Contemporary Poetry Reading". *Close Listening: Poetry and the Performed Word*, ed. Charles Bernstein, Oxford UP, 1998, pp. 262–299.

Millay, Edna St. Vincent. "Recuerdo". *PennSound at the University of Pennsylvania*, https://media.sas.upenn.edu/pennsound/authors/Millay/Millay-Edna-St-Vincent_02_Recuerdo_New-York-1961.mp3.

Ong, Walter J. *Orality and Literacy*. 1982. Routledge, 2002.

Pinsky, Robert. *Democracy, Culture and the Voice of Poetry*. Princeton UP, 2002.

Smith, Stephen James. "My Ireland". *Fear Not*. Arlen House, 2018, pp. 110–121.

———. "'My Ireland', recorded February 15, 2017". *St. Patrick's Festival 2017*, https://www.youtube.com/watch?v=tqEZBOzC3e4.

Wakoski, Diane. *Toward a New Poetry*. U of Michigan P, 1980.

Williams, William Carlos. "To a Poor Old Woman". 1935. *The Collected Poems of William Carlos Williams, Volume 1: 1909–1939*, eds. A. Walton Litz and Christopher MacGowan. A New Directions Book, 1986, p. 383.

———. "'To a Poor Old Woman', recorded January 9, 1942". *PennSound at the University of Pennsylvania*. https://media.sas.upenn.edu/pennsound/authors/Williams-WC/01_Columbia-Univ_01-09-42/Williams-WC_04_To-a-Poor-Old-Woman_Columbia-Univ_01-09-42.mp3.

Yeats, William Butler. "The Lake Isle of Innisfree". 1893. *The Collected Poems of W.B. Yeats*, ed. Richard J. Finneran. Scribner Paperback Poetry, 1996, p. 36.

———. "On 'The Lake Isle of Innisfree', recorded October 4, 1932". *PennSound at the University of Pennsylvania*. https://media.sas.upenn.edu/pennsound/authors/Yeats/Yeats-WB_Lake-Isle-of-Innisfree_1932.mp3.

Notes

1 A free download of the album is available at https://experimentalwords.com/.

2 All three versions are accessible through the University of Pennsylvania's PennSound archive: https://writing.upenn.edu/pennsound/x/Yeats.php

72 *Jessica Bundschuh*

3 The recording is accessible through the University of Pennsylvania's Penn-Sound archive: https://media.sas.upenn.edu/pennsound/authors/Williams-WC/01_Columbia-Univ_01-09-42/Williams-WC_04_To-a-Poor-Old-Woman_Columbia-Univ_01-09-42.mp3

4 The video is accessible through the St. Patrick's Festival channel: https://www.youtube.com/watch?v=tqEZBOzC3e4

Section 2

Poetic Forms

7 The Ballad

Catherine Charlwood

I

What do we mean by 'ballad'? Such a simple question, but with a complex answer. This one word, this concept which has asserted itself in many European cultures is harder than you think to pin down. Mark Strand and Eavan Boland's effort in their *Anthology of Poetic Forms* sees them designate five statements to define ballads broadly:

1 It is a short narrative, which is usually – but not always – arranged in four-line stanzas with a distinctive and memorable metre.
2 The usual ballad metre is a first and third line with four stresses – iambic tetrameter – and then a second and fourth with three stresses – iambic trimeter.
3 The rhyme scheme is *abab* or *abcb.*
4 The subject matter is distinctive: almost always communal stories of lost love, supernatural happenings, or recent events.
5 The ballad-maker uses popular and local speech and dialogue often and vividly to convey the story. This is especially a feature of early ballads. (73)

So far, so good. However, I want to problematise this definition. Before I do so, though, I want to focus attention on certain aspects of Strand and Boland's definition.

There is some kind of "narrative" impulse driving the ballad; we can, at most, agree on what is "usually but not always" the case. Ballads are "memorable": I'll return to this in earnest below, but keep in mind the importance of mnemonic devices to oral cultures. Ballads feature rhyme and metre strongly – in that sense they are among what is commonly, or traditionally, thought of as 'poetry'. "[C]ommunal stories": ballads are a format employed by multiple generations for sharing content with each other. While novelty might be prized in artistic creation, the ballad form stems from the familiar and recognisable. In their attention to "local speech and dialogue", ballads reveal something about regional identity and a sense of place, and also might have a lower register and sound more colloquial than

DOI: 10.4324/9781003244004-9

76   *Catherine Charlwood*

other forms of poetry. Finally, we are back to "story": a ballad may spin us a yarn, but that is not to say that the story will necessarily be linear, complete, or lacking in enigma.

This chapter is split into three sections. First, I'll attempt to define a loose – and it is necessarily loose – perimeter around the word 'ballad', then I'll look in-depth at the forms which ballads take through examples, before turning to the possibilities within and beyond that structure. Throughout, I'm interested in using ballads to consider the vexed question of poetic form in general.

If we look at the etymology of the word 'ballad', music and dance are strongly implicated. Ballads were originally sung aloud and were not written down – ballads owe their origins to preliterate, oral culture. Sure enough, the *Oxford English Dictionary*'s first definition pertains to song: "A light, simple song of any kind" ("ballad, n."). If we add in definitions 1b ("A popular, usually narrative, song, *spec.* one celebrating or scurrilously attacking persons or institutions") and 1c ("A narrative poem in short stanzas, esp. one that tells a popular story"), a sense of ballads builds up as something "popular", and – in the case of 1b – perhaps satirical.

To understand how ballads used to operate, you need to imagine that you live in a pre-technological, preliterate society. As Alan Bold puts it:

> The modern reader has lived so long with ballads as a permanent feature of every library that it requires an imaginative leap to conceive of a time when the ballads had no fixed texts and were simply and fondly remembered by those who enjoyed singing them. Critics have constructed such a massive academic apparatus around these beautiful songs that there are times when the direct power of the ballads is obscured. When topics like modality and musical morphology are being debated, it is salutary to remember that many of the songs under critical scrutiny were sung, not by sophisticated musical performers, but by milkmaids and nurses and ploughmen. (2)

While not ignoring the "academic apparatus" around balladry, I want to emphasise the varied lives ballads have lived both within and beyond published poetry. Up until the end of the nineteenth century, ballads were still a popular and ubiquitous form of street entertainment. 'Popular ballads' is the term designated to those ballads sung live which were handed on without any recourse to text: you heard a ballad-singer's performance and perhaps replicated the song. Popular ballads, then, could last in a largely stable form for generations, without being written down. Conscious of balladry's contributions to both regional and national culture, but also their vulnerability, ballad collectors sought to capture in print those ballads which were passing out of living memory (for myriad reasons including print technology, increased literacy, and increased movement for work, meaning that people left their local communities). Examples of ballad collections include Thomas Percy's *Reliques of Ancient English Poetry* (1765), Sven Grundtvig's *Danmarks gamle Folkeviser* (1853 onwards), and Francis James Child's *English and Scottish Ballads* (1860 onwards).

A much more ephemeral form than the popular ballad is the broadside ballad. These singable verses were cheaply printed on a single-sided sheet of paper (often with an indication of which 'tune' you should sing it to at the top). A single song (a 'slip') would cost a halfpenny, with a 'broadside' sheet with several songs costing a penny. The broadside tradition in England lasted c.1550–1900, and these songs and subsequent sales could be found on streets, but also at events like fairs, markets, and races. Imagine a nineteenth-century London street: it's crowded, it's noisy, and everywhere sellers and street hawkers are vying for your attention. The nineteenth century also saw the rise of advertising, and a boom in patent medicines – individual preparations which made various (spurious) claims to being a miracle cure. A brief example of a broadside ballad would be "The Wonderful Pills" which pokes fun at such a medicine. Across ten sung verses, this ballad promises that the pills can cure "a dog with a broken nose" and "make an ugly woman fair" alongside many more outlandish claims (Morgan). The Bodleian Libraries Broadside Ballads Online is an invaluable resource to explore this tradition of balladry.

Broadside ballads, although printed, were much more ephemeral than popular ballads. They often responded to, or poked fun at, contemporary situations which had a very brief cultural half-life. Formally, they are similar to the larger ballad tradition, but their content sits slightly at odds. Due to their popularity and lowbrow status, scholars have traditionally seen broadsides as lesser than popular ballads. When ballad collectors travelled their respective countries preserving ballads in text for posterity, they tended to collect those ballads which had never previously been committed to paper (and because of this, ballad collectors needed to record several variants).

To make things confusing, there is another spelling of 'ballad' as 'ballade'. This is related in many ways to the broader definitions of 'ballad' with which we began, but refers to a more tightly constructed poem, more common to French since it relies on having a multiplicity of rhyme words (which English doesn't readily provide). Wendy Cope's "Proverbial Ballade" is a modern-day example. The ballade stanza is longer at seven or eight lines (with a repeated last line), and a ballade has lines of equal length and usually ends in an envoy (the concluding lines of the poem). Cope opts for eight-line stanzas of iambic tetrameter in an *ababacbc* structure. She structures her poem out of a series of ludicrous, proverbial-sounding statements or, as she writes, "adages like these" (l. 25). The final line of each stanza – the refrain "So say I and so say the folk" (l. 8) – links to the idea of a ballad's communal nature: this is rehearsing "folk" wisdom, and thus is (apparently) not to be questioned. Part of the comedy is that while these statements are patently ridiculous, they are also demonstrably true:

78 *Catherine Charlwood*

"who has two legs *must* wash two knees", but it's so obvious as to be banal (l. 5, emphasis mine). Cope re-routes existing proverbs into rhymed lines which will meet the demands of the ballade structure, offering amusing alternatives to such well-known phrases as 'you can't teach an old dog new tricks' and 'Rome wasn't built in a day'.

II

Having suitably exploded the meaning of the word 'ballad', let's look at what is most commonly thought of in terms of poetic ballads, rather than popular or broadside ballads, which tend to be studied as a historical or socio-cultural phenomenon rather than a literary one. The most obvious touchstone for poetic ballads is that poetic precedent altogether, the publication of Wordsworth and Coleridge's *Lyrical Ballads* in 1798, and the second volume in 1800 with the famed "Preface". While this is taken as poetry proper, one of the reasons I mentioned popular ballads earlier is because there is a false dichotomy between popular ballads and poetic, or literary, ballads: Wordsworth and Coleridge were heavily influenced and inspired by Percy's ballad collection *Reliques of Ancient English Poetry.* Given that Wordsworth famously asserted that the *Lyrical Ballads* constituted "fitting to metrical arrangement a selection of the real language of men in a state of vivid sensation" (287), we might see this work as a meeting point between two types of ballad tradition which criticism often tries to separate.

"Fitting to metrical arrangement" announces the question of poetic form, and whether in versifying words, that is in setting them within verses, poets are doing something unnatural to language. That is certainly what the proponents of *⟳* free verse – those poets at the turn of the twentieth century who eschewed the bonds of rhyme and metre – would argue, with Ezra Pound noting

> Don't chop your stuff into separate *iambs*. Don't make each line stop dead at the end, and then begin every next line with a heave … . you may fall victim to all sorts of false stopping due to line ends and caesurae … . If you are using a symmetrical form, don't put in what you want to say and then fill up the remaining vacuums with slush. (204–205, original emphasis)

This is an argument against allowing the form to overtake the poem. The violence of "chopping" and the lumbering "heave" characterise the writer as unwieldy, or as wielding words badly. One risk of metre is "filling-in" – adding extraneous words merely to fit the metre. Pound here presents form as a negative external force, forcing poets into "all sorts of false stopping", but as we shall see the ballad form holds more flexibility than might appear at first glance. I mention free verse partly to remind us of that

The Ballad 79

against which ballads stand in stark contrast, but also because sung ballads or street ballads die out around the turn of the century, and the rise of free verse coincides in some ways, understandably, with the demise of ballads: a form which is particularly informed by rhyme and metre.

Certainly, Wordsworth's "fitting to metrical arrangement" makes it sound as if he is forcing words to fit into a framework, and at its worst, that is exactly what ballads sound like: that the content exists purely to suit the container. A good example of contained content is found in Wordsworth's "The Thorn", where the description of a pond notes "I've measured it from side to side: / 'Tis three feet long and two feet wide" (ll. 33–34). The problem with those lines is that they are too predictable: "side" awakens "wide" long before we get to it; the monosyllabic last line drums out the expected metre. But this is also exactly what gives ballads their power: the expectation of a particular beat, such as that in Wordsworth's "The Tables Turned".

A very regular line in ballad metre would be the first of the fourth stanza: "And hark! how blithe the throstle sings!" (l. 13), but what do we mean by 'ballad metre'? It's a metre that's so often used that it also goes by 'common metre' (or CM), and is used in a wide range of poems and songs from ancient hymns and carols ("O Little Town of Bethlehem" is a well-known example) to Madonna's "Material Girl".[1] Stanzas in a ballad have four lines, alternating iambic tetrameter and iambic trimeter built on the iamb, a poetic foot consisting of an unstressed syllable followed by a stressed syllable. While we usually describe poems in terms of feet, ballad metre is also often known by the shorthand 8686, counting the number of syllables per line. Even within this tight structure, though, Wordsworth allows the individual poem, rather than the form, to determine the sound. The above line pauses (instead of drumming on) after the first foot to mark the exclamation "And hark!" The same stanza ends "Let Nature be your teacher" (l. 16). Regular ballad metre aside, Wordsworth noticeably manages to marry "Nature" and "teacher" – a tenet of Romantic ideals – through the use of the same stressed-unstressed rhythmic unit's being placed similarly within the iambic line.

About a hundred years later, a poet heavily influenced by Wordsworth, English novelist and poet Thomas Hardy wrote "In Time of 'The Breaking of Nations'". This brief three-stanza ballad watches what seems a fairly innocuous scene: "Only a man harrowing clods" (l. 1) in a quiet, pastoral scene with a young couple passing through at the end, hinting at young romance. However, written in 1915, published in 1916, this sees the ballad form used to comment on war. While we can read this as a product of its specific contemporary context – the First World War – there is little in the poem that dates it, beyond its being a scene of pre-mechanised farming. While the same ballad form underlies the poem, and the language is relatively simple (if slightly archaic-sounding for 1916), it is not a simple, easily dismissed poem. That war is "harrowing" has become somewhat

80   *Catherine Charlwood*

of a commonplace, but here it is "only" the meaning of "harrowing" as 'ploughing'. "Only" is an unlikely word on which to begin a poem about "The Breaking of Nations", a phrase which is a quotation from the King James Bible: Chapter 50 verse 21 of the Book of Jeremiah – "Thou art my battle axe and weapons of war: for with thee will I break in pieces the nations, and with thee will I destroy kingdoms". So a poet who had very famously lost his faith and become an atheist entitles his poem with a Biblical quotation – thus setting up a high register – and then opens it on "only", bringing the reader back to a homely, workaday scene of one man ploughing. "Only" also challenges the reader to shirk their imagined version of what "the breaking of nations" might constitute, to avoid what other kinds of fires might be burning beyond the flameless one in the poem.

Moreover, while the poem fits within the frame of ballad metre, it doesn't have regular line lengths: the syllable counts are 8696 7685 7585. The first stanza is the most regular, but from there Hardy lapses increasingly into cataleptic lines, ones with a final beat missing, which fail to reach their full potential. While the poem ultimately ends on the positive idea that love continues, that life will go on, the form suggests a backdrop of loss which resonates beyond and around these quiet, perhaps complacent, figures.

As well as writing his own ballads, Hardy was known to be interested in balladry. His friend Edmund Gosse enquired about "Let's go a shooting, said Richard to Robin" and following a question about the ballad used in the novel *Under the Greenwood Tree,* Hardy replied:

> I have been unable to meet with a person who remembers the song about which you inquire; though some old people still sing it in this county … . [T]he song, as sung in this neighbourhood, has always been … as far as I know – orally transmitted only. (*Collected Letters* 198–199)

Hardy's experience of ballads is actual as well as textual: these are songs he has heard first-hand.[2] In this letter, as in several others, there is the sense of ballads passing out of existence as their singers die off. That they are "orally transmitted only" gives ballads an immediacy and vibrancy, but also makes them susceptible to loss. In October 1924, Hardy showed his second wife "the old barn at the back of Kingston Maurward. Here, as a small boy, he had listened to village girls singing old ballads" (*Life and Work* 460). Memory is evidently implicated in writing ballads for Hardy, in passing on textually those traditions he received aurally. Although ballads played a role in Hardy's life, Hardy was also attentive to the textual tradition of ballads: "balladry was consistent with his interest in other metrical forms which were undergoing historical development or exploration in the later nineteenth century" (Taylor 55).

The power of ballads derives from the near-incantatory metre. A ballad-singer relates stories; 'to tell' might be considered the bard's verb. Yet this verb breaks down under pressure. Ballads have a peculiar relationship with revelation: formally, they appear simple, yet their content asks to be deciphered – even as they may ultimately suggest there is no conclusion to be found. In this way, ballads both anchor the memory (with their known structure) and also insist on further memory work (as the reader engages with what is being handed on). While the ballad-maker tells, they neglect to tell all, asking the reader to provide part of the message. Deceptively simple, ballads are usually enigmatic rather than revelatory: writing about Hardy, Thom Gunn notes how central omission is to the form, that "we get a paring-down to essentials, and the greater the paring the wider and richer the implications" (26). Again, the emphasis is on what is absent, on what is heard only by the imagination. Noticeably, "In Time of 'The Breaking of Nations'" looks at first glance to be an inconsequential ballad in which nothing much happens. Yet Hardy sets this (in)activity against the passing of "Dynasties" – a huge geographical and temporal vista (l. 8). Moreover, while the young people's "story" will apparently outlast "war's annals" (ll. 11–12), it is not a story to which the reader is privy: the significance is emphasised, but not explained.

III

What we have seen in the ballads of Wordsworth and Hardy is their adherence to formal principles which come from a tradition of oral poetry, one which had to rely heavily on mnemonic devices in order for the poem (or at least identifiable variants of it) to survive:

> An unlettered person had to rely on conventions and a contemptibly familiar structure in order to retain a large number of stories. The evolution of the form made memorization easier, made it possible for the mind to lock on to a definite conceptual shape. It was this shape that was fixed in the brain, and when it passed from mind to mind, via the oral tradition, incidental variations were inevitable … . So ballads are schematic story-containers sturdy enough to retain their basic shape despite repeated usage by different people. (Bold 14–15)

The ballad only offers a "contemptibly familiar structure" when judged by the standards of literary works: this mnemonic property is purposeful and valuable within oral culture. What interests me here is Bold's notion of a "shape that was fixed in the brain" which could be "passed from mind to mind". Ballad tradition has long been part of cultural memory, with its long-rehearsed narratives and ability to bind an audience, but because of the form, there is also a cognitive aspect to ballads.

In his monograph, psychologist David C. Rubin examines the cognitive psychology of 𝔥 epics, ballads, and counting-out rhymes: three forms derived from oral culture. Rubin writes at length on the importance of 'rhythm', though he does not make the literary-critical distinction between rhythm and metre, that the former is the variability of individual words, whereas the metre is the stable, underlying pattern of stresses: he uses the term 'rhythm' for 'metre'. Rubin's Theory of Remembering for Oral Traditions marks metre out as the most significant constraint:

> The poetic devices of rhyme, alliteration, and assonance work locally within lines and between nearby lines. Of all the constraints ... rhythm is the most effective globally because the specific rhythm being used in the line or stanza being sung is usually the same specific rhythm that is used in all lines or stanzas. The local organization is the global organization. (177)

Here, Rubin stresses the pervasiveness of the metrical constraint as a constant (and "constraint" here is non-pejorative, meaning more a stabilising principle). Metre provides a framework upon which other constraints may be overlaid. Readers naturally latch onto this "organization" of ballad metre. As Rubin is specifically discussing oral traditions, he points out that

> A verbatim text is not being transmitted, but instead an organized set of rules ... that are set by the piece and its tradition. In literary terms, this claim makes the structure of the genre central to the production of the piece. In psychological terms, this claim is an argument for schemas that involve imagery and poetics as well as meaning. (7)

The stabilising effect of the form, though, means that poets can take advantage of the fact that both culturally and cognitively a reader feels they know what is coming next in a ballad. This is how you get an experimental form like Hardy's "The Voice" (346), where the *abab* quatrain is extended from 8-6-8-6 to 12-10-12-10 across three stanzas, and only when the reader is habituated to this elongated ballad stanza does Hardy pull the form from under us for a final stanza bereft of the pattern, shortened to 6-7-10-6. The power of the ballad is in its possibilities, not blind allegiance to its standard form.

Ballads have long provided poets with a ready structure to both adopt and adapt. Their longevity from oral culture to an age of mass literacy and their pervasiveness across different cultural mediums (poetry, popular song, hymns, and more) is testament to the lasting power of this form to offer something meaningful to its audiences. Ballads can be read or heard; tell us about a momentary happenstance, or the character of an entire epoch; transmit memories or fade upon the air; lead us to expect patterns and thus to be surprised when those predicted are not realised. The form offers a series of possibilities to the poet, a framework which can be fashioned to the individual poem: countless poets have already taken up the challenge, and many more will continue to do so.

The Ballad 83

> **NOW READ ON…**
>
> – You can access a host of broadside ballads through Bodleian Libraries Broadside Ballads Online, a collection of material provided by the University of Oxford: ballads.bodleian.ox.ac.uk
> – This chapter opens up a contrast between ballads and the use of ⊘ free verse.
> – Ballads are narrative poems, which may put them in close contact with (or at a significant distance to) ⊘ epics. Make sure to investigate the differences between these two forms.
> – If you want to further explore the role of the speaker in various stages of the development of the ballad, also consider the chapter on the ⊘ dramatic monologue and the chapter on the ⊘ long poem.

Notes

1 While "ballads" remain a popular music genre today, this refers to a slow(er) song with generally romantic content. The musical comparisons above are in terms of their adherence to ballad form rather than being ballads in musical terms ("Material Girl" demonstrably not being a ballad).
2 I stress the real-life experiences of ballads for Hardy to distinguish him from those "Middle-class poets from Tennyson to Kipling [who] often seized upon (and plundered) the ballad as a way of reaching a popular audience" without any personal connection to this tradition (Isobel Armstrong, *Victorian Poetry* 161).

References

Armstrong, Isobel. *Victorian Poetry: Poetry, Poetics and Politics.* Routledge, 1993.
"ballad, n." *OED Online.* Oxford UP, December 2021. www.oed.com/view/Entry/14914. Accessed 28 December 2021.
Bold, Alan. *The Ballad.* Meuthen, 1979.
Cope, Wendy. "Proverbial Ballade". *Making Cocoa for Kingsley Amis.* Faber and Faber, 1986, pp. 24–25.
Gunn, Thom. "Hardy and the Ballads". *Thomas Hardy,* special issue of *Agenda,* ed. Donald Davie, vol. 10, no. 2–3, 1972, pp. 19–46.
Hardy, Thomas. *Collected Letters, Vol. 1:1840–1892,* eds. Richard Little Purdy and Michael Millgate. Clarendon P, 1978.
———. "In Time of the Breaking of Nations". *The Complete Poems: Variorum Edition,* ed. James Gibson. Macmillan, 1978, p. 543.
———. *The Life and Work of Thomas Hardy,* ed. Michael Millgate. Macmillan, 1984.
———. "The Voice". *The Complete Poems: Variorum Edition,* ed. James Gibson. Macmillan, 1978, p. 346.

Morgan, John. "The Wonderful Pills". *Ballads Online.* Bodleian Libraries, U of Oxford. http://ballads.bodleian.ox.ac.uk/view/edition/19293. Accessed 15 November 2021.

Pound, Ezra. "A Few Don'ts by an Imagiste". *Poetry*, ed. Harriet Monroe, vol. 1, no. 6, 1913, pp. 200–206, *The Modernist Journals Project.* Brown U and The U of Tulsa. http://modjourn.org/. Accessed 4 February 2013.

Rubin, David C. *Memory in Oral Traditions: The Cognitive Psychology of Epic, Ballads, and Counting-out Rhymes.* Oxford UP, 1995.

Strand, Mark, and Eavan Boland. *The Making of a Poem: The Norton Anthology of Poetic Forms.* Norton, 2000.

Taylor, Dennis. *Hardy's Metres and Victorian Prosody.* Clarendon P, 1988.

Wordsworth, William, and Samuel Taylor Coleridge. "Preface". *Lyrical Ballads*, eds. R. L. Brett and A. R. Jones, 2nd ed., Routledge, 2007, pp. 287–314.

———. "The Tables Turned". *Lyrical Ballads*, eds. R. L. Brett and A. R. Jones, 2nd ed., Routledge, 2007, pp. 149–150.

———. "The Thorn". *Lyrical Ballads*, eds. R. L. Brett and A. R. Jones, 2nd ed., Routledge, 2007, pp. 115–123.

8 Blank Verse

Calista McRae

I

Blank verse is relatively straightforward to sum up: unrhymed iambic pentameter. 'Blank' might seem to define the form through a deficiency: that it does not have the interplay of likeness and unlikeness that rhyme continually promises, satisfies, and surprises. But the lack of rhyme foregrounds the interest of the five-beat line itself and its variations. These variations are driven by the rhythms of English, on several levels: speech – dramatic speech, colloquial speech, internal speech – animates blank verse. And in addition to the interactions of speech and abstract pattern within a poem, blank verse takes part in a much larger conversation, too: one of replies and allusions and parallels between blank verse works across centuries. This chapter traces a few of the form's many developments in John Milton's *Paradise Lost*, Samuel Taylor Coleridge's "Frost at Midnight", and Gwendolyn Brooks' "In the Mecca".

While blank verse first appeared in English in the Earl of Surrey's translations of the *Aeneid* (c. 1540), as part of Surrey's attempt to imitate a rhymeless classical ♫ epic, it was refined on the stage. The dramatic heritage of blank verse is crucial to its later possibilities for metre and speech. In the plays of Marlowe, Shakespeare, Jonson, and Webster, blank verse became an elastic, expressive form, able to support just about any kind of monologue or dialogue. In Webster's early seventeenth-century play *The Duchess of Malfi*, when the murderous de Bosola tells the Duchess that "The manner of your death should much afflict you: / This cord should terrify you" (IV.ii.203–204), the beginning of the Duchess' swift, defiant retort is all the swifter and more defiant for slipping into the last three syllables of de Bosola's pentameter: "Not a whit", she answers (IV.ii.205). She doesn't need any time to collect herself.

We would probably not consciously notice this effect while watching a performance: one reason blank verse becomes so prominent both in early modern drama and in later poetry is that its rhythms work fairly naturally in English – the language of the two lines above feels like something real people could say. But even such brief exchanges are drawing on tensions that are central to blank verse. De Bosola's quite regular pentameter, for

DOI: 10.4324/9781003244004-10

86 *Calista McRae*

example, offers scope for an actor (and later, for a reader): to adhere to the metre with creepy, menacing uniformity, giving even "of" a little stress? Or to read the line more as one might speak it normally, with four main stresses? While nearly any accentual-syllabic metre can elicit such decisions, blank verse – because of its relative closeness to everyday English – heightens the relations between poetry and talk, between syllables and stresses.

II

The expressive opportunities that flourish in early modern drama carry over into *Paradise Lost*. In general, Milton's blank verse calls to mind a powerful, all-encompassing form that can carry a sentence for twenty lines or longer, accumulating force as it goes; since this blank verse is encountered not in live performance but on a page, the syntactic demands made on comprehension can be much more elaborate. Milton's blank verse can glide from one planet to another in a single long periodic sentence (II.1034–1053), or can gradually pan over the vegetation in Adam and Eve's bower (IV.689–705). It tends to connote grandeur and strength. But it is worth looking at the effects not only in verse paragraphs as wholes, but in specific five-beat lines, and even individual feet.

Countless examples of local effects occur in the revealing and manipulative speeches of Book II. Satan has gathered the fallen angels to debate possible courses of action: what he calls "open Warr" (II.41) or a stealthier approach. Moloch speaks up right away; in an extremely blunt first sentence, he argues for that same "open Warr" (II.51). Legions of his comrades, he claims, wait for a chance to fight and recapture Heaven: if they fail, nothing could be "worse" (II.85) than their current predicament. Blank verse intensifies Moloch's rage, despair, and vengefulness: given his explicit attitude, his short clauses and frequent caesuras seem to create a rough, stop-start rhythm expressive of his vehemence. And in this context, his trochees and spondees – like "Black fire" at the start of one line (II.67) and "strange fire" at the end of one nearby (II.69), both kinds of fire being weapons he wants to use against Heaven – seem rough and violent. His many enjambed lines (for instance, II.63–69) seem apt for a speaker who wants revenge, right away. Admittedly, metre does not have effects in and of itself; rather, it builds on what language establishes. Nevertheless, much of the interest of blank verse lies in teasing apart the diverse ways metre interacts with meaning.

Moloch's blank verse, for example, seems to spring from his fury: it expresses intense feeling. But after he ends, the more controlled, devious Belial begins to speak, and his blank verse reflects his character in another way. Pointedly returning to the phrase that both Satan and Moloch used, that of "open Warr", Belial tells his colleagues that he "would be much for open Warr" (II.119), an iamb ensuring that his slightly unctuous "much" gets

Blank Verse 87

stress. And the parallel goes further: in both Moloch's and Belial's speeches, "for open Warr" occupies the third and fourth feet of the line, and is followed by a caesura. The word-for-word, rhythm-for-rhythm repetition exposes two key differences. First, unlike Moloch, Belial is using a counterfactual subjunctive: he "wóuld" support war, just not in this case. Second, and almost comically, these two opening lines part ways in their fifth and last feet: whereas Moloch uses that space to dismiss strategic "wiles", Belial takes up those wiles by smarmily addressing his "peers" (II.119).

Through his echoes, Belial both dutifully indicates that he has listened to Moloch and shows just what the "open Warr" that Moloch fullthroatedly supports would look like. For Belial, there is something to be said for their current situation, and more to be said against battle. As he reminds his associates, their recent past was (*pace* Moloch) certainly "worse" than their present (II.163). He then sketches what could be worse in the future, beginning with an ominous "What if" (II.170) that opens an eighteen-line cascade of what God could visit upon them. "What if the breath that kindl'd those grim fires" (II.170) – the fires they recently fled – were to return? Here blank verse has a persuasive effect: it lightly mimics the terror remembered. When the last foot expands into a spondee at "grim fires" (or at least into two hefty syllables that receive significant weight), the pentameter itself seems to enact how a single exhalation can lead to a massive blaze.

Across Book II, blank verse can imitate not only strong feeling or artful elocution but objects, or actions – plummeting, hovering, bombarding, and so on. When the former angels fan out through Hell, they must clamber through ten monosyllables, a bare list of various hostile landforms that make up one of the poem's most striking lines (II.621). Stony regions, swampy regions, cavernous regions: all these and more push up against each other, seemingly jumbled together in no order, two whole landscapes to a single metrical foot. This intensely freighted, protracted line suggests both how laboriously the fallen angels make their way across the hellish terrain and how vast that terrain is. The blank verse of *Paradise Lost* can be showy and subtle; it can convey rhetoric and emotion, and the objective realms beyond.

To this day, blank verse tends to be used in long poems, perhaps in part because its modulations of metre and syntax take some time to develop a context and become evident, and in part because *Paradise Lost* solidifies the link between blank verse and serious, ambitious poems. Henry Weinfield argues that Milton links blank verse and intellectual freedom, a link that then runs through the Romantic and Victorian eras into Modernism. Because blank verse exists between the guaranteed pattern of rhyme and the absence of such pattern in prose, it offers freedom to wander in thought between these realms – and between all the contrarieties of subject they might encompass. More broadly, blank verse comes to promise scope, whether in a dramatic or narrative or meditative work.

III

Across the eighteenth and nineteenth centuries, while blank verse retains the complexity and breadth exemplified by Milton, it is also increasingly welded to ordinary language and situations. It can seem intimate and confiding, as in Coleridge's 1798 "Frost at Midnight". When Coleridge's speaker, after remembering his own childhood, turns to the future of the infant son sleeping in a cradle near him, blank verse helps convey a moment of intense conviction and wishfulness within a soft, introspective speech. This blank verse is quiet. It furthers a sense of simplicity: Coleridge seems to address a young child directly, though the child is not yet old enough to understand.

"Frost at Midnight" ends with a single ten-line sentence describing how the natural world will welcome the son in "all seasons" (l. 65). That spondee (or at least, those two metrically prominent syllables, depending on how you scan) gives "all seas|ons" emphasis but not aggressive, italics-style emphasis: it is so decisive that it can be left understated. The remaining clauses build gently, moving from season to season, and from a night with gale-force winds to one so still that the only movement is the drip and freeze of an icicle. Over this last sentence, blank verse – with intermittent, unobtrusive substitutions – guides the reader.

Several lines, for example, end with the pyrrhic-spondee combination, as part of a gradual building of momentum. On a morning poised just between winter and summer, a robin might sing "on the bare branch" (l. 68); a pyrrhic-spondee pair fleetingly calls attention to that bit of branch not covered by the lingering snow. The next cluster of substitutions, over the last two feet of line 69 and the first two feet of 70, calls attention to a cold, damp roof meeting the warmth of the morning sun. At the same time, these and other substitutions also work up a contrast to the last four lines, which are more iambic and which, on the whole, produce a sense of calm. The last line is especially interesting: Coleridge ends with an image of stillness epitomised by icicles "Quietly shining to the quiet Moon" (l. 74). This line is close to what would be a four-stress line in speech, and it has at least two effects. On the one hand, breaking the line into two symmetrical halves underscores the otherworldly mirroring described (that the icicles seem to be "shining" back at what shines on them); on the other hand, four stresses sounds natural, even slightly homespun.

IV

Over the 250 years after Milton announced blank verse as revolutionary in its freedom, the iambic pentameter constituting blank verse came to dominate English poetry. And by the early twentieth century, given this dominance, pentameter is seen by one strain of modernist poets as an outdated husk, as unable to reflect contemporary speech or life. But this revolt ends up extending the possibilities of blank verse. As Robert Shaw observes, for those younger poets who "did decide to give iambic pentameter a try, the stylistic developments of the early twentieth century gave them disparate models" (132).

The results range over a huge amount of ground, but one way of roughly categorising recent blank verse is to divide it into two currents. In stricter blank verse, the five-beat pattern remains audible and variations are limited to those of a standard set; in looser blank verse, variations are sometimes many and so unorthodox that the pentameter becomes an abstraction, a remote idea. In practice these two approaches are not always separate. The blank verse of Robert Frost, for instance, is both adventurous and usually strict: though some lines can be initially difficult to scan, they almost always can be broken down into inventive substitutions, frequently ones that can clarify implication. With Robert Lowell's ⏀ sonnets in blank verse, there often is no way to scan the majority of lines, which can have fifteen or more syllables – but at least once in every sonnet, Lowell reinstates blank verse with an entirely scannable five-stress line, often one that comes to sound epigrammatic because syntax and metre align so neatly.

Additionally, blank verse can arise in putatively ⏀ free verse – not just in glancing, unintentional snippets of pentameter, but as a deliberate device. Brooks' markedly experimental "In the Mecca" (1968) is a good example: it consists of just over 800 lines of intermittent free verse, metrical rhymed verse, and blank verse. One of Brooks' first works influenced by the Black Arts movement, the poem demonstrates how blank verse can be central to meaning even when not the exclusive metre. At times Brooks seems to be asking: how much can blank verse take in? Where does it have to give way to another form, whether rhymed verse or free verse? One way of reading "In the Mecca" is as a wary consideration of blank verse – of its power, and of what or who it has historically not made space for.

The poem winds through the rooms of the Mecca Flats (a large, decaying apartment complex in Brownsville, Chicago) in search of Pepita Smith, a young girl who has gone missing. The narrative is manifestly fractured: the normal priorities of plot give way to passage after passage describing neighbours' memories or hopes or preoccupations. With every new verse paragraph, Brooks' omniscient speaker changes perspectives, sketching the lives and recording the words of residents. It is not clear whether only the speaker and reader discover Pepita's body under a bed in another apartment, in the final passage. There is little solace of closure; instead, the poem is defined by its fleeting vignettes, its glimpses at the various people who care or do not care about the lost girl. Rendering an individual disaster against others' hard lives and differing concerns, the poem spans a strikingly wide array of registers; its blank verse provides strands of cohesion in an often jagged, unpredictable poem. Thus blank verse relates to Brooks' exploration

90 *Calista McRae*

of sympathy – of both the residents' varying levels of sympathy for the family and their lost child, and the narrator's and readers' sympathy for the Mecca's inhabitants as a whole.

"In the Mecca" is also a reminder that formal effects are entwined with culture and history. For example, blank verse's associations with spaciousness – and dignity – are relevant to this enormous and once impressive but now overcrowded and decrepit complex, whose inhabitants must live in close proximity to roaches and rats. Brooks links pentameter to the building from the outset: as it happens, the very first prose epigraph is a description from a *Harper's* magazine article. Its opening words have been cut, so that the epigraph begins simply with "... a great gray hulk of brick, four stories high" (p. 2, ellipses in original).[1] That phrase makes a striking line of expressive pentameter, with two especially loaded feet: the "gray hulk" and "four stor|ies". Building and blank verse are fused from the start, and establish yet another effect of blank verse in "In the Mecca": to provide a distant reminder of scope, behind literally and figuratively cramped, limited circumstances.

More generally, "In the Mecca" – the poem itself, though also the larger book that takes its title from the poem – is a turning point for Brooks, a move away from the fixed Anglo-European forms (like ⟨ sonnets) that she had begun twisting and flexing years before. At some moments in the titular poem, to return to pentameter when free verse is available can have an ironic edge. For instance, when six lines of extremely regular pentameter announce the arrival of "the Law" (p. 18), they seem stiff; they call to mind connotations of blank verse as imposing, as related to heroic genres, as conventional, as a white form, as not fitting the actual lives and speech of the Black residents. At other moments, however, pentameter conveys the unexpected crisis that Pepita's mother and family are facing, and the difficult lives of others in the Mecca.

Blank verse begins in the poem's second verse paragraph, which introduces "Mrs. Sallie" (p. 5). Admittedly, this pentameter looks more like free verse on the page. Within its thirteen lines are two short ones which combine to make a five-stress line, one three-syllable line on its own and two others that would fit perfectly into iambic pentameter except that the initial unstressed syllable of one has been appended to the end of the line before it. These tiny, mainly visual changes present interpretive difficulties: why evoke blank verse to this particular degree? Such lines deviate only trivially from a completely regular pattern – were one to just move a few syllables to one or the other side of a line break, they would fall into regular iambic pentameter. To the ear, they would still sound like solid blank verse, but to the eye they are somewhat unsettled.

Over the next few pages, Brooks follows Mrs. Sallie up four flights of stairs, down a hall, and eventually into her kitchen, passing neighbours in the Mecca and then meeting eight of Mrs. Sallie's children. Throughout these introductions, pentameter functions as a base for lines that frequently

Blank Verse 91

expand and contract. Given these frequently shifting line-lengths and units, the traditional associations of blank verse – its recollections of sublimity or tragedy or literary prestige, or of a 'civilised' style – are mixed with something much more spikier, or flatter. Through both its lofty, heavily metaphorical diction and its erratic pentameter, "In the Mecca" calls up a high style that it draws on for force but also for irony and exhaustion and disappointment.

About a third of the way into the poem, Mrs. Sallie notices that one of her children is not in their apartment. She does so in the only two upper-case lines of the poem (p. 13). The urgency here is marked; these lines are isolated on the page. Brooks might have been expected to turn to free verse to register this alarm, where the bottom starts to drop out of Mrs. Sallie's world, but she does not: it is blank verse. If you hear the two all-caps lines out of context, they do not sound like iambic pentameter – the first line in particular creates what seems to be an aggressively falling rhythm with a lurch in the middle. But its substitutions are in fact traditional: a trochee in the first foot for "SÚDDEN|LY" and an equally common extra syllable in the last foot. The mother's panic fits in the framework of iamb-dominated pentameter; but while real speech and blank verse exist in literally the same space, they do so at times uneasily – an unease that Brooks probes.

The blank verse of "In the Mecca" can simultaneously suggest how a line is spoken, and push the rhythms of speech against palpable artificiality. After realising she has no idea where her daughter has gone, Mrs. Sallie turns to her children, asking them one by one if they know. Her first address – "Càp, whére | Pepít|a" (p. 13) – has a tentative feel to it: both syllables in that first foot require emphasis, with a pause in between, as if Mrs. Sallie might hesitate, just for a second, to give voice to her fear. But once she does, she repeats the same two-word question to each of her children, each time landing on "where", until the narrative voice takes over; that voice then paraphrases the question in the more elevated, periphrastic style of formal written English, asking where "may" the daughter "be" (p. 13). In this passage, the strain between blank verse and the rhythms of Black vernacular speech, and stylised language and verisimilitude, is audible.

At other moments, though, pentameter and speech seem meant for each other, as when blank verse captures the memories and speech habits of an aged neighbour – a great-great grandmother and former slave. After briefly telling Mrs. Sallie that she hasn't seen Pepita, this neighbour describes her childhood in a cabin with a leaking roof and dirt floor. In one of the poem's longest passages of direct speech, she remembers an unnamed "Something", a pest that "creebled" and "squished" on the floor (p. 15), and which she and her siblings used to "stomp" (much as the children in the Mecca stomp cockroaches, eighty years later). The blank verse of the great-great grandmother's speech is different from the uncanny, austere,

92   *Calista McRae*

more formal passages described above: its short, tight, enjambed sentences seem to fall into pentameter effortlessly, as if to assert that suppressed histories and experiences have a right to this form.

Blank verse can be warped or wielded; it can shine or hide. In the poem's second-to-last paragraph, the one that reveals Pepita's death, Brooks continues to gesture towards and frustrate pentameter. She begins with a declaration that seems jarringly, awkwardly, haltingly trochaic (p. 31). Traditionally, you can scan it as a headless line, one beginning with what is known as a 'defective foot' (a single syllable missing its other half), but the initial reading is disorientating. Just under half of the lines that follow – of tragic, gruesome disclosure – are very rough pentameter, with late caesuras and harsh enjambments that force syntax against metre. Several other lines have too many syllables, or too few. Take the middle two lines of the sixteen-line passage: one is textbook pentameter with no substitutions, almost too perfectly summarising Pepita's death; the next, however, cuts off at nine syllables, refusing the neatness and epigrammatic power and closure of pentameter.

In 1965 – just a few years after Brooks' "In the Mecca" – the critic Paul Fussell estimated that approximately three quarters of English poetry was in blank verse (63). In the fifty-five years since, that proportion has changed. Partly in reaction to twentieth-century waves of attack on and defences of blank verse, blank verse has become largely the realm of formalists and more recently of neoformalists. One thread of contemporary blank verse tends to position itself as seamlessly joining a centuries-long tradition. Another thread seeks out ways of binding this traditional form to new kinds of wildness or roughness – sometimes through metrical interference, but also through indecorous subject matter, or even through typography. For instance, blank verse loses most appearance of conventionality when relaying a Ouija board's snarky all-caps pronouncements in James Merrill's epic *The Changing Light at Sandover* (1982).

In Amit Majmudar's "The Miscarriage" (2005), about the hours just after a pregnancy loss, the needed edge of unpredictability comes from leaving out all punctuation: the poem is made of several paragraphs of run-on sentences. Majmudar documents a barrage of emotions: the bitter knowledge that "some species lay / a purple froth of eggs and leave it there" (ll. 2–3) with more success, the partly shared sorrow, the eventual return of hope. The prosody is quite regular, but because Majmudar forgoes the tonal guidance of commas and semicolons, the statements of "The Miscarriage" remain difficult to pin down. We have seen blank verse sound dramatic, domestic, and uncanny; this blank verse feels desolate, a bit numb, a bit as if it is on autopilot. It is one more extension of blank verse's ever-adapting form.

Blank Verse 93

NOW READ ON…

- As blank verse is often associated with longer forms, you will find discussions of blank verse in use in the chapters on the ⏥ epic, the ⏥ dramatic monologue, and the ⏥ long poem.
- On the surface, they may be easily confused as neither form employs rhyme, but it may be well worth comparing and contrasting blank verse with ⏥ free verse.
- For other famous works making conspicuous use of blank verse, see, for instance, John Keats, *The Fall of Hyperion*; Robert Frost, *North of Boston*; Robert Browning, "Fra Lippo Lippi"; Robert Hayden, "Middle Passage".

Note

1 Since "In the Mecca" extends over thirty pages, and since its lines are occasionally broken and spaced in ways that make counting them ambiguous, for this poem the information given in brackets refers to page numbers.

References

Brooks, Gwendolyn. *In the Mecca*. Harper and Row, 1968.

Coleridge, Samuel Taylor. "Frost at Midnight". *Poetical Works*, ed. Ernest Hartley Coleridge. Oxford UP, 1969, pp. 240–242.

Fussell, Paul. *Poetic Meter and Poetic Form*. Rev. ed. Random House, 1979.

Majmudar, Amit. "The Miscarriage". *Poetry*, October 2005. https://www.poetryfoundation.org/poetrymagazine/poems/46348/the-miscarriage.

Milton, John. *Paradise Lost*, ed. Barbara K. Lewalski. Blackwell Publishing, 2007.

Shaw, Robert. *Blank Verse: A Guide to Its History and Use*. Ohio UP, 2007.

Webster, John. *The Duchess of Malfi*. New Mermaids, ed. Brian Gibbons, 4th ed. Methuen Drama, 2001.

Weinfield, Henry. *The Blank-Verse Tradition from Milton to Stevens: Freethinking and the Crisis of Modernity*. Cambridge UP, 2012.

9 The Blazon

Jordan Kistler

I

The *blazon* (sometimes 'blason') is a form of love poetry popular in the late medieval and early modern periods. Its name is taken from the French for 'coat of arms' or 'shield' in traditional heraldry. 'To blazon' was to describe arms or other heraldic devices; it is a tradition of describing or cataloguing parts. The literary blazon, too, offers a catalogue of the physical attributes of a subject, usually a woman. The device was made popular by the Italian poet Petrarch (Francesco Petrarca) in the fourteenth century, and was used extensively by Elizabethan poets in England, including William Shakespeare.

Petrarch's *Il Canzoniere* ('Song Book'), a collection of 366 poems, describes his unrequited love for Laura, a married woman. This sequence was highly influential, establishing conventions of love poetry that would remain in use for hundreds of years. In sonnet 157 of the sequence, we find a good example of the blazon. Sonnet 157 is a 'Petrarchan' or 'Italian' sonnet, which divides the fourteen lines of a ⌀ sonnet into an octave (first eight lines) and a sestet (final six lines). In the sestet of this sonnet, we find the elements of the blazon: a catalogue of Laura's body parts described through simile. Her hair is like "gold" (l. 9), her eyes are like "stars" (l. 10), her cheeks like "snow" (l. 9), her mouth like a "rose" (l. 12), her teeth like "pearls" (l. 11). The conventional blazon compares the beloved woman's body parts to natural objects, like the rose, or objects of great value, like gold or pearls. Petrarch also establishes the conventional parts described in the blazon: eyes, lips, teeth, cheeks, hair, and brow. This poem, and the others in *Il Canzoniere*, set the standard for amatory poetry for much of the next several hundred years across Europe.

Petrarch's work was very influential on sixteenth-century sonneteers in England, including William Shakespeare, Philip Sidney, Michael Drayton, and Edmund Spenser. As Nancy J. Vickers argues, "his portrayal of feminine beauty became authoritative" (265). This influence is evident in Spenser's *Amoretti* (1595), a series of eighty-nine sonnets and six songs devoted to his wife, Elizabeth.[1] In the fifteenth poem of the sequence, we find a typical example of the English blazon. In this sonnet, Spenser

DOI: 10.4324/9781003244004-11

The first six lines of the poem establish the metaphor, in which Elizabeth
will be compared to earthly treasures traded by "Merchants" (l. 1) around
the globe. The next six lines compare the traditional body parts of the
blazon – brow, hair, lips, eyes, and teeth – to various precious metals and
gems such as "Saphyres" (l. 7), "Rubies" (l. 8), and "Yvorie" (l. 10), re-
peating the hair of gold and teeth of pearls exactly from Petrarch.

II

While the blazon was still at the height of its popularity, the tradition of
the *contreblazon* developed; these poems mock or parody the blazon. The
most famous example of a contreblazon is likely Shakespeare's sonnet 130,
"My mistress' eyes are nothing like the sun". Dedicated to a 'dark lady',
this poem satirises the clichés of love poetry found in the blazon. Shake-
speare insists that his dark lady is not as lovely as the beauties of nature; her
lips are not so red, her skin not so white. By refusing to compare her to
the sun, coral, snow, or roses (ll. 1–5), Shakespeare rejects the hyperbole of
the blazon tradition, suggesting that it is possible to love a woman who is
merely human. Thus, the sonnet concludes: "And yet, by heaven, I think
my love as rare / As any she belied with false compare" (ll. 13–14).

Yet, Shakespeare's blazon is not as different from Petrarch's and Spens-
er's as it might initially seem. All three poems demonstrate a core problem
with this form of amatory poetry: "the act of praising the woman is an act
of self-fashioning" (Baker 9). Spenser and Shakespeare write English rather
than Italian sonnets, but both follow a similar formula, which includes a
'turn' that reverses the poem's opening position. Traditionally, the octave
of an Italian sonnet introduces a problem, expresses a desire, or presents a
troubling situation, while the sestet offers a solution or resolution of some
kind. In this form of the sonnet, the ninth line is known as the *volta* (Ital-
ian for 'turn'). This is where the poem turns from problem to solution. An
English sonnet, in contrast, is divided into three quatrains (four lines) and
a couplet. In this form, the 'turn' comes at the couplet, which traditionally
presents the moral of the poem or summarises its content in an axiomatic
fashion. Looking closely at the turn in each of these sonnets reveals that
these blazons are only *ostensibly* about the woman they describe; all three
are, in fact, far more about the poet than his beloved.

The problem posed by Petrarch in the octave of sonnet 157 is a problem
about poetry, not love. These eight lines introduce doubt about the power of
poetic expression, claiming that "no genius" (l. 4) could successfully portray
Laura's beauty. Yet, the sestet (the solution) goes on to do just that, in terms
that proved highly influential on poetry for hundreds of years. In these six
lines, Petrarch demonstrates both the power of poetry and his own mas-
tery of poetic expression. Though the sonnet describes Laura, what it really
showcases is not Laura or her beauty, but Petrarch's skill as a poet.

96   *Jordan Kistler*

The turn that comes in Spenser's *Amoretti* 15 is a turn from the external to the internal. In the final couplet, Spenser undermines the form of the blazon by arguing that Elizabeth's real value is internal; that which is "fairest" is her mind. The sonnet thus more widely chides those who focus only on external beauty. Yet, again it could be argued that this poem is more about Spenser than his beloved. We actually learn very little about Elizabeth in this poem, except that she seems to have the identical golden hair and red lips of all other women ever addressed in love poetry. The final couplet, in which the moral or the message of the poem is contained, is not really about Elizabeth at all. It is about Spenser, and his ability to see her for what she is really worth. He favourably contrasts himself with the "Merchants" of line 1 and, implicitly, the rest of mankind. He is one of the "few" who "behold" (l. 13) the real treasure that Elizabeth has to offer. It is, therefore, his own "vertues" (l. 14), rather than hers, that become the focus of the sonnet.

Similarly, Shakespeare's sonnet 130 ends with a couplet that presents the moral of the poem; Shakespeare argues his love is not less real than other poets' simply because he refuses to write in the false style they favour. Again, the turn is from the beloved to the poet. It is the quality of *his love*, rather than *her beauty*, that is his subject. All three sonnets, therefore, praise the poet far more than the beloved, lauding his talents and virtues, over her mere beauty.

In fact, feminist critics of the blazon tradition note that the female beloved is more of an absence than a presence in these poems. As a collection of pearly teeth, golden hair, and rosy lips, none of the women are individual or unique. They are, rather, just the idea or the *ideal* of a beautiful woman. The fact that much of the love poetry of this period is addressed to generic female names – like 'Stella' and 'Celia' – rather than specific women intensifies the impression that these poems are not about the beloved at all. Rather, as Moira Baker argues, the woman serves as a mirror which "reflects back to the speaker his own act of self-creation as a master-poet" (10).

III

This is not the only fault that feminist critics have found with this poetic tradition. The blazon is a form of praise poetry and courtship poetry; the poet flatters the female beloved with the extensive description of her beauty in an attempt to woo her. However, feminist critics in the twentieth and twenty-first centuries have suggested that the idea of 'cataloguing' a woman's body is not actually flattering to the beloved, as it reduces her to her a set of body parts to be displayed to the reading audience – with or without her permission. These critics, then, have challenged us to consider issues of consent and autonomy in these poems. As we will see, however, the earliest writers of blazons were aware of these potential objections, as

Thomas Campion's "There is a Garden in her Face" (1601) demonstrates. Campion's eighteen-line lyric poem conforms to the conventional blazon in the parts of the woman's face he describes – lips, teeth, eyes, and brows – and the similes employed, like pearl teeth and rose lips. Yet, the theme he develops is one of consent, through the refrain of "cherry ripe": "There cherries grow which none may buy / Till 'Cherry ripe' themselves do cry" (ll. 5–6). Though this beloved is beautiful like pearls, flowers, and fruit, which can all be picked out of nature by anyone who wants them, she is still a person with agency and thus is not for sale. Campion resists the logic of these conventional similes and thus resists the commodification of women common to the blazon tradition. Furthermore, he grants the beloved quoted speech. "Cherry ripe" are her words, not his. This is unusual in the blazon form, which normally represents the beloved as the silent and passive object of the speaker's active love.

Despite this, we may still question how much agency this beloved is granted in a poem that centres on her 'ripeness'. This word choice conjures the image of a young girl on the cusp of maturity, suggesting that her readiness to be bought or plucked is signalled by a physical change in her body, the 'ripening' of puberty and sexual awakening. This physical change is not something she has control over and is not necessarily indicative of emotional or intellectual readiness. Moreover, the very existence of the poem undermines its message. Campion enjoins his audience to wait for her consent, but the poem itself refuses to do so. The final stanza details her attempts to divert sexual attention, of "hand or eye" (l. 16), away from herself, but the "eye" of the poem is fixed steadily upon her, displaying her to the reading public, despite her wishes.

The blazon is a display: display of poetic skill and display of the beloved. Many twentieth and twenty-first century critics, therefore, have pointed to the blazon as a poetic enactment of the 'male gaze'. Coined by the film critic Laura Mulvey in the 1970s, the 'male gaze' describes the objectification of women for male pleasure. Mulvey discussed cinema specifically, but the concept of the male gaze has since been extended to other media – including poetry. Mulvey writes:

> In a world ordered by sexual imbalance, pleasure in looking has been split between active/male and passive/female. The determining male gaze projects its phantasy on to the female figure which is styled accordingly. In their traditional exhibitionist role women are simultaneously looked at and displayed, with their appearance coded for strong visual and erotic impact so that they can be said to connote *to-be-looked-at-ness*. (11)

Mulvey draws our attention to the power imbalance embedded into the male gaze, in which the male subject is rendered active while the female object is passive. She further notes the meaning that is mapped onto that

98 *Jordan Kistler*

female object through the male gaze. Displayed for men's erotic fantasies, she is not a person with thoughts and feelings of her own, but merely a receptacle for male fantasies. We find a similar power imbalance built into the conventions of the blazon. The nature of the blazon, a record of a man's love for an unattainable woman, necessarily presents the male speaker as an active, feeling subject, while the beloved is merely the *object* of his affections. While the male poet addresses sometimes hundreds of sonnets to her, she is completely silent and passive. She does not respond. His thoughts, his feelings, and his desires define her. She has none of her own.

Seen in these terms, blazons enact male fantasies. As Baker insists, "the subject of much of [this] erotic verse is not woman's body at all, but the male poet's power to appropriate that body and manipulate it in language to create delicious fantasies for himself" (17). The blazon allows the poet access to the female body that he would not otherwise be granted (since she spurns his love). Yet, as Mulvey notes, women are "simultaneously looked at and displayed". The blazon is not a private fantasy, but a public display; these poems have an audience. Though the blazon is categorised as a form of courtship poetry, the implied audience of this form of poetry is not the beloved. Blazons are rarely addressed directly *to* the woman, and when they are, they still present her as an object to be admired, in part by the reading audience. Pleasure in looking, as Mulvey argues, is coded male. Thus, the implied audience for the blazon can be assumed to be other men. Within this framework, the female beloved is reduced to a commodity traded between men.

The objectification and commodification of the beloved is readily apparent in Spenser's *Amoretti* 15. The parts of the beloved described in the poem – eyes, lips, teeth, forehead, hair, and hands – are placed explicitly within an economic market. They are like the "pretious things" (l. 2) bought and sold by "tradefull Merchants" (l. 1). Rather than conceiving of romance as an exchange between a man and a woman, the poem reduces the beloved into a 'thing' that can be traded between men. Furthermore, Spenser sets this sonnet against a backdrop of British maritime exploration, expansion, and empire, introducing not just trade but exploitation to his extended metaphor. The merchants of the first line seek treasure in "both the Indias" (l. 3). This poem was published in 1595; British merchants were granted royal permission to trade in India in 1591. The British East India Company, which would go on to seize large parts of the Indian subcontinent, establishing British rule in the region that would last until 1947, was officially established just five years after the poem's publication. Empire and conquest underpin the poem and its description of the beloved, implying not just that she can be bought and sold, but that she could also be forcibly taken. While these are "tradefull Merchants", Spenser also says that they "spoile" India of its treasures. In the early modern period, 'spoil' means to rob or plunder; to take by force, rather than by trade. It further carried connotations of disrobing or unclothing. Thus, Spenser raises the spectre of rape in this poem. Though some of the beloved's virtues are 'hidden' and safe from spoile, her beauty is brazenly displayed, and thus at risk of plunder. The threat of sexual violence haunts this sonnet.

Though considered a form of love poetry, therefore, the blazon can be seen to objectify, commodify, and dehumanise women through the 'male gaze', which grants power to the active male voyeur and renders the woman silent, passive, and powerless. Reduced to "a collection of exquisitely beautiful disassociated objects" (Vickers 266), blazons develop the subjectivity of the male poet at the expense of the female beloved.

IV

After enjoying enormous popularity in the fifteenth and sixteenth centuries, the blazon's fortunes waned in the seventeenth and eighteenth centuries. Yet, it was revived again in the nineteenth century by poets who were fascinated by the past and by past forms of art. This period saw a 'medieval revival' in architecture, fashion, and literature; poets revived several medieval and early modern forms of writing, including the ⟋ sonnet sequence, the ⟋ ballad, and the blazon. The criticism of the gendered power dynamics of the blazon outlined in this chapter began with second-wave feminist literary criticism in the 1970s. However, we find similar criticism in the Victorian revivals of the early modern form. Victorian poets did not simply revive the blazon; they used the form to critique the gender roles that underpin it and that were being reinscribed within their own society in ideologies like 'separate spheres' and 'the angel in the house'.[2]

The most explicit critique of both male artists and the blazons they write comes from Christina Rossetti in the sonnet "In an Artist's Studio" (composed in 1856). In this sonnet Rossetti describes the studio of her own brother, the pre-Raphaelite painter and poet Dante Gabriel Rossetti, where "One face looks out from all his canvases" (l. 1). In the 1850s, Dante Gabriel's work was dominated by his 'muse' and fiancée, Elizabeth Siddal. Yet, like modern critics of the blazon, Rossetti highlights the way this form of 'worship' obscures individuality, reducing the beloved to a conventional ideal instead of a fully realised person; she becomes "one selfsame figure" (l. 2) who is somehow less than whole, less than human. She is "hidden" (l. 3), "nameless" (l. 6), with only "one meaning" (l. 8): her beauty in the eye of the male artist.

As Slavoj Zizek argues, in the conventional blazon "the Lady functions as a mirror onto which the subject projects his narcissistic ideal" (96). Rossetti levels this same critique at the male painter, accusing him of failing to see the female beloved "as she is" (l. 13). The octave of the sonnet describes the paintings, but the sestet turns to the real woman behind these images, revealing her to be far different than what the artist paints. She is "wan" and "dimmed" by sorrow (l. 12). Yet, he sees only his own fantasy, his "dream" (l. 14).

100 *Jordan Kistler*

Like the feminist critics that would deconstruct this genre of poetry in the twentieth and twenty-first centuries, Rossetti recognises objectification as a form of violence. As Norman Bryson has argued,

> [t]he etymology of the word *regard* points to far more than the rudimentary act of looking: the prefix with its implication of an act that is always repeated, already indicates an impatient pressure within vision … its epithets tend toward a certain violence (penetrating, piercing, fixing). (Bryson 93)

Rossetti makes this clear in the *volta*, which dramatically shifts the tone of the poem: "He feeds upon her face by day and night" (l. 9). Rossetti casts the male gaze as vampiric. His art doesn't just reflect her beauty, it consumes it. Rossetti suggests this is not the unfortunate by-product of art, but rather its *purpose*. By draining the life from her, he renders her silent, passive, and submissive, remaking her into the ideal beloved of the blazon.

This theme is taken even further in Algernon Charles Swinburne's "The Leper" (1866). Swinburne situates his lengthy ♫ dramatic monologue explicitly within the tradition of medieval and early modern amatory poetry. Adopting a medieval setting and metre, the poem purports to be based on a manuscript from 1505, and depicts the worshipful devotion of a lowly clerk to a high-born lady. The first three stanzas of the poem conform closely to the conventions of the blazon: the beloved is a cruel and uncaring mistress, whom the clerk watches devotedly from afar, admiring her lips, hair, and brows. Yet, in this poem, not all is as it seems. Like Rossetti, Swinburne peels back the attractive surface of the blazon to reveal the reality of the situation, which is particularly horrible here. Swinburne takes Rossetti's critique of the conventions governing the blazon to its natural conclusion, insisting that the ideal woman of the blazon is not just silent and passive: she is dead.

Swinburne literalises the figurative fragmentation of the beloved inherent to the blazon, in order to forcefully argue that the reduction of a woman to her body parts is dehumanising. Over the course of the poem, we learn that the beloved contracted leprosy and was expelled from her aristocratic home. The clerk took her in and cared for her in her illness – and continues to keep her body, six months after her death. Swinburne chose leprosy specifically because of the popular belief that the disease causes the body to fall apart before death. Early in the poem the clerk watches the lady, and talks of her lips, her hair, her brow, her eyes, and especially her feet. The figurative dismemberment enacted by his dissecting male gaze, which reduces her to the "eroticized part" (Baker 19), becomes all too real later in the poem. For instance, in lines 32–36, the clerk fantasises about holding the lady's dainty feet in his hands. This image returns in line 102, except now she is dead. Even more, she is leprous and rotted, confronting the reader with the suspicion that the "two cold feet" he holds in his hands might no longer be attached to her body. Similarly, in the first half of the poem, the clerk fantasises about what the lady was like in bed with her former lover, picturing her "body broken up with love" (l. 62). This image returns later in the poem, but has become literal: she has "shed life out by fragments'" (l. 97), helped along by the clerk's 'love' and obsessive handling of her rotting body. These are deliberately grotesque images that serve to remind us that the beloved was *already* "broken up" and "fragment[ed]" long before the disease took hold, by the clerk's gaze and by the form of the blazon. She was nothing but lips, hair, brows, and feet to begin with. Swinburne exposes the toxic nature of this kind of poetry and the form of romance it reifies. "The Leper" is an inversion of love poetry: all the acts and tropes are the same, but the outcome is death rather than love.

The blazon as a form is easy to spot; any poem that contains a catalogue of body parts, especially when those parts are the hair, lips, brow, teeth, eyes, and hands of a woman, is a blazon. It can be used to explore a number of different topics, from the earliest blazons which functioned as both love poetry and a celebration of the poet's own 'genius', to later works which use the form in order to deconstruct the gender norms of their time. The blazon can be used to praise or condemn; it can be about the beloved or the poet or art itself. It can be misogynistic or feminist, conventional or utterly surprising. It is both a very simple form of poetry, with few rules, and a liberating one, which can be used to any number of poetic ends.

NOW READ ON...

- This chapter emphasises the role that Petrarch and the ⟳ sonnet tradition played in early modern literature.
- The present chapter discusses Swinburne's "The Leper" in terms of the blazon but also points out that it is a ⟳ dramatic monologue.
- Further examples of the Victorian deconstruction of the blazon can be found in Christina Rossetti's *Monna Innominata*, as well as Elizabeth Siddal's "Love and Hate" and "The Lust of the Eyes".

Notes

1 This sequence differs from the Petrarchan tradition in that it doesn't depict unrequited love. Rather, it details the successful courtship and eventual marriage of Spenser to his wife Elizabeth.

2 'Separate spheres' dictated that the public, commercial, and political world was the domain of men, while the domestic (the home) was the proper sphere for women. This was reinforced by the veneration of the ideal wife in the form of the 'Angel in the House', taken from Coventry Patmore's 1854 poem of the same name. The Angel in the House was maternal, self-sacrificing, and morally pure.

102 *Jordan Kistler*

References

Baker, Moira P. "'The Uncanny Stranger on Display': The Female Body in Sixteenth- and Seventeenth-Century Love Poetry". *South Atlantic Review* 56.2 (May 1991), pp. 7–25.

Bryson, Norman. *Vision and Painting: The Logic of the Gaze.* Yale UP, 1983.

Campion, Thomas. "There is a Garden in her Face". *The Norton Anthology of Poetry*, eds. Margaret Ferguson, Mary Jo Salter and Jon Stallworthy, 5th ed. W. Norton, 2005, p. 282.

Mulvey, Laura. "Visual Pleasure and Narrative Cinema". *Screen* 16.3 (Autumn 1975), pp. 6–18.

Petrarca, Francesco. "Sonnet 157". *One Hundred Sonnets: Translated after the Italian of Petrarca with the Original Texts, Notes, and a Life of Petrarch*, ed. Susan Wollaston. Edward Bull, 1841, p. 119.

Rossetti, Christina. "In an Artist's Studio". *The Norton Anthology of Poetry*, eds. Margaret Ferguson, Mary Jo Salter and Jon Stallworthy, 5th ed. W. Norton, 2005, p. 1129.

Shakespeare, William. "Sonnet 130". *The Norton Anthology of Poetry*, eds. Margaret Ferguson, Mary Jo Salter and Jon Stallworthy, 5th ed. W. Norton, 2005, p. 267.

Spenser, Edmund. "Amoretti 15". *The Norton Anthology of Poetry*, eds. Margaret Ferguson, Mary Jo Salter and Jon Stallworthy, 5th ed. W. Norton, 2005, p. 191.

Swinburne, Algernon Charles. "The Leper". *The Broadview Anthology of Victorian Poetry and Poetic Theory*, eds. Thomas J. Collins and Vivienne J. Rundle. Broadview P, 1999, pp. 987–989.

Vickers, Nancy J. "Diana Described: Scattered Woman and Scattered Rhyme". *Critical Inquiry* 8.2 (Winter, 1981), pp. 265–279.

Zizek, Slavoj. "From Courtly Love to *The Crying Game*". *New Left Review* 1.202 (November 1, 1993), pp. 95–108.

10 Concrete Poetry

Tymon Adamczewski

I

Often synonymous with typographical experimentation, concrete poetry is a multifaceted literary form which explores the relationship between words, images, and sound. The texts included under this rubric literally come in various shapes and sizes as they fuse the form with the meaning they attempt to convey. This frequently includes spatial and graphic practices associated with the layout of words or letters as recorded both on the printed page and beyond. In this sense, concrete poetry can be regarded as an attempt at testing the audience's conventional expectations of a literary work, which testifies to an intriguing linguistic creativity that probes the very limits of communication, especially by means of visualising the language and its most minute building blocks (words or letters).

Drawing on various past sources of inspiration, which go back at least to modernist avant-gardes like Dadaism or Futurism, and indirectly even to the renaissance (e.g. pattern poetry) or much earlier forms of problematising textual materiality (e.g. carmina figurata), concrete poetry might also be thought about as a fairly recent occurrence in a much longer tradition of thinking through the consequences of print and writing. While these technologies allowed for material and visual recording of speech and verbal communication, they also imposed various rules and limitations for authors and audiences (like the Western custom of reading from left to right or from top to bottom). Concrete poetry challenges many such customary regulations. It does not only employ unusual layout or unconventional typeface, colour, and printing procedures but frequently places disparate elements of language (from letters through inscriptions to whole stanzas or poems) *physically* outside the printed page (e.g. in various public spaces like parks, walls, tube stations, etc.). Additionally, many texts deliberately play around with literature's overlapping with other media so it also includes artistic installations, performance art, or digital work. Despite the reliance on the very physicality of inscription and writing, some concrete texts point to the musical qualities of words, speech, and communication itself which is often lost in print. Many such works, often conceptual in nature and execution, contain a strong sonic component which brings them closer to sound poetry.

DOI: 10.4324/9781003244004-12

104　*Tymon Adamczewski*

As a literary and artistic current, the practices associated with concrete poetry have a convoluted history, especially since many of the exponents (and critics) had very different notions of this poetic form. It originated in German-speaking countries, roughly around the 1950s, although it is frequently considered an international movement owing to the prominent founding work of the Brazilian Noigandres group (est. in São Paulo in 1952) and following a particularly welcoming reception and academic attention in the anglophone world, which became home to a lot of important anthologies (e.g. Bann 1967, Solt 1968, Williams 1967). Having subsequently flourished in various places around the world (from Austria, Czechoslovakia, and Poland, through Japan, Turkey, or Finland, to Portugal or Iceland), it is no small wonder that in the introduction to her anthology, which includes artists from even more countries, Mary Ellen Solt expresses the difficulties in actually defining the form.

Marked with a need to return to the concrete materiality of words, many works from the period between the 1950s and the 1970s can be seen as a general response to post-war politics and share similar sentiments to versions of modernism, like the Dadaists, for example, for whom the conventional language was compromised by ideology (see Thomas). Among other important contexts for this poetic form are the 1960s dematerialising tendencies in art, especially in conceptual or minimalist practices popular at the time. These are perhaps most pronounced in the case of concrete painting which intended to deliberately draw attention to its own material in an orderly, clear, and deliberate fashion, instead of aiming to represent something external to the medium of artistic expression. For concrete poets, language, with its very materiality, was often both the medium *and* the content. Paradoxically, such thinking generally opposed the abstract form of artistic expression and was supposed to manifest 'concrete' meanings (hence the name) which would take the audience beyond thinking about art as figurative or representational.

II

But how does concrete poetry work exactly? One way in which this might be illustrated is a comparison between a seemingly conventional text and a more experimental one. Most people's associations with what a 'typical' poem is (assuming for a moment the validity of such a term), or, more importantly, the way such a traditional text works may be easily illustrated with William Wordsworth's famous poem known as "The Daffodils" (1807). This is also known by its incipit line "I wandered lonely as a cloud", which already stages the classical Romantic understanding of a poetic text – one which places the speaker at its forefront and right from the start signals an interest in recording one's experiences with the object that is being described (in this case, the flowers). Symptomatically, much of what is stereotypically associated with lyrical texts is modelled on such a subjective perspective:

the daffodils (object of description) are just an excuse for the speaker (the subject) to dwell on their emotions and experiences. The eponymous flowers in this case are personified and serve as a springboard for remembering past moments in life. Such literariness, understood as a deliberate 'estrangement' of language from its everyday (functional) use, achieved by the employment of poetic devices like metaphors and similes can be further contrasted with the dry, factual, and data-driven diction of an encyclopaedic definition. In this case, the daffodils (Lat. *Narcissus pseudonarcissus*) can be described as a perennial plant which "grows to about 41 cm (16 inches) in height [featuring] five or six linear leaves that grow from the bulb and are about 30 cm (12 inches) long" (Britannica). Without a doubt, such language choices are intended to produce an objective description – one which avoids literary ambiguity and the personal (subjective) colouring of the literary description. The seemingly universalising language, including physical dimensions of the flowers and the Latin-based scientific wording of the whole definition, is absent from Wordsworth's rendering, where the flowers are personified as dancing and animated. This, in turn, centres more on the romantic, highly sensitive speaking subject channelling their emotions into the language, for whom the flowers are just an occasion to dwell on the importance of collecting personal experiences.

If both the encyclopaedic definition and romantic poetry employ language in a fairly conventional way – to record and use expressive conventions and for unambiguous communication, respectively – concrete poetry draws more on the poetic tradition which is more ambiguous to take its elements even further. E.E. Cummings' "Grasshopper" (1935) might be a good example here as it is much closer to a visual manifestation of its content and the formal features of language. Starting with the poem's title, often actually spelled as "r-p-o-p-h-e-s-s-a-g-r", the readers are faced not with the traditional aim to *record* experience but more with the aim of staging the occasion to *enact* it. Instead of providing a lyrical account of *seeing* the grasshopper, the letters are scattered around the page in a seemingly random order. Thus, already at the first glance, the reader's gaze has to literally 'jump' from one place to another in a desperate attempt to make some sense of the marks which seem to randomly pepper the page, perhaps to imitate the fidgety movement of the insect itself. This certainly acts against the Western customary rules of reading (top down, left to right) and further contributes to viewing the whole poem as a visual work. Breaking the semantic content of texts like this one down to a minimum, such poems do not tell a story in a traditional sense (there's no narrative element) and are self-referential since they speak about, or enact, the possibilities of language, verse, and literary forms. Additionally, instead of adopting an authoritative position (that of an author or a speaker) to produce a description of a given object chosen for artistic/verbal rendering, concrete property aims to effect conditions for the audience to experience this, thus privileging the role of the reader in making meaning.

106   *Tymon Adamczewski*

III

It is precisely such activating features that might be seen in early concrete work of the influential Brazilian Noigandres group. Their members often aimed at achieving a unified aesthetic expression that was to stem from a bare-bones aesthetics of the deceptively simple graphic arrangement of words. "Silencio" (1953), by the Bolivian-born Swiss author Eugene Gomringer, a key figure for the movement, is a good example, as it successfully merges verbal and visual language while gesturing towards a sonic effect announced in the title. The poem is made up of the Spanish word for 'silence' which forms a rectangle filled with fourteen identical words surrounding an empty space in the middle. The austere form of the work (black font on a white background), with its blank central space not only alludes to the auditory effect achieved by the sudden absence of language, but also formally enacts it. This further interacts with the literary poetic tradition (e.g. of the fourteen lines to a ∅ sonnet) and with the limitations imposed by particular forms, but also fits into other contemporaneous tendencies, like John Cage's famous minimalist composition *4′33″* staging silence in musical terms which premiered only a year before. A similar case of spatial and typographical wordplay that fuses language, images, and differing meanings can be seen in Augusto de Campos' "Sem Um Numero" ("Without a Number") (1957). This visual poem, composed of a series of modifications to the title phrase, effects an almost physical sensation of rotation and twisting around the central 'nought' – a key zero-point of the text, as we trace how subsequent lines gradually contract and expand to manifest the changes in length and spelling of the words that form the title. The eponymous three-word phrase, indicating a lack of number, is transformed into "Um Sem Numero" ("numberless") as the phrase explores the ambiguities of language (grammar, phonetics) and at the same time conceptualises the main idea of numberless*ness*, further evoking emptiness or even infinity.

On the one hand, such multilayering of semantic ambiguities with visual and connotative wordplay accounts for the popularity of such works, but, on the other, it also documents a historical line of typographical experimentation. Running at least from George Herbert's early modern verse, through Stéphane Mallarmé's or Guillaume Apollinaire's typographical experiments, to modernist avant-garde aesthetics or works by poets like Dylan Thomas to name but a few significant stages, the coupling of linguistic and material elements in writing brings to mind a long-lasting and widespread preoccupation with materiality and meaning visible not only in the use of the 'international' sans serif font but also in concrete poetry's universal appeal. Following the influence of Futurism or Dadaism, the emphasis on modifying the language according to the constructivist rules of simplicity and clarity resulted in such concrete staples as various modifications to grammatical forms, spelling, and non-standard graphic distribution on the page resulting in deliberate shifts of meaning, which in many cases aimed at subverting the established, routine linguistic (common) sense.

While certainly intriguing, the examples above may render concrete poetry as a merely intellectual or even elitist practice detached from any social or cultural concerns. Such arguments can be refuted fairly easily, for example, when we look into texts like Décio Pignatari's "Bebe Coca Cola" (1957).

A subversive reworking of the power of advertising, the poem ironically comments on the use of language for persuasive purposes. The Portuguese version of the "Drink Coca Cola" slogan, rendered in the company's familiar colour coding (red and white), is dissected in subsequent lines into separate items: Cola (Engl. 'glue') and Coke (cocaine) to indicate the captivating yet deceptive allure of marketing practices. The message is, however, much more pessimistic as further lines hint more directly at the consequences of substance abuse, particularly with words "babe" and "caco" (Eng. 'drool' and 'shard', respectively) that lead on to the final line with a standalone word "cloaca" ('sewer' or 'cesspool') effectively evoking the dire consequences of addiction. Since similar rules for meaning making, relying on shifts or slips in spelling, have already been in operation for some time in the media and public discourse, Pignatari's work can be seen as criticising the incessant capitalist imperative of pumping up sales with advertising campaigns. These are seen as polluting language and communication with ideologically charged clichés. Interestingly, the poem carries

Figure 10.1 "Bebe Coca Cola" (1957) D. Pignatari, file authored by Vinicius Nacif, licensed under the CC 4.0 International, available at https://commons.wikimedia.org/wiki/File:Bebococapoema.gif.

out its semantic deconstruction by employing a similar play with connotations and phrasing that usually serve to boost sales. It further shows how such strategies, when employed by concrete poets and informed by modernist or avant-garde poetics, could address "the possibility of globally coherent modes of communication" otherwise perceived as only "tangentially responsive to the emergence of a global consumer-capitalist culture" (Thomas 5).

A similar sense of disillusionment with contemporary life and its waning spirituality can be seen in the works of one of the most recognisable artists associated with concrete poetry, Ian Hamilton Finlay. This Scottish poet, publisher, and designer of neoclassical gardens often transgressed disciplinary boundaries only to receive praise for his unfailing ability "to create poem-objects, inscriptions and sculpture" now largely regarded as prime examples of "the possibility concrete poetry represented" (Cockburn and Finlay 19). Minimalistic in his early compositions, Finlay also played around with the materiality of the book (cf. loose sheets of *Rapel* [1963]), effectively incorporating a personal dimension to the otherwise impersonal and cool concrete poetics. *Tea-leaves and Fishes* (1964), for instance, is printed on various landscape oriented sheets of pale-coloured, grainy paper many of which are of varying density and thickness but marked with visible (and palpable) texture. Thus, they not only appeal to the haptic sensations, making the whole interaction more sensual, but also give an impression of an accidental access to an intimate space for recording thoughts and feelings, giving off the impression of being jotted down in a diary-like volume. Similarly personal and corresponding to Hamilton's life-long fascination with seafaring culture is a humorous take on the topic which opens the book. Page 3, entitled "Landman's tea", displays a single letter t (at the same time resembling a fishing hook) and is immediately contrasted with "Fisherman's tea": a page containing the word 'tea^2' printed nine times and arranged in a 3×3 square. What looks like a mathematical formula turns into a witty play with the t/tea homophone allowing for a condensation of meaning, to a degree similar perhaps to the potency of the actual infusion brewed by the seasoned sailors and opposed to the weak 't[ea]' drunk by regular land-dwellers.

Concrete poetry, in this form, allows for stripping the language of the (unnecessary) expressive and subjective features of traditional communication. It allows one to introduce order and clarity, ideals celebrated by Finlay as reaching back at least to the classical culture, into the hazy, schizophrenic subject-driven, ego-culture of the contemporary world. Significantly, the international scope of such sentiments about the deliberate and minimalistic expressionism teased out from single typographical characters was shared around the globe. It is enough to look at Seiichi Niikuni's "Kawa mata wa Shu" (1966) to notice a similar approach to explorations of Japanese written symbols (ideographs), which stand for 'river' and 'sandbank', arranged in such a way to graphically represent the

Concrete Poetry 109

landscape and evoke the image of a riverbank. Symptomatically, the work successfully renders its semantic content already at the level of its visual form and through its links with landscape and writing may be used to introduce another spatial dimension to thinking about concrete poetry.

Indeed, Finlay takes these qualities even further by placing them beyond the printed page. While his works encompass various original variations on books, print, sculpture, and painting, his installations and terrain design usually incorporate linguistic elements: text, words, and letters. His works, near the Max Planck Institute in Stuttgart, Germany, for example, are a good illustration of such spatial understanding of concrete poetry. One of these is the 'Schiff' monument, which consists of

Figure 10.2 A wall poem in Leiden, the Netherlands, in Japanese, by Seiichi Niikuni. Photograph by David Eppstein, licensed under CC 3.0, available at https://commons.wikimedia.org/wiki/File:NiikuniSeiic hiShuKawaLeidenWallPoem.jpg.

two neatly rectangular stony slabs, symmetrically placed at opposing ends of a little similarly shaped pool. The German word for 'ship' is inscribed onto the internal surfaces of both blocks in such a way that one of the carvings can only be read when reflected on the water's surface. This work fuses the linguistic form with its referent, since the word itself, just like a ship it signifies, literally floats on water. In a way, it also develops the themes continuously important for the artist, like the idea of a distorted symmetry and perverted order, while exhibiting the awareness and significance of the surroundings and the natural environment in shaping the artistic message.

More work like this can be found in the neoclassical garden Finlay designed in the late 1960s together with his wife Sue. Located near Edinburgh, Little Sparta, formerly known as Stonypath, includes sculptures, poem-objects, garden temples, and ponds, all of which testify to the interest in ascribing cultural meaning to physical space. "The Present Order Is the Disorder of the Future" (1983) is a good example of this approach, which consists of granite slabs etched with an expression taken from the French revolutionary Louis Antoine de Saint Just.

Like many other objects in Little Sparta, this could be seen as a concrete poetry sculpture physically functioning within an artistically altered environment. Each word is inscribed onto a separate monumental piece of stone which, together with the classical capitalised font, evokes a sense of historical gravity of the message. The solemnity effected by the combination of matter, form, and language is perhaps made even graver when we recall that Saint Just was one of the fiercest and most dogmatic agents responsible for the terrors and executions during the French Revolution. Thus, Finlay's work offers not only a bitter comment on the fate of radical ideals but also problematises the textual, poetic, and aesthetic orders, rules, and dogmas. Ideas of clarity, minimalism, and purity become tainted with the awareness of history, which necessarily needs to include not only the fate of turning into revolutionary violence when ideals are blindly followed, but also the invasive terraforming practices materially changing the surface of inscription, just like the author himself when digging the pond which can be seen just behind the place from which the poem can be read.

In this way, concrete poetry can be seen as an important language of addressing the past and the present. Owing to Finlay's versatile artistic skills, the questions of classical heritage reach out beyond the spaces of the garden or the printed page. While these issues can be identified as uncomfortable for contemporary society, the artist's version of concrete poetics, in most cases, managed to successfully translate such questions into the language of form, language, and style. By transcending both the physical limitations of the page and the immediacy of the fluctuating contemporaneous political affairs, concrete works can poignantly reference the repressed elements of cultural history, including the present-day neoliberal

Figure 10.3 Sculptures/objects in the sculpture park *Little Sparta* by Ian Hamilton Finlay in Scotland/UK. Photograph by yellow book ltd, licensed under the CC 2.0 Generic, available at https://commons.wikimedia.org/wiki/File:Little_Sparta_-_The_present_order_is_the_disorder_of_the_future_(St_Just).jpg.

tendencies to flatten out spiritual dimensions. Additionally, like in the case of Edwin Morgan (1920–2010), another renowned Scottish poet, critic, and academic, the critique may also be directed at the growing domination of seemingly universal standards. In fact, an important portion of Morgan's oeuvre explores concrete poetry's sonic dimension, notably because it allows to preserve and recall oral traditions. His work "expresses a more self-conscious desire than Finlay's to subvert the grammars of concrete poetry itself, turning it to a new range of expressive, descriptive, and polemical ends and to fantastical scenarios of communication ranging from outer space to the animal kingdom" (Thomas 15). Correspondingly, while "The Loch Ness Monster Song" (1990) at first glance may look like

112 *Tymon Adamczewski*

gibberish, Morgan's presentation of "Nessie, that most Scottish of clichés, in a sound poem" (Cockburn and Finaly 15), unfolds its true linguistic potential in a reading out aloud. Full of nonsense words and seemingly impossible to pronounce letter clusters in print, in an oral delivery the poem masterfully evokes Scottish sounds, consequently drawing attention to the political dimensions of language, accent, speech, and communication in a "refusal to endorse notions of universal linguistic value" (Thomas 15).

IV

While the examples chosen to represent concrete poetry in this chapter are mostly those by male authors, this gender bias stems more from the history of this form than a deliberate choice. Thus, it is important to note the active presence of people like Mary Ellen Solt, who influenced the reception and academic interest in concrete poetics by translating poems, editing influential anthologies and who, at the same time, contributed to the movement by composing works that take the form of the objects they refer to (cf. her anagrammatic poem "Forsythia" from the aptly titled collection *Flowers in Concrete*, 1966). A recent collection, entitled *Women in Concrete Poetry 1959–1975* (Balgiu and Torre), makes an important case for acknowledging how

> gender inequality was often explicitly denounced by the artists and poets in this anthology. They proved that questions of identity, gender, and power were not only *not* antithetical to concrete poetry, but also could be made intelligible – and could be activated – through the process of the materialisation of language. (Balgiu and Torre 14)

Concrete poetry as a poetic form which privileges the role of the reader in constructing meaning is thus also capable of recording both the past and future problematisation of the limitations and possibilities of writing, materiality, and reading as both experience and practice. Its continuous attempts at coupling form and content in linguistic, visual, and sonic means continue to act against a stale and routinised standardisation of language and communication. While certainly intellectual and demanding on the audience, it nevertheless opened many gateways for future works (e.g. in hypertext or born-digital works) which likewise fuse form with content. More importantly, it seems concrete poetry can still offer stimulating work, like, for instance, J.R. Carpenter's project entitled *This Is a Picture of Wind* (also published in book form in 2020) which uses her poetic descriptions of wind with actual weather readings and wind reports from from the South West of England southwest of England to generate lines of verse. Accessible online, these are as immaterial as they are fleeting and mutable, perhaps like the gusts of the very element that propels them into momentary linguistic being.

> ### NOW READ ON...
>
> - In creating its own forms, concrete poetry can in some senses be likened to ⏎ free verse.
> - The addition of a pictorial element means that concrete poetry can feature superficial overlaps with ⏎ ekphrastic poetry. That said, the chapter on ekphrastic poetry argues that word and image are never fully reconciled, which is exactly what concrete poetry sets out to achieve.

References

Balgiu, Alex, and Mónica de la Torre, eds. *Women in Concrete Poetry: 1959–1979.* Primary Information, 2020.

Bann, Stephen, ed. *Concrete Poetry: An International Anthology.* London Magazine Editors/Shenval P, 1967.

Britannica, The Editors of Encyclopaedia. "Daffodil". *Encyclopedia Britannica*, 22 June 2021. https://www.britannica.com/plant/daffodil. Accessed 1 December 2021.

Carpenter, J. R. *This Is a Picture of Wind.* Longbarrow P, 2020.

Cockburn, Ken, and Alec Finlay, eds. *The Order of Things: An Anthology of Scottish Sound, Pattern, and Concrete Poetry.* Polygon, 2001.

Solt, Mary Ellen, ed. *Concrete Poetry: A World View.* Indiana UP, 1968.

Thomas, Greg. *Border Blurs: Concrete Poetry in England and Scotland.* Liverpool UP, 2019.

Williams, Emmett, ed. *An Anthology of Concrete Poetry.* Something Else P, 1967.

11 The Dramatic Monologue

Gabriella Hartvig

I

The dramatic monologue is a distinct form of poetry, a poetical genre. This chapter begins with a definition of the term and how you may best recognise it through its main characteristics by which we can distinguish it from other poetical forms. A brief historical overview will follow in which some of the best-known critical approaches in the twentieth century will be mentioned which further refine our understanding. The poems that will be discussed in some detail show the evolution of the genre: I will discuss "Ulysses" (1842) by Alfred, Lord Tennyson, "My Last Duchess" (1842) by Robert Browning, "The Love Song of J. Alfred Prufrock" (1915) by T.S. Eliot, and, to also offer a contemporary example by a living Poet Laureate, Carol Ann Duffy's "Mrs Lazarus" (1999). Largely relying on the reader's understanding, the dramatic monologue invites a more intellectual and more psychological reading, which likens it to metaphysical poetry: in eliciting its meaning, much depends on the reader and on current cultural traditions. Therefore, we will also see how, over time, changing cultural norms and different literary conventions have shaped the form and carried additional meanings and purposes.

The dramatic monologue is a speech given by a fictional persona, a speaking voice, to an imaginary audience which is always present but never responds to it. Its distinctive elements were established by Ina Beth Sessions. These are: the speaker, a silent audience, the occasion on which the speech is given, revelation of character, interplay between the speaker and the audience, dramatic action, and that the action takes place in the present (508). In the latter half of the twentieth century, those formal features were complemented with further elements and given critical reassessment (e.g. in terms of psychological or political aspects of interpretation). The dramatic persona or speaker may be historical, mythical, or entirely fictional but this voice is never identical with the poet. The audience, the addressee of the speaker's monologue, is often identified with the reader, who can see behind the speaker's meaning and takes a critical attitude towards what is said. There is always an occasion, usually a life-changing event, or some kind of crisis, which bears great weight on the life of the

DOI: 10.4324/9781003244004-13

speaker. The words of the *dramatis personae* in any dramatic monologue are always indicative of their character; therefore their speech reveals more of their true nature than they intend to tell. Although the audience does not respond to the speaker's speech, yet its presence influences the speaker whose words are targeted at the silent listener. Thus, an exciting interplay develops where the reader often takes the position of the audience and judges the speaker's intentions. All this creates a dramatic action in the present between the speaker and the listener. The monologue of the persona, which has some reference to the poet's present, reveals a new, previously unheard of or disregarded, aspect of the speaker, which clashes with our historical knowledge and teaches us to look at well-known subjects from a new perspective.

II

Although the term itself was not used by them, the dramatic monologue was first widely employed by two Victorian poets, Alfred, Lord Tennyson and Robert Browning (Culler 366). Earlier examples of the form do exist, for example in metaphysical poetry, but it was after the largely lyrical voice of the Romantics that Tennyson turned to a more objective, staged form of poetry where he could distance the speaker from the poet: his poetical personae usually adopt the characters of mythical figures such as "Ulysses", "Tithonus", or "The Lotos Eaters". Many of Browning's speakers are historical characters such as Johannes Agricola, the Protestant theologian from the sixteenth century who features in "Johannes Agricola in Meditation", or Andrea del Sarto, the Italian Renaissance painter who inspired the eponymous poem. Some of Browning's dramatic monologues introduce imaginary characters who may represent a type such as the corrupted Catholic prelate of "The Bishop Orders His Tomb" or the murderous Duke of "My Last Duchess". The story is sometimes based on a real or probable event from the past as the unexpected and mysterious death of Lucrezia, the Duke of Alfonso II's very young wife who died soon after their marriage: the Duke of "My Last Duchess" may be modelled on the sixteenth-century Duke of Ferrara.

The term itself was coined in 1857 by George W. Thornbury, who referred to his own poems as "dramatic monologues" and by doing so established a new school of poetry (Culler 366). Browning did not use the actual term but he used similar expressions such as 'dramatic lyrics', 'dramatic romances and lyrics', or 'dramatis personae': in the advertisement to *Dramatic Lyrics* (1852), he refers to the shorter poems in the collection as "always dramatic in principle, and so many utterances of imaginary persons, not mine" (Browning, *Selected Poems*, 6, 884). Speaking of his *Dramatic Idyls* (1879), he explains that they are called dramatic because "the story is told by some actor in it, not by the poet himself" (qtd. in Culler 366). Tennyson's and Browning's use of the new poetic form gave

116 *Gabriella Hartvig*

rise to a critical history of the genre: around the turn of the century and in the following decades, many scholars discussed the main elements of the dramatic monologue. In his book *Browning and the Dramatic Monologue* (1908), Samuel S. Curry, recognising the readers' difficulty in understanding the dramatic form of many of Browning's poems, suggests that we read the poems as "one end of a conversation" and pay attention to its distinctive components: "We must realize the situation, the speaker, the hearer, before the meaning can become clear", he writes (7). Curry also points out that the dramatic monologue in its more lyrical form appeared long before it could gain a wider critical recognition; early examples are of lyrical monologues which, although they show "one end of a conversation", focus on emotions rather than the presence of a speaker or listener: "The Lover's Appeal" by Sir Thomas Wyatt, Christopher Marlowe's "The Passionate Shepherd to His Love", or Robert Burns' "John Anderson, My Jo" reveal not merely the speaker's emotions but they are also dramatic representations (115–117).

After the early critical discussions, Sessions clarifies the formal features of the genre in the 1940s. In her article on "The Dramatic Monologue" she examines the seven distinctive elements of "My Last Duchess", which she calls the most perfect embodiment of the poetical form (508). Her working definition is the most often used approach to the formal rules of the dramatic monologue.

What may distinguish earlier poems such as Romantic conversation poems from the Victorian dramatic monologue is that in earlier monologues the dramatis persona may have represented the poet's voice, whereas in the latter the speaker is clearly not the poet but someone else, there is a discrepancy between the poet and the speaker; the poet is distanced from the viewpoint and alleged purpose of the speaker, and so is the audience. After Sessions' formal analysis, studies in the latter half of the twentieth century started to pay more attention to psychological effects. In his book on *The Poetry of Experience* (1957), Robert Langbaum focuses on how the reader interprets the speaker's monologue whose attitude can be either sympathetic or judgemental. It is the reader's relation to the speaker, to the content of the poem, and to the speaker's audience which results in the singular meaning of the dramatic monologue (83). Langbaum calls attention to the importance of the non-formal elements of such poems: "Arguments cannot make the case in the dramatic monologue but only passion, power, strength of will and intellect" (86).

From the latter half of the twentieth century, critical approaches have concentrated more on an analysis of the mental state of the dramatic persona and how speakers view themselves, as set against the poet's own implied judgement. In his study on the *Dramatic Monologue* (1977), Alan Sinfield examines the "divided consciousness" that exists between the speaking voice and the poet's mind (32). He originates the dramatic monologue in an ancient poetical exercise, well known among Victorian poets, the

The Dramatic Monologue 117

prosopopoeia, or impersonation, as elaborated by Quintilian in his *Institutio Oratoria*. It was a rhetorical task in the study of public speaking given to young orators who had to adopt the imaginary character of famous historical persons such as Caesar or Cicero, and speak in their name (92).

More recently, the psychological and political aspects of oratory have been explored in twenty-first-century approaches. In *The Psychology of Victorian Poetry* (2012), Gregory Tate examines how the Victorian poem, especially Tennyson's poetry, is engaged with the study of the mind, and is informed by the latest discoveries of the newly born discipline of psychology. In the discussion of Carol Ann Duffy's poetry we will see that, in contemporary poetry, the dramatic monologue often serves a political as well as moral function by touching upon pressing issues such as social injustice, or the unequal treatment of sexes in contemporary society.

III

Both Tennyson's "Ulysses" and Browning's "My Last Duchess" take an incident and make it the central theme of their poem (Langbaum 91). Tennyson borrows the story of Ulysses after his return from the Trojan war from Homer and from Dante; Browning wrote a book review of Richard Henry Wilde's *Conjectures and Researches Concerning the Love, Madness, and Imprisonment of Torquato Tasso*, which is about the supposed love of the sixteenth-century Italian poet for Princess Leonora of Este; this might have given him the idea of creating the character of the Duke. In both cases, it is the reader's task to judge the speaker's purpose by setting the original context against the present of the poems. In *The Divine Comedy,* Ulysses does not return to Ithaca but persuades his mates to travel on: in *The Inferno* (Canto XXVI, 90ff.) Dante and his guide Virgil find Ulysses among the false counsellors and he tells the story of his disastrous last voyage to the Southern Hemisphere when a giant wave smashed the ship and killed everyone. In *Odyssey* (xi, 100–137), Ulysses is in Ithaca with his son and his wife Penelope and there is only a passing reference to his death by sea. Tennyson's Ulysses is an ageing hero, who has become a name, and who does not accept his old age and fragility but longs to explore the world. He speaks to his crew at the port and tries to convince them to set out to sea again, to go forward and not give up, even if they are old and may have to face death. The point he makes is that although his mariners and he may have been made weak by their age, inside they are as strong in their will as they have ever been, so it is not too late for them to seek out a new world. Written in unrhymed iambic pentameters, the poem appeared after the sudden death of Tennyson's close friend Arthur Hallam. It demonstrates the poet's intention to carry on and face the hardships of life after the shock of the early death of his friend. Listening to Ulysses, his audience experiences the disparity between his impossible desire and the fragility of his old age. The reader's attitude oscillates between sympathy for the one-time legendary hero and judgement of his willfulness and the infeasibility of his plan, which is also evidenced by Ulysses' prophesied failure and his ensuing death at sea. Ulysses' character is revealed by his persuasive speech, which is a beautiful rhetorical achievement. We understand his curiosity, the reasons why he cannot stay any longer, and why this moment is a turning point in his life: he despises his people, and is bored with the task of being a ruler; nothing holds him back from this new journey; he is not attracted to his ageing wife any longer, and he believes his son Telemachus is better suited for the duties of a king. But we also learn from his words which reveal hesitation that he is not fit for travelling – and he knows it. This introspection of the poetic voice shows the tension between one's noble desires and what values one would like to cling to among the calamities of life, which evokes our sympathy for Ulysses. On the other hand, the absurdity of his wish to travel beyond the physical world which is out of reach for the living also shows his great courage and fearlessness, which raises him above the living.

IV

Unlike Tennyson's Ulysses, Browning's Duke does not invoke much sympathy in the listener. His speech reveals his true character, his cruelty towards his late Duchess. This sixteenth-century Italian Duke was probably modelled on the fifth Duke of Ferrara, Alfonso II d'Este, who married the fourteen-year-old daughter of Cosimo I de' Medici: three years later she died under suspicious circumstances, presumably from poisoning. Browning's Duke intends to marry another Duke's daughter who sends his envoy to discuss the details of the wedding and the new Duchess's dowry. Instead, the Duke shows his late wife's portrait behind a curtain and talks about her supposed misbehaviour which had to be stopped. The fatal error she committed, and for which she had likely been ordered by her husband to be killed, was that she did not respect the very ancient name of the Duke and smiled at everyone and was too kind to others. We learn from the Duke's speech that it was beneath him to warn his wife. Showing the late Duchess's portrait to the envoy is an act of warning as regards the behaviour of the future wife: she must subject herself to her husband otherwise she may become just another picture in the Duke's portrait gallery.

"My Last Duchess" is a perfect illustration of the seven formal features of the dramatic monologue established by Sessions. The speaker is the Duke, who unknowingly reveals his true character, his dark personality, through his monologue. The envoy listens to the Duke's words, and we can imagine what message he will carry home. The occasion on which we hear the monologue is a significant event, the discussion of the details of the Duke's next marriage, which, as it gradually turns out, conveys a serious threat. The way he talks about his late wife reflects his self-possession, egotism, and cruelty. The dramatic action, the Duke's showing his artistic collection with a purpose, his portrait gallery, and a statue of Neptune taming a sea-horse, is the poem's present but it also involves past and future, the late Duchess's death and the impending wedding. The dramatic effect of the poem is carried by the tone of the Duke's speech, by which his character unfolds before our eyes. Readers are invited to interpret the Duke's powerful words in their own way. One effect of the dramatic monologue is the tension created by the two opposing readerly attitudes, sympathy and judgement. Sinfield argues that, in order to understand the Duke's personality, we must briefly try and understand the Duke's own perception of events and his motivation: "we must look through the speaker's eyes and enter his mind" (Sinfield 6). We cannot disregard the Duke's social standing either: he is a Renaissance nobleman bound by the rhetorical conventions of the decorum of his time. Baldassare Castiglione provided guidance for the courtier and the perfect lady in his *The Book of the Courtier* (1528) which Browning knew well (see Dimitrijevic 32–34). In this context, the late Duchess violated the protocols of expected behaviour of ladies of the court and committed unforgivable indiscretion by smiling at strangers. Browning's intentional irony is also manifested in his choice of heroic couplets which are often enjambed, strengthening the impression of spontaneity, which, in return, deepens the gap between the speaker's intended meaning and the reader's understanding of his character. Browning develops dramatic irony further in his later poems: his great dramatic narrative *The Ring and the Book* (4 vols., 1868–1869) employs a dozen voices, offering different accounts of a criminal case.

V

Early twentieth-century modernist poetry further complicates the role and function of poetic dialogue. "The Love Song of J. Alfred Prufrock" is an early poem of T.S. Eliot: it was first published in the 1915 issue of *Poetry: A Magazine of Verse* and in *Catholic Anthology 1914–1915*, and then in Eliot's first collection of poems, *Prufrock and Other Observations* (1917). The allusiveness of the poem offers an interplay between the literary allusions and their current context. Such is the epigraph which serves as the motto of the poem; Eliot cites the words of Guido da Montefeltro from Dante's *Inferno* (27.61–66): Montefeltro was a false counsellor who tells his shameful life to Dante believing that his confession will never be known since no one has returned from Hell alive. The reader is invited to make out how the analogy of Montefeltro's voice from Hell, his secret revelation, contributes to the meaning of Prufrock's monologue.

Eliot shapes the Victorian dramatic monologue into a modernist poem. His use of intertextual allusions and references to classical poetical conventions such as troubadour lyric or the metaphysical conceit point to the discrepancy between those rhetorical strategies as we know them and Eliot's transforming them into new meanings. Langbaum explains this transition in Eliot's modernist use of the dramatic monologue by turning the aspect

120   *Gabriella Hartvig*

of the audience into an internal dialogue which Prufrock is having with himself, as with a second voice which reflects on itself. The poet's purpose is not so much to reveal the character of the speaker to the listener or to the reader; instead, "the style of address gives the effect of a closed circuit, with the speaker directing his address outward in order that it may return with a meaning he was not aware of when sending it forth" (Langbaum 190–191). We cannot even decide whether what Prufrock talks about, his passing the foggy streets in an October night to a tea party, is happening or whether Prufrock is just imagining the situation where he is expected to stand up and give a toast. His hesitation occupies his mind and he finally decides not to sing the promised love song in the title.

Prufrock, after he invites his company, referred to as "you" in the poem, to go with him, wanders through deserted streets on a "soft October night" (l. 21) to a drawing-room where he meets the ladies who walk around. He ponders about how much time he has before his performance at dinner, whether he dare sing his song, and what the song would be about – because he can only tell the ladies how he passed the streets covered with yellow fog, and that is a subject not worth singing. He then retreats into himself imagining what the future holds for him: he will be defined by his sartorial choices (l. 57) and choice of haircut (l. 62). In the Biblical allusions he sees his head on a platter like John the Baptist, and he is Lazarus who is raised from the dead or he might also be the beggar Lazarus. All these references to well-known sources modify our image of the speaker while his overarching hesitation blurs and also relativises our understanding of the established roles of the speaker, the audience, and even the occasion, which reveals much on the real subject of the poem, crisis, alienation, and a resulting frustration experienced by the modern individual in a God-forsaken and troubled society. The unheroic existence of the speaker is also underlined by the ⊘ free verse employed in the poem: the colloquial nature of Prufrock's speech and his indecision allow no regular rhyme scheme. The poem's ending line brings together the ultimate failure of the speaker who is drowned by the voices of the party, and the structuring element of the final literary allusion to the sirens in Homer's ⊘ epic poem who lured sailors with their seductive songs into jumping into the sea to find their death.

VI

Dramatic monologue in contemporary poetry can be employed to serve specific purposes through its social agenda. Carol Ann Duffy uses the form to point out the controversial nature of major narratives told from a dominantly male point of view, leaving out other possible aspects of the story.

"Mrs Lazarus" was published in Duffy's collection of poems *The World's Wife* (1999) together with other pieces which are also dramatic monologues often personifying the wives of famous historical or mythical people such as "Mrs Darwin", "Frau Freud", or "Mrs Midas". These poems tell the untold stories of their married life. Duffy wants to call attention to the female point of view, the feminist perspective: in "Ann Hathaway", for example, Shakespeare's widow remembers the time she and her husband had spent in the "second-best bed" that Shakespeare bequeathed to his wife in his will.

The source of "Mrs Lazarus" is the Biblical story of Lazarus of Bethany from the Gospel of Saint John (Chapter 11) who, after he was entombed for four days, is raised from the dead. In the poem more time passes, possibly months: Mrs Lazarus remembers how she grieved for her husband, how she wept, repeated his name endlessly, and associated it with death. Lazarus' resurrection happens when she is reconciled to her new situation, when his image has vanished, and he becomes a legend. Their meeting is devastating for both: Mrs Lazarus' new relationship makes a cuckold out of Lazarus. The villagers share the shock of the encounter.

The aspect of time is perhaps the most critical vehicle in carrying the poem's meaning: the occasion of Lazarus' return, the present situation seems to be wrong, so much out of place and time, and disturbing the order of things. The irregular, ⬀ free-verse stanzas adhere to Mrs Lazarus' revolt against the unworldly act of Lazarus' resurrection, which seals her destiny: she is married to someone who came back from the dead. Mrs Lazarus is a woman of our time; thus the discrepancy between past and present cannot be bridged.

As has been shown in this short survey, the dramatic monologue has gone a long way to carry the thought processes of dramatic speakers whose minds are moulded by changing cultural circumstances. It is the rhetorical strategies that the poet employs which make the meaning of these poems sometimes puzzling and certainly more intriguing than many other poetical forms. The dramatic monologue attempts to accomplish an impossible task: it purports to playfully, often ironically, reconstruct and recognise the unheard voices of male and female personae, thus shaping our cultural memory of the past.

NOW READ ON...

- This chapter references additional poems by Tennyson, Browning, Eliot, and Duffy that merit further reading.
- The form of the dramatic monologue features many interesting overlaps with that of the modernist ⬀ long poem, as witnessed by the fact that the chapters on both forms reference T.S. Eliot's poetry.
- Both the dramatic monologue and the modernist long poem may be composed in ⬀ free verse, so a look at that chapter may also prove rewarding.
- As pointed out above, the dramatic monologue may take some of its themes from a look into the past – at either history or ⬀ epic poetry, so the chapter on the latter may have additional insights to offer.

References

Browning, Robert. "My Last Duchess". *Selected Poems,* eds. John Woolford, et al. Routledge, 2013, pp. 197–200.

Culler, A. Dwight. "Monodrama and the Dramatic Monologue". *PMLA* 90.3 (1975), pp. 366–385.

Curry, Samuel S. *Browning and the Dramatic Monologue.* Expression, 1908.

Dimitrijevic, Emilija. "Noblesse Oblige: The Act of Rhetoric in 'My Last Duchess'". *The Journal of Browning Studies* 2 (June 2011), pp. 32–43.

Duffy, Carol Ann. "Mrs Lazarus". *The World's Wife: Poems by Carol Ann Duffy.* Faber and Faber, 2001, pp. 50–51.

Eliot, Thomas Stearns. "The Love Song of J. Alfred Prufrock". *Prufrock and Other Observations.* The Egoist, 1917, pp. 9–16.

Langbaum, Robert. *The Poetry of Experience: The Dramatic Monologue in Modern Literary Tradition.* The U of Chicago P, 1957.

Sessions, Ina Beth. "The Dramatic Monologue". *PMLA* 62.2 (1947), pp. 503–516.

Sinfield, Alan. *The Dramatic Monologue.* Methuen, 1977.

Tate, Gregory. *The Poet's Mind: The Psychology of Victorian Poetry 1830–1870.* Oxford UP, 2012.

Tennyson, Alfred Lord. "Ulysses". *Tennyson: A Selected Edition*, ed. Christopher Ricks. Routledge, 2014, pp. 138–145.

12 Ekphrastic Poetry

Anja Müller-Wood

I

The adjective 'ekphrastic' is today mainly used as a label for poetry inspired by visual artworks, although the actual presence and significance of the visual stimulus varies from poem to poem. Many poems ostensibly take inspiration from specific and clearly identified paintings or sculptures, but that inspiration often serves goals other than mere description, which is the actual meaning of 'ekphrasis' (from Greek 'ekphrázein', 'to proclaim or call an inanimate object by name'). In practice, ekphrastic poetry thus often challenges the claim, by some of its theorists, that visual and verbal forms of representation are compatible, and the one can be translated into the other. Leo Spitzer links his definition of ekphrasis as "the poetic description of a pictorial or sculptural work of art" with the notion, by the nineteenth-century French writer and critic Theophile Gautier, that ekphrasis entails a "'transposition d'art,' the reproduction through the medium of words of sensuously perceptible objets d'art (ut pictura poesis)" (207). The Latin phrase *ut pictura poesis*, by the Roman poet Horace, means 'as in pictures so in poetry' and assumes that the two media are fundamentally comparable. The idea survived into Renaissance and Neoclassicism, notably in the concept of the 'sister arts', as in Charles Alphonse du Fresnoy's *De arte graphica* (1668), translated by John Dryden (1695): "Painting and Poesy are two sisters; which are so like in all things, that they mutually lend to each other both their Name and Office. One is called a dumb Poesy, and the other a speaking Picture" (84).

However, as I will show in this chapter, ekphrastic poetry itself often foregrounds the limitations of this analogy, expressing the understanding that the visual arts and poetry are discrete aesthetic forms relying on fundamentally different representational procedures: While the former are analogical, seemingly representing things 'as they are', the latter relies on the symbolic system of language and requires decoding (for that reason, visual signs are often called 'natural', linguistic signs 'conventional' and arbitrary). This recognition dates to the eighteenth century, one seminal source being "Laokoön oder Über die Grenzen der Malerei und Poesie" (1766), an essay by the German Enlightenment poet G.E. Lessing. Laocoon

DOI: 10.4324/9781003244004-14

124 *Anja Müller-Wood*

is a figure from Greek mythology: a priest killed by gigantic snakes at the behest of the goddess Athena. His agony is the topic of an ancient marble statue (whose date is as uncertain as is the myth's plot) around which Lessing's discussion revolves. It concludes that visual and verbal representation differ in that they have different 'objects': while the object of the visual arts is to depict bodies, that of poetry is to depict actions. By implication, visual representation is static, whereas representation in language can show movement and change in ways that ultimately stir the reader's emotions: this, in fact, is poetry's particular purpose (cf. Krieger 44–49).

Lessing's claims point to the origins of ekphrasis in classical rhetoric, where the term identifies "a self-contained description … inserted at an appropriate place in a piece of oratory so as to enhance its *persuasive* powers" (Verdonk 232; emphasis mine). More precisely, the aim of ekphrasis is to show an immobile object in a 'state of activity', to endow it with what Aristotle calls *enargeia* ("being-at-work", "at-work-ness"; Sachs n.p.) and thereby "enabl[e] the silent figures of graphic art to speak" (Heffernan 304). Yet as works of art including the statue of Laocoon show, every visual stimulus is likely to contain an "embryonically narrative impulse" (Heffernan 304) in that it usually depicts a "pregnant moment" that deserves to be recounted. To render "explicit the story that graphic art tells only by implication" (Heffernan 301), then, is *one* goal of ekphrastic poetry.[1]

The view that poetry can achieve that goal ostensibly forms the basis of John Keats' "Ode on a Grecian Urn" (1819), in which the speaker sets out to recount the stories depicted on the frieze of an ancient Greek vase (which vase precisely inspired the poet is unknown). Although the urn as such is mute, as the speaker emphasises, his own poem provides the mouthpiece for the stories that adorn it, as well as their 'protagonists': a handsome young man (l. 15) sitting singing in an idyllic grove, another courting the beautiful object of his desire (l. 17), a "priest" (l. 32) leading a sacrificial calf to a communal ritual. He also claims that the urn's decorations emit sound, even though it remains inaudible (l. 13; l. 14); in fact, these silent sounds (l. 12) are more delightful than those that can be heard. In the end, the urn's wordless message as articulated by the speaker is a cryptic proclamation about the permanence of art in a world of change and destruction that has been puzzling generations of scholars: "Beauty is truth" (l. 49).

Yet the urn is clearly not uttering these words, and in the poem the speaker's distance from the object is foregrounded from the outset. First of all, the urn triggers *questions* about the characters and actions depicted on it, for instance, at the end of the first stanza (ll. 8–9). Similarly, in the fourth stanza, the speaker enquires about the identity of the participants in the ritual and their place of origin (l. 35; l. 37). These questions are never answered and seem unconnected to the speaker's assertive exclamations about the urn's time-transcending significance with which they alternate. This incongruence is also underlined by the poem's hyperbolic style: the aforementioned metaphoric flourishes at the opening of the first stanza and the vexatious repetitions ("happy" is repeated six, "for ever" five times) in the third (Aske 111; 118), which highlight the speaker's inability to redeem his representational promise. Defeated by the urn's "irresistible alterity" (Aske 119), the speaker presents at best an associative (and grammatically incomplete) "incantation" (Aske 118) of subjective claims which, quite apart from being unrelated to the object described, is "discontinuous and fragmentary, radically unaccomplished" (Aske 111). In fact, the poem contains *two* stories: the urn's silent tale and the speaker's discourse that fails to put its story into words, even is supplementary to it (cf. Aske 115).

Where this discourse is not a form of projection, it seems to merely reiterate the stasis of the visual object, freezing the world depicted on it in an ideal state in which the youth will always sing, the lover always pine for the object of his desire and the sacrificial calf always be on the way to the altar. This "*story* of changelessness" (Heffernan 306, emphasis in original) is of course the precondition for the comforting permanence promised at the end of the poem. However, while Keats' "Ode" thereby corroborates Heffernan's definition of ekphrasis as "the verbal representation of graphic representation" (299), it also illustrates that ekphrastic poetry, precisely in exploring the intersection between visual and verbal modes of representation, confirms their fundamental separateness.

II

The disclosure of the inevitable gap between the visual object and its poetic representation links Keats' "Ode" to a poem written almost half a century later by the British aestheticist poet and critic Algernon Charles Swinburne: "Before the Mirror", published 1866 in the collection *Poems and Ballads*. Unlike Keats' poem, however, Swinburne's is based on a clearly identified visual model, a picture by the American artist J.A.M. Whistler with whom the poet was close at the time. Entitled "Symphony in White, No. 2: The Little White Girl" (1864),[2] the painting shows a young woman in a white dress leaning against a mirror-topped mantlepiece in a fashionably decorated interior; instead of looking at her reflection, however, she contemplates the wedding band on her left hand. The poem Swinburne wrote in response was affixed to the picture's frame at its first exhibition in 1865 by Whistler himself (Dickey 37, Spencer 1998, 311) in what appears to be a public gesture of acknowledgement and approval. This should not lead us to conclude that the two works are identical, however, and indeed Swinburne diverts from his model in ways that foreground the difference between, perhaps even the incompatibility of, verbal and visual modes of representation.

Swinburne's poem consists of three distinct sections of three seven-line stanzas each, joined by the topics of transitoriness and permanence that also compel Keats' "Ode"; here, these are underpinned by a conventional analogy of feminine beauty and a rose. Like the older poem, too, "Before the Mirror" remains vague and implicit, and although this stance interacts productively with the several references in the poem to dream visions and ghosts (which evoke the notion of narrative content 'haunting about' the urn in Keats's poem), it ultimately leaves readers in the dark about its story.

At the opening of Section I an unidentified speaker invokes the image of a "rose" (l. 1), which subsequently is linked to an unspecified luminous "face" (l. 7). Although the face is introduced with the deictic pronoun "this", which suggests familiarity, it remains unlocated, unreadable and mysterious: it is placed "behind the veil" (l. 8) and neither the nature of this veil nor the emotions the face behind it might betray can be determined. This impression is underlined by the fact that the speaker invokes these emotions through questions (ll. 10–11). The topic of death provides a lingering backdrop to this mysterious face, manifesting itself in an extended metaphor of a garden exposed to "a hard East [wind]" (l. 5) of winter, in which flowers first tremble and finally take "flight" (l. 18).

Section II is composed in direct speech/thought (highlighted by citation marks), in which another speaker – an "I" only identified as female in the second stanza of this section – echoes the interconnected themes established in the previous section as she contemplates herself and her reflection (l. 24). This line provides the only hint at the actual situation invoked by the poem's title. The analogy between rose and female beauty is reiterated when the speaker imagines her hand as "a fallen rose" (ll. 34–35); later, she identifies flowers (and implicitly the rose) as the quintessence of beauty (l. 42). In the third stanza of this section the speaker responds to the (rhetorical) questions asked in Section I, confirming that she sees neither pleasure nor pain (l. 41). Her listlessness and passivity are directly related to the confrontation with her reflection, which leads her to contemplate the possibility that she and her mirror image might be interchangeable phantoms (ll. 31–33).

Section III returns to the outside perspective of, presumably, the initial speaker, who now has insight into the mind and feelings of the poem's female protagonist. But this ostensible transparency does not make that figure any more tangible, as she is not the owner and agent of those thoughts and feelings, but merely their conduit (cf. Dickey 45). In the same way, the sensory verbs "to see" and "to hear" used in lines 54 to 55 do not equip her with agency, but underline that she is a mere passive recorder of a nebulous vision of suffering that finally obliterates her as an experiencing individual (cf. Dickey 44).

The three sections of Swinburne's poem, then, oscillate between the general and the specific; in doing so, the poem also oscillates in terms of perspective – from the outside to the inside and back. This feature can be connected to the poet's very modern interest in human consciousness and the inaccessibility of the mind to both the self and others; it also presents a no less modern attempt at representing mental processes in text.

While the limited and uncertain points of view of the speakers in the first two sections are underlined by the questions they ask, Section III "vastly expands the consciousness of the poem", not only granting the young woman "access to 'all past things' and 'all men's tears'" but also giving the viewer "access to her thoughts" (Dickey 45). Nevertheless, at the end of the poem the reader only *appears* to have had a glance into the female character's mind, as this is already in the process of being "absorbed into the vastness of time" (Dickey 45) that she is witnessing passively. Although the poem's shifting perspectives might seem to have the effect of endowing the impassive protagonist of Whistler's painting with *enargeia*, the process is an entirely interior one that condemns the protagonist to a situation of stillness and inaccessibility not unlike that described in Keats' "Ode".

Recreating the impression of interiority requires a modification of the visual source, and Swinburne alters Whistler's painting in a number of significant details: The carefully orchestrated decorative objects in the picture – two paintings on the wall behind the young woman's reflection, two vases on the mantlepiece and the fan in her hand, all Japanese in style – are not mentioned in the poem at all; instead, Swinburne exchanges the painting's elegant indoor setting for a vision of a garden that has no source in the picture. Even more obviously, neither is the young woman's hair "bright" (l. 25), nor does she look at her reflection, as the poem suggests. In fact, in the painting she "seems not to see anything" (Dickey 39). The changes undertaken by Swinburne eroticise the model in a way that suggests an entirely different visual influence on his poem than the painting in question: the English Pre-Raphaelite artists, whose romantic medievalism often revolved around the depiction of a particular (seductive) type of female beauty (cf. Maxwell 241; see also Dickey 37).

Swinburne seemed to be aware of the disparities between his visual source and the poem he based upon it, as he felt the need to assert, in a letter to the painter, that "the metaphor of the rose and the notions of sad and glad mystery in the face languidly contemplative of its own phantom and all other things seen by their phantoms" (qtd. in Spencer 1999, 62) were presented to him by the picture itself. Yet Whistler's work contains nothing of the kind and Swinburne's poetic response might have been occasioned by very different considerations, amongst them his own aesthetic agenda. Indeed, the trajectories that structure Swinburne's poem – the shift from vagueness to transparency and from an internal to an external perspective – are directly related to his own avant-garde poetics. For Thain, Swinburne "represents clearly a turning point" in nineteenth-century poetry, marking the onset of aestheticism (190; cf. also Lyons; Spencer 1999). Often falsely reduced to the maxim "art for art's sake", aestheticism was a complex artistic phenomenon in response to the moralistic realism of contemporary poets such as Tennyson and Browning. Inspired by the idealisation of classical paganism and secular sensuality, in combination with a commitment to formal experimentation and exuberance,

128 *Anja Müller-Wood*

aestheticism anticipated the concerns of later, modernist poetry (cf. Lyons, esp. Introduction).

An important aspect of Swinburne's aestheticism is the concept of the lyric, which is here not to be taken as a genre category like 'epic' and 'drama', but as a poetic mode associated with sensuous authenticity and emotional intensity, subjective experience rather than objective analysis. Swinburne himself associates lyric poetry in general with song (Thain 190), a term he also used for "Before the Mirror" (Spencer 1999, 63). The song-like quality of the poem manifests itself in the way he manages and manipulates poetic *voice*. On the surface, two distinct voices are juxtaposed with one another: that of the speaker describing the female figure before the mirror in Sections I and III and that of the woman herself in the middle section. Regarding voice, that middle part is complex in itself, however, and skews what appears to be a neatly contrastive arrangement between interior and exterior perspectives. It might be considered a small-scale ♫ dramatic monologue: a popular mid-nineteenth-century genre of poetry, in which a character clearly distinguished from the author, in recounting a momentous event to an implicit listener, unintentionally reveals her or his character (Abrams 70–71). This encounter with the speaker's mind might not only turn out to be unsettling, but also draws attention to fundamental questions about the nature of poetic voice: Who is speaking these words, the character or the poet? If there are two voices, are they independent or connected? And how does their interplay impact the matter of the poem?

Swinburne's dramatic monologue *en miniature* interacts productively with other moments in "Before the Mirror" in which self and other merge, most strikingly of course when the female figure mysteriously blends with her "white sister" (l. 32) in the mirror. In that, of course, the poem lends its thematic interest a linguistic dimension: In Section II, Swinburne has the female speaker repeat individual formulations from the previous section verbatim, as if in dialogue with the first speaker and his external perspective. In turn, this dialogical quality is underlined aurally by the echoes created by the poem's evocative rhyming keywords (e.g. "white"/ "light" / "night"/; "air"/ "hair"/ "fair"; "die"/ "sigh"/ "sky") that resound hauntingly across the stanzas.

The choral or polyphonic effect of these echoes takes the overt multi-perspectivity of the poem one step further, blurring the boundaries between its different speakers and supporting the notion – also apparent in other poems from *Poems and Ballads* (cf. for instance Thain's discussion of "Anactoria", esp. 194–195) – that for Swinburne lyric poetry was "inherently multi-vocal" (Thain 196). Whistler's visual scene of reflection provided a particularly rich source of inspiration for the poet, suggesting a world of indefinite mirrorings, a "universe of terrifying correspondences" (cf. McGann 176–177) in which meaning is a matter of relations and nothing seems real.

III

Just like Swinburne's poetry, Whistler's art represents an aesthetic turning point, albeit one motivated by opposite concerns. While Swinburne was committed to creating sensual experiences, Whistler was working towards ever greater abstraction. Although "Symphony in White, No. 2" is in the tradition of time-honoured artistic genres – portraiture and the *vanitas* tradition (Spencer 1999, 66) (paintings, that is, whose specific goal is to remind the viewer of her or his mortality) – its main title, which was only added as an afterthought (Spencer 1998, 310–311), indicates that Whistler's concerns lay elsewhere. The painting hints at the influence of Japanese art on his style and already points to his later explicit rejection of the premise – still powerful in late-nineteenth-century portraiture – that the human face reveals a person's 'soul'. Instead, he increasingly considered the persons portrayed as no more than elements in a painting's overall composition (an assumption explored in much of his work after "Symphony in White, No. 2", most famously in the notorious portrait of his mother, provocatively entitled "Arrangement in Grey and White") (cf. Petri 122–123).

The painting's topic of 'reflection' is germane to this principle of abstraction, treating the human figure as just another double amongst the many other "repetitions and mirrorings" (Dickey 41) that manifest themselves in the picture in various ways: in the form of objects (e.g. the two paintings on the wall), thematically (one of these paintings is a landscape repeated by the scene depicted on the young woman's fan) and in the use of colours (the same fan repeats the blue and red of the Japanese vases on the mantlepiece) and basic shapes and structural principles (i.e. the large rectangles in neutral colours that subdivide and pattern the painting). This assemblage of "optical reflections" absorbs the painting's apparent protagonist "into [its] matrix as an aspect of light and design" (Dickey 40); she, too, is no more than a white shape set against other coloured shapes on the canvas.

However much these multiple reflections might superficially chime with Swinburne's own poetic principle of polyvocality, they ultimately serve a goal of abstraction that the poet rejected. Although Swinburne, too, treats the female figure like an (aesthetic) object that receives its meaning through its relationship with the surrounding world (cf. Dickey 42; 18), thereby depriving her of animation and agency, he differed from Whistler's commitment to abstraction in his (rather traditional) insistence that a work of art is supposed to affect its recipient. Swinburne eventually would criticise Whistler's idea that "art ... should stand alone, and appeal to the artistic sense of eye or ear" and be judged for its "arrangements and harmonies" (Whistler 128) – not least because he believed that the painter's own work, in containing "qualities which actually appeal ... to the intelligence and the emotions, to the mind and heart of the spectator" (qtd. in Whistler 252), failed his principle of abstraction and aesthetic distance.

"Before the Mirror" can be seen as Swinburne's attempt to distil sensual effects from a painting that purposefully eschews them. In the process, rather than proving the painter wrong, Swinburne merely reinforces the differences that exist between his poem and the visual model. He thereby not only reveals himself to be steeped in an effect-driven aesthetic that looked back to a romantic poet like Keats, but also documents ekphrastic poetry's inevitable failure to speak for the visual source by which it is inspired.

NOW READ ON…

- Another one of Keats' famous odes is discussed in the chapter on the ⟋ ode.
- The speaker's role in "Before the Mirror" is likened to that in a ⟋ dramatic monologue, so the chapter on that form might make interesting reading.
- Perhaps the most famous example of modern ekphrasis is to be found in W.H. Auden's "Musée des Beaux Arts", but, as the present chapter demonstrates, the relation between pictorial arts and literature at the heart of ekphrasis is never an uncomplicated one.
- The chapter on the ⟋ elegy discusses a poem based on a photograph, Wisława Szymborska's "Photograph from September 11". See if you can make sense of that poem as an ekphrastic work.

Notes

1 The term 'narrative' is, strictly speaking, inappropriate in the context of poetry, but is used here in the sense of 'content'.
2 The painting can be found at Tate Britain: https://www.tate.org.uk/art/artworks/whistler-symphony-in-white-no-2-the-little-white-girl-n03418

References

Abrams, Meyer Howard. *A Glossary of Literary Terms*, 8th ed. Wadsworth, 2005, pp. 70–71.

Aske, Martin. *Keats and Hellenism: An Essay.* Cambridge UP, 2008.

Dickey, Frances. *The Modern Portrait Poem: From Dante Gabriel Rossetti to Ezra Pound.* U of Virginia P, 2012.

Dryden, John. *The Works of John Dryden.* Vol. XX: Prose 1691–1698, ed. George R. Guffey, et al. U of California P, 1990.

Heffernan, James A.W. "Ekphrasis and Representation". *New Literary History* 22.2 (1991), pp. 297–316.

Keats, John. "Ode on a Grecian Urn". *The Poems of John Keats*, ed. Jack Stillinger. Harvard UP, 1978, pp. 282–283.

Krieger, Murray. *Ekphrasis: The Illusion of the Natural Sign*. 1991. Johns Hopkins UP, 2019.

Lyons, Sara. *Algernon Swinburne and Walter Pater: Victorian Aestheticism, Doubt, and Secularisation*. Modern Humanities Research Association and Taylor & Francis, 2015.

Maxwell, Catherine. "Algernon Charles Swinburne (1837–1909)". *The Cambridge Companion to the Pre-Raphaelites*, ed. Elizabeth Pretterjohn. Cambridge UP, 2012, pp. 236–249.

McGann, Jerome J. *Swinburne: An Experiment in Criticism*. The U of Chicago P, 1972.

Petri, Grischka. "Whistlers 'Arrangement in Grey and Black: Portrait of the Painter's Mother'. Meisterwerk Zwischen Karriere und Kritik". *Kanon Kunstgeschichte: Einführung in Werke, Methoden und Epochen, Bd. 3: Moderne*, eds. Kristin Marek and Martin Schulz. Wilhelm-Fink Verlag, 2015, pp. 113–131.

Sachs, Joe. "Aristotle: Motion and Its Place in Nature". *Internet Encyclopaedia of Philosophy*. https://iep.utm.edu/aris-mot/

Spencer, Robin. "Whistler, Swinburne and Art for Art's Sake". *After the Pre-Raphaelites*, ed. Elizabeth Pretterjohn. Manchester UP, 1999, pp. 59–89.

———. "Whistler's 'The White Girl': Painting, Poetry and Meaning". *The Burlington Magazine* 140.1142 (1998), pp. 300–311.

Spitzer, Leo. "The 'Ode on a Grecian Urn', or Content vs. Metagrammar". *Comparative Literature* 7.3 (1955), pp. 203–225.

Swinburne, Algernon Charles. "Before the Mirror". *The Poems of Algernon Charles Swinburne*, vol. I: *Poems and Ballads*. Chatto & Windus, 1904, pp. 129–131.

Thain, Marion. *The Lyric Poem and Aestheticism*. Edinburgh UP, 2016.

Verdonk, Peter. "Painting, Poetry, Parallelism: Ekphrasis, Stylistics and Cognitive Poetics". *Language and Literature* 14.3 (2005), pp. 231–244.

Whistler, James Abbott Mc Neill. *The Gentle Art of Making Enemies*. 1967. Dover, 1990.

13 The Elegy

Patrick Gill

I

Like many other poetic genres, the elegy is a form of poetry whose function it is to transform the reader's state of mind, to transport the reader from one mood to another. In concrete terms, an elegy is a poem of mourning concerned with a recently deceased person or persons.[1] Elegies come in various shapes and sizes: they can be as long as Alfred, Lord Tennyson's book-length *In Memoriam* or as short as W.S. Merwin's single-line poem "Elegy". They can concern themselves with the death of a public figure like Percy Bysshe Shelley's "Adonais" on the death of fellow poet John Keats, or they can represent acts of private mourning as in Thomas Hardy's elegies to his wife, collected in the volume *Poems of 1912–13*. But whatever form they take, elegies will usually mark the passing of a person, bemoan their sudden absence, and then find a way towards consolation by perhaps commemorating their deeds or their importance in the lives of the mourners. In their closing, elegies traditionally offer a future outlook, some inkling of how or with what renewed purpose life may go on for the bereaved. Elegies thus trace a development from initial loss via a full appreciation of that loss towards a state of acceptance and consolation. While it may be tempting to think of elegies as a direct imitation of the mourner's psychology, the mental stages they go through as they try to process grief and loss, I agree with Peter M. Sacks in arguing that "the elegy, as a poem of mourning and consolation, has its roots in a dense matrix of rites and ceremonies" (2), meaning that traditional elegies follow a fairly conventional path of mourning and commemoration towards consolation. What these poems represent is the movement towards a letting-go – an acceptance of the separation between the living and the dead.

As such, elegies – even though they are a non-prescriptive form of poetry and thus all look very different – tend to contain a number of key elements: the life and virtues of the deceased are usually evoked; sorrow at their loss is expressed; an outlook on a sadder, emptier future for the survivors is given; yet still some sense of consolation is arrived at, usually by means of an insight of transcendence – the life of the deceased will carry

DOI: 10.4324/9781003244004-15

on in some way, either in a happier afterlife or by virtue of their living on in the hearts and minds of the community of mourners.

In some way, then, the elegy would appear to be formulaic, heavily reliant on conventions. But this chapter will argue that the elegy changes as the world around us – or, more importantly, our experience of it, our knowledge about it – changes. Without expressly going out of their way to do so, elegies absorb ideas of their respective time and culture much more immediately than other forms of poetry because elegies are concerned with the central problem of what it means to be human: coming to terms with mortality. And the response to that existential quandary will be very different if you mourn death in, say, seventeenth-century London or in New York in 2001. What they all do, even if they refuse to participate in the formulaic, the clichéd, is to seek out a relation to the standard form. An elegy written for victims of the First World War, for instance, will implicitly refer back to the elegies written about heroes of previous wars, even if it ends up contradicting them in some way. In the following, that change of the key elements of commemoration and consolation will be traced along with the changing role of the speaker. In limiting itself to a discussion of these aspects, this chapter will of necessity leave out a great number of other aspects that may well be just as interesting, for the simple reason that these are not as consistently present in all elegies.

II

John Milton's "Lycidas" (1638) is one such example of an elegy that contains a number of aspects we would not necessarily expect to discover in the poetry of mourning. Written to commemorate his fellow student, Edward King, the poem is used by Milton to criticise in strident terms what he sees as the failings of the Anglican church of his day. The main strategy the poem pursues, however, is that of a mingling of Christian elements with those of ancient mythology by means of its pastoral mode: fellow students at Cambridge, Milton and King are both represented here as young shepherds growing up in a landscape imbued with classical motifs, from the invocation of the muses at the beginning of the poem to the Greek name Lycidas given to the recently drowned Edward King and to the presence of ancient deities. The ancient form of the pastoral is seen as apt by Milton because while it refers back to ancient Greek and Roman times, its imagery is also employed in Christian similes when Christ is referred to as the lamb of God, or when bishops tending to their congregations are likened to shepherds herding their flocks. "Lycidas" thus begins with references to the ancient world and much of its commemoration and mourning is undertaken in those terms: nymphs looked on helplessly as Lycidas drowned (ll. 50–51), and nature itself mourns the young man's death (ll. 136–151) as his lifeless body is tossed about at the bottom of the sea (ll. 154–155). The ancient world is powerless to do anything but

134   Patrick Gill

bewail Lycidas' passing, it seems. Then suddenly, stanza ten exhorts the shepherds to stop their crying (l. 165) because "Lycidas ... is not dead" (l. 166). How has his salvation been wrought? Through his Christian faith (ll. 172–173): he has been granted eternal life and is in Heaven (ll. 177–178). Having witnessed and described the rise of Lycidas from an ancient world of pagan deities – helpless onlookers all – to the salvation of a Christian afterlife, the speaker of the poem can turn "to fresh woods, and pastures new" in the poem's final line. This "leap from plaintive helplessness to authoritative consolation" (Pigman 1) may strike us as facile, but it is a part of the underlying structure of the poem and its championing of the Christian Resurrection. With Lycidas in Heaven, he has ceased to be the responsibility of the speaker of the poem: Lycidas is taken care of, the separation of living and dead can take place, and the poem's speaker can move on with his life. While its tirades against the Anglican church (ll. 113–131) and its contemplation of the vagaries of a literary career (ll. 64–84) are not elements we would usually expect to find in a poem commemorating a recently deceased friend, "Lycidas" represents a typical use of the elegy in its movement from mourning to consolation.

III

That movement presents itself as something more complicated in W.B. Yeats' "In Memory of Major Robert Gregory" (1918), in which the poet mourns the death of the son of his friend Lady Gregory in the First World War. While the title of the poem seems straightforward enough, the poem proper does not once name the person it is supposedly designed to commemorate. Instead, Yeats uses his move to a new house to remember all those dead friends who will no longer be able to come and visit him there. Across twelve eight-line stanzas, he gives us a litany of friends, praising each for a distinct quality: one was particularly bookish (ll. 17–24), the other widely travelled (ll. 25–32), the next was a great horse rider in his youth (ll. 33–40). Praising each of his dead friends in turn, turning them into a pantheon of almost superhuman strength, dexterity, intelligence, Yeats approaches the real subject of his poem by means of indirection: the man his poem is supposed to commemorate remains unnamed but was of such brilliance that he outshone all the others. The poem's penultimate stanza considers that it was foolhardy to expect a man of such brilliance to "comb grey hair" (l. 88), i.e. grow old, and the final stanza simply admits defeat: faced with the tragic death of this young hero, words fail Yeats, and he cannot continue. In choosing this strategy for his elegy, Yeats can have it both ways: he praises Gregory and commemorates him while at the same time leaving the eulogy incomplete, suggesting that his loss (and Lady Gregory's) is too great for words. Easy consolation is thus resisted, no promise of transcendence is offered. Instead of relying on Christian ideas of salvation, or invoking a thankful nation in whose service Robert

Gregory gave his life,[2] Yeats chooses silence over explicit consolation. Robert Gregory was the greatest, the poem tells us, and his loss is beyond words. Any attempt at finding consolation would seem cheap and contrived when contrasted with the dignity of the man himself and the life he led. Yeats' tendency to mythologise his friends in death is still in evidence in his praise for the other men mentioned in the poem, but he is aware that it would fall short of what is required in this instance.

Yeats' rejection of traditional forms of consolation in the context of the First World War is shared by war poets such as Wilfred Owen and Siegfried Sassoon. Witnessing at first hand how – rather than the result of a heroic contest between brave individual combatants – the war with its use of machine guns, mortars, and poison gas makes death "obscene, meaningless, impersonal" (Sacks 299), these poets go even further than Yeats in rejecting tried and tested ideas of commemoration and consolation. Looking beyond the horrors of the Great War, several factors work together to reinforce the notion that consolation is not as uncomplicated a matter as it was for Milton. Death and dying are increasingly seen as phenomena taking place outside of the family home (in hospitals and retirement homes). Increasing secularisation means that religion is not as immediate and natural a recourse for mourners. And conflicts become ever more bloody, spreading anonymised killing from the world of combatants to the home front. In such a climate, making sense of death becomes increasingly hard, and the idea that a few lines of poetry would have the power to provide an explanation as well as adequate consolation seems in danger of breaching basic decorum. As a consequence, poets work harder and harder to dissociate themselves from pat ideas of providing consolation while at the same time still trying to convey a sense of dignity on the deceased. This development has such far-reaching consequences for the writing of elegies that some critics see in the further course of the twentieth century the rise of what they term "*anti*elegy", a form of elegy that "cannot accept traditional religious and ethical certainties" (Rae 247).

IV

One of the most famous examples of such an anti-elegy is Dylan Thomas' "A Refusal to Mourn the Death, by Fire, of a Child in London" (1945). Commemorating the young victim of a German bombing raid during the Second World War, the poem is a careful exercise in avoiding two possible pitfalls: that of becoming a piece of wartime propaganda and that of offering clichéd and uncomplicated consolatory formulae. The first aim is achieved by not mentioning the enemy responsible for the child's death, nor the war itself. The poem's speaker explicitly vows not to exploit the child's death for political ends (ll. 14–18), choosing instead to set the scene of his poem in a timeless and universal environment rather than in any recognisable portrayal of wartime London. The avoidance of clichéd and outdated notions of consolation is achieved by means of an intricate interweaving of biblical and scientific or natural imagery. The first sentence of Thomas' poem is a thirteen-line adynaton,[3] a vow on the part of the speaker not to mourn until the end of the universe – and that end of the universe is described in terms that can be read as either religious or scientific, or both. From the very start then, the poem avoids the certainty of religious faith by intermingling religious language with concepts of cosmology, physics, and biology. This ambiguity is upheld up to and including the poem's final line, "After the first death, there is no other". Read from a religious point of view, this could mean that the innocent child has had to suffer death once but can now enjoy a life eternal – a traditional religious sentiment not that far removed from Milton's "Lycidas … is not dead". Read from a less hopeful point of view, though, the line could just mean that death is final and the child's suffering is over. Given its cryptic phrasing (why is it called the "first death" if "there is no other"?), the line – the shortest sentence in the entire poem – leaves room for doubt. The speaker's certainty, expressed in the poem's thirteen-line opening sentence, concerns the stance he will take vis-à-vis the child's death. What happens to the child after death is not expressed in certainties but in this highly ambiguous closing statement. As has been demonstrated, Thomas' reticence in providing consolatory certainties is not matched by any reticence on the part of the speaker in making himself the master of ceremonies in this mourning ritual. Thomas' persona possesses a bardic, priestlike quality in his wartime elegies that automatically foregrounds the role of the speaker while the dead are often quite anonymous (we only find out in the final stanza that the child was a girl, never learn her name, and are generally kept ignorant of any of her personal traits).

That foregrounding of the speaker is seen rather differently in the second half of the twentieth century and is problematised in a number of more recent elegies. In a way, it is unavoidable that the commemorator takes on a central role in an age of diminished faith, when the handing over of responsibility to an omnipotent being does not provide a simple means of consolation. If elegies can no longer end with the deceased having gone to a 'better place', the burden of remembering and finding cause for consolation rests squarely on the shoulders of the mourners themselves, first among them writers of elegies. At the same time, poets become more self-conscious about their role when they write about human tragedy for the simple fact that they are furthering their careers by turning those less fortunate than themselves into content, into material to be published to their financial benefit. A prominent example of this new type of reticence to take on the role of elegist is Geoffrey Hill's "September Song" (1968) in which the persona approaches a memorial to a victim of the Holocaust whose date of birth happens to coincide with his own. The identification of the persona with the deceased is not new – we have already observed it in Milton's "Lycidas", where the speaker points out that both he and the deceased grew up together. But while Milton's speaker can find closure in the knowledge that his friend Lycidas is now in Heaven, Hill's persona has no such solution to offer and is plagued by a sense of survivor's guilt: this could have been me, he seems to say, acknowledging the horrors of the Holocaust and his own luck in not having been caught up in the "coldly calculating efficiency of the Nazi death machine" (Reeves 585). Compared to the nameless victim, his was by far the luckier path, and he is acutely aware of it. The resultant sense of guilt and responsibility permeates the short poem to such a degree that it ends quite abruptly with the ambiguous statement "This is plenty. This is more than enough". "This" being a deictic word, it can mean many things depending on the context in which it is used. It might refer to the speaker's surroundings which, however modest, at least guarantee a safe and comfortable existence. It could also refer to the poem itself, thus expressing the idea that enough has been said on the matter, and any further elaboration would only serve to exploit the misery of others for art. His identification with the victim is what lends the poem such an emotional validity, and yet, it is also an aspect he is reticent to spell out as it would unfairly equate his fate with that of the victim. Paradoxically, then, Hill is so reluctant to turn others' suffering into art that he ends up talking about himself and his hesitancy rather than commemorating the victim or offering any sense of consolation. But what is there to say in terms of commemoration when you are faced with a plaque or gravestone commemorating one victim among millions? And what possible consolation could you offer that would not sound cheap and undignified in the face of such suffering? In facing these unanswerable questions, the form of the elegy finds itself confronted with certain limits: consolation cannot be offered, commemoration sounds trite and clichéd, and every act of writing implicates the speaker in the fate of the victim, turning him into a gawper at the scene of the accident, observing human tragedy for profit or titillation. While Hill's poem can have a tremendous emotional effect, the recipe it is based on seems an unrepeatable experiment, a poetic dead end.

V

There are two distinct ways in which poets react to this dead-end situation. The one, most applicable to occasions of public mourning, foregrounds the impotence of poetry to bring about a real sense of consolation and closure. The other, a preferred mode in cases of private acts of mourning, is for the speaker of a poem to take on the task of remembering the deceased, thus making unnecessary the separation of living and dead so common in earlier elegies. The first of these avenues is followed by Wisława Szymborska in her poem "Photograph from September 11". Observing a photographic image of victims of the 9/11 attacks jumping out of the windows of the Twin Towers, Szymborska's speaker describes what she sees: the frames of people jumping from different floors (ll. 1–3), seemingly suspended in mid-air (ll. 4–6). But as, in the further course of the poem, the speaker focuses on many small details which mark these victims out as individuals, as people you might meet in the street, people with individual features (l. 8), their keys falling from their pockets (ll. 12–13), gradually the horror of the situation sinks in: we are all joined in the communal activity of watching living people plummeting to their deaths. The art of photography can capture and preserve them in mid-air. But literature is a sequential art form, and so there is always the question of what happens next. Do we really want to witness the horror of that? Would that not turn us into gawpers, bystanders enjoying the horror and misery others experience? What is a decorous way out of this altogether indecorous situation? Szymborska knows that to follow literature's sequential nature would be to remember the victims in the least dignified way, and so she refrains from doing so, instead ending her poem by saying that she will "not add a last line" (l. 19). As in Yeats' poem, in the absence of consolation, silence is seen as more appropriate than any other alternative.

Where personal mourning and remembrance are concerned, the lack of an obvious outlet, an authority to whom care of the dead can be delegated, leads to an obligation on the part of the living to continue to carry the burden. Where Milton's speaker could turn "to pastures new", secure in the knowledge that Lycidas would be looked after in Heaven, modern elegists feel that the dead have nowhere to go, and so it falls on them to keep them alive in their memory, painful as that may sometimes be. That aspect of the contemporary elegy is illustrated by Simon Armitage's poem "The Shout" (2002) in which two boys are sent out into the school yard to conduct an experiment in acoustics: shouting to each other while gradually increasing the distance between them (ll. 1–9). A sudden jump in time takes us from schoolboy reminiscence to the present, where we discover the 'you' of the poem to have died twenty years before, probably by taking his own life. And even though the poem's speaker has reiterated that his memory of his school friend is incomplete, he knows that he will carry it with him for the rest of his life: "Boy with the name and face I don't remember, / you can stop shouting now, I can still hear you" (ll. 19–20).

Modern grievers' inability to let go, to find a new and comforting home for their dead, challenges the erstwhile function of the elegy itself: where it was once designed to celebrate and bring about a transition from this life to the next, as well as a separation between living and dead, increasing secularisation has meant that rather than leaving their dead in the care of God, rather than merely fashioning a ritual transition, writers of elegies now have to bemoan the relative powerlessness of their own art (as Szymborska does, for instance) or have to create vessels of remembrance themselves, vows never to forget the deceased (as Armitage does). While the former case is represented by a number of highly prominent and visible poets, the latter reaction may be the more common. In fact, so widespread

The Elegy 139

has the phenomenon become that one critic sees in it not a natural extension of the elegy, but a wholly new form of poetry: "The unwillingness of ... elegists to abandon their dead ... has been replaced by a desire for the dead to continue to walk among us. Indeed, reading many contemporary elegists, it almost seems as if we need a new generic term for a literature of the undead" (Kennedy 145–146).

VI

If we take a step back from the terminological wrangling over 'elegy', 'antielegy', and 'literature of the undead', we can see that elegy as the poetry of mourning is one of the few genres still in everyday use at the hands of everyday people. Peruse the pages of any local newspaper and you will probably find someone publishing their personal elegy in memory of their grandmother or other recently deceased relative; online forums offer a place to share personal poems of mourning: in the hands of non-professional writers, the elegy still has a role to play in our culture, as people endeavour to make sense of mortality and find consolation for their losses. Professional poets, however, have struggled with the traditional patterns and functions of elegy. As outsiders looking at public bereavements, they cannot offer any consolation that has not been earned, that might strike readers as facile. Simply saying "she's in a better place now" may constitute a sincerely held consolatory belief at the end of a personal poem commemorating a relative, but it would strike readers of an elegy on a public tragedy as wooden, clichéd, unearned. To avoid these stock responses (untenable in a mostly secular age anyway), elegists of the past hundred years have tended to resist consolation, to avoid the conclusion that at the end of their poems everything is back to normal and sadness has been overcome. With reference to the early twentieth century, Rae calls this type of writing "*antielegy*" – by the beginning of the twenty-first, we can call it the new orthodoxy of elegising

---

NOW READ ON...

- Some famous poets use the term 'elegy' or its derivatives in the titles of works that are not strictly concerned with the recent death of a specific person. If you look up works such as Thomas Gray's *Elegy Written in a Country Church-yard* (1751) or Charlotte Smith's *Elegiac Sonnets* (1784), you might see in how far that usage is still justified, how these works do or do not relate to the concept of elegy outlined in the present chapter.
- In commemorating the deceased, elegies are often also poems of praise written in a formal style, and as such they may feature interesting overlaps with the ⯈ ode, another form characterised

140　*Patrick Gill*

not so much by rhyme scheme and metre but by an argumentative structure, a sequence of ideas.

- "Photograph from September 11" is an instance of ⊘ ekphrastic poetry, emphasising once more that – in contrast to the traditional notion of that technique being a celebration of the commonality of literature and the visual arts – these poems consciously or inadvertently end up outlining the categorical differences between the forms.
- The same poem also happens to be written in nineteen lines of ⊘ free verse. The only poetic form discussed in this book that habitually features nineteen-line poems is the ⊘ villanelle. With its emphasis on repetition and, thus, stasis, maybe the villanelle (though usually written in rhyming tetra- or pentameter) is a useful reference point for a discussion of "Photograph from September 11".
- For another act of public mourning that turns into an ostensible questioning of the power of literature, look up Carol Ann Duffy's "Last Post", a poem she wrote as Poet Laureate to commemorate the last two British veterans of the Great War.

Notes

1　In discussing the origins of elegy, encyclopaedias and dictionaries frequently go back to classical Greek times. However, in ancient times, the term was used to describe a particular type of *metre* employed in the writing of lyric poetry rather than defining the subject matter of a poem.
2　This avenue available to many elegists of soldiers killed in action is further complicated by the fact that Robert Gregory, like many Irishmen, died fighting for Britain while many in his home country were engaged in a struggle for independence from the colonial power.
3　An adynaton is a hyperbolic figure of speech in which something very unlikely is stipulated as a condition for an action to express the idea that that action will never be taken. Popular idioms in this regard are "when hell freezes over" or "when pigs learn to fly".

References

Armitage, Simon. "The Shout". *The Universal Home Doctor*. Faber and Faber, 2002, p. 3.

Hill, Geoffrey. "September Song". *The Norton Anthology of English Literature*, eds. Meyer Howard Abrams et al., 6th ed., vol. 2. W.W. Norton, 1993, p. 2383.

Kennedy, David. "Elegy". *The New Critical Idiom*. Routledge, 2007.

Milton, John. "Lycidas". *The Poetical Works of John Milton*, ed. Helen Darbishire, vol. 2. Clarendon P, pp. 163–170.

Rae, Patricia. "Double Sorrow: Proleptic Elegy and the End of Arcadianism in 1930s Britain". *Twentieth Century Literature* 49.2 (2003), pp. 246–275.

Reeves, Gareth. "'This Is Plenty. This Is More Than Enough': Poetry and the Memory of the Second World War". *The Oxford Handbook of British and Irish War Poetry*, ed. Tim Kendall. Oxford UP, 2007, pp. 579–591.

Sacks, Peter M. *The English Elegy: Studies in the Genre from Spenser to Yeats*. Johns Hopkins UP, 1985.

Szymborska, Wisława. "Photograph from September 11". *Monologue of a Dog: New Poems*, trans. Clare Cavanagh and Stanisław Barańczak. Harcourt, 2005, p. 69.

Thomas, Dylan. "A Refusal to Mourn the Death, by Fire, of a Child in London". *Deaths and Entrances*. Dent, p. 8.

Yeats, William Butler. "In Memory of Major Robert Gregory". *W.B. Yeats: The Poems*, ed. Daniel Albright. Dent, 1990, pp. 181–184.

14 The Epic

Rachael Sumner

I

The epic is a poetic form which boasts an astounding longevity, stretching back via the Homeric narratives of *The Iliad* and *The Odyssey* to the 4,000-year-old Babylonian tale of *Gilgamesh*. It morphed out of systems of oral narrative which embraced an encyclopaedic view of myth, geography and history, often with the intention of celebrating the origins of a particular culture. Epics frequently harked back to a golden and heroic age, thereby defining and reinforcing a distinct belief system or set of values. While it aimed for linear narrative, ancient epic required vast leaps in time and space in order to tell its stories. Furthermore, its narrators had an omniscient eye, capable of following their heroes across the perilous landscapes of the known world. The epic has survived because it lends itself to adaptation and re-contextualisation – from those early incarnations of the form mentioned above, to its appropriation in the twentieth century by postcolonial poets such as Derek Walcott in his work *Omeros* (1990). This chapter will examine that process of change and transformation in the epic tradition, concentrating on the Old English poem *Beowulf*, before considering the way John Milton adapted the form in *Paradise Lost* to express the worldview of seventeenth-century English Protestantism.

Perhaps one of the most interesting aspects of epic is the way it transcends boundaries between oral traditions and the written word. This is as true of the earliest English epic – *Beowulf* – as it is of ancient Greek and Babylonian exponents. In this respect, certain lexical or metrical formulae served a mnemonic function, helping the rhapsodist – as the Greek narrator was called – or the Old English *scop* to navigate the poem. This might occur through the use of repeated phrases or metaphors, or of devices such as alliteration. It is conceivable that such techniques were effectively memory aids, and later contributed to the systematisation of poetry as it became a written form.

Also of interest is the way the epic existed as a kind of palimpsest, with the myths and tales of one culture reworked into the poetic structure of a later one. In the case of *Beowulf*, for example, the poem's espousal of Christian values is superimposed upon the laws and beliefs of a much older

DOI: 10.4324/9781003244004-16

culture. This epic sees the eponymous hero rid the Danish King's mead-hall of two vicious monsters – Grendel and his mother – accruing glory and honour as a result. Beowulf dies in combat as an old king fighting a third monster – a dragon. While we might associate monsters with lost systems of pagan belief, the narrator informs us that they have been exiled to the peripheries of human society by a very Christian God (ll. 102–108). There is a conceptual merger, then, between earlier permutations of the poem – as a product of oral tradition – and this later version, written and recorded in a now Christian reality. This is a fusion of oral and written modes of communication which the epic has never really abandoned.

The perception of epic as being, in some sense, innately nostalgic is outlined by Paul Merchant, who argues: "Those who transmitted *The Iliad, Odyssey, Aeneid, Beowulf,* and *Mahabharata* were both literally and figuratively singing to an Iron Age audience the lays of a lost Bronze Age, with behind it the even more shadowy myths of a Golden Age" (Merchant 246). The epic, then, often refers to a mythic past in order to draw attention to the weaknesses or cultural decline which is perceived in the poet's own times. Paradoxically, this has led writers throughout history to proclaim the death of epic on the grounds that epic time is over – ironic, given the fact that it presumably never existed. Milton's ⏷ mock-heroic descendants such as Alexander Pope, for example, were adamant that satire, not epic, was the only option in an England as degenerate as the one they inhabited.

An epic frequently espouses an idealist worldview. The *Beowulf* poet, for example, devotes considerable space to detailing the feasting and gift-giving that take place after Beowulf slaughters the monster Grendel. The narrator informs us that "there was nothing but friendship. The Shielding nation/was not yet familiar with feud and betrayal" (ll. 1016–1018). The implication in these lines is surely that the mutual respect between the Danes and the Geats – their systems of reward and reliance – has contributed to this brief sense of harmony, shortly to be shattered by Grendel's mother. Alliance, courage and not a little cunning are required in order to preserve order and peace. It is, the poet notes, human feuds and betrayal which have led to the dark times in which the poem is composed.

As Karl Reichl claims with regard to *Beowulf*, the epic becomes a way of reinforcing collective belief systems: "[T]here can be little doubt that *Beowulf* can be viewed as a normative epic, a narrative in which the values of heroic behaviour are presented within the cultural value system of the society depicted in the epic" (68–69). In this respect, Anglo-Saxon epic served a similar purpose to ancient iterations of the form, reminding its audience of their origins and value systems. Furthermore, as will be argued later in this chapter, Milton's *Paradise Lost* would prove the ultimate attempt to take the Puritan project back to its very roots.

Beowulf provides us with a classic example of the way martial themes and acts of bravery are central to epic, with its emphasis on the hero's

144   *Rachael Sumner*

prowess in combat and instinctive courage. Furthermore, it is necessarily a narrative rather than an abstract poem, tracing Beowulf's rise to glory and his eventual death, and breeding new stories as it gathers pace. The protagonist's extended boast of his swimming competition with Brecca provides just one example of the way epic refutes chronology in its urge to embrace as many narratives as possible. The reader (or audience) is unexpectedly transported from the horrors of Heorot and plunged into the monster-infested depths of the seas beyond (ll. 529–581).

The role of the narrator is another significant aspect of the form. Centuries before the omniscient voice comes into force in the prose form of the novel, it can be found in epic. The narrator may carry his audience from the camps of the Greeks to the besieged walls of Troy. He can accompany Odysseus on his traumatic voyage back to Ithaca, and watch Beowulf grow from young warrior to mature king. To a large extent, the narrator remains an impassive observer, accompanying the audience or reader as they witness the trials and tribulations of the characters.

As stated at the beginning of this chapter, however, the epic has survived through acts of creative adaptation. It is a highly self-conscious genre which pays homage to its literary predecessors while morphing across historical periods and cultures. This propensity for adaptation has proved intrinsic to the form's ability to function across literary epochs. The remainder of this chapter will examine ways in which John Milton both consolidates and interrogates the epic tradition in *Paradise Lost*.

II

Paradise Lost sets out to dramatise the fall of man: to establish the origins of evil in Satan's disruption of the cosmic order that God has ordained for his newly created world. Suspended between Heaven and Hell, humans should find themselves on the side of the angels, but that route is lost to them when the devil tempts Eve into taking fruit from the tree of knowledge. It is of course this single act of disobedience which consigns the human race to perdition unless the son of God intervenes, offering to take on the burden of human sin and effectively presenting an opportunity for redemption. The story of Genesis is not the most obvious point of departure for an epic, since it locates its site of conflict in the human conscience rather than on a physical battlefield. Furthermore, it is hard to imagine how a seventeenth-century English writer could regard Genesis as a foundational myth for the English nation. Nor is there any obvious space for an epic hero in a story which would seem to reduce everything to abstractions: good and evil; sin and salvation. Finally, given its publication in the seventeenth century, we might be inclined to question the way it echoes oral traditions.

On a fundamental level then, it is difficult to see how Milton could have translated such material into an epic format. Nevertheless, the poet is explicit in his claim that this particular project should be considered within the context of the epic tradition, referring to his poetry as song (III.29): a clear acknowledgement of epic poetry as an oral form. Milton also invokes his muse – a classic epic device – although she appears far more amorphous in character than the classic invocations to the Olympian muses. At times she is named Urania (the goddess of astronomy), indicating the cosmic reach of *Paradise Lost* (VII.1). Alternatively, she is reincarnated as a muse in the Judaeo-Christian tradition, rather than the classic Pagan one (I.6–7). That equation of poetry with song rather than the written word is later confirmed when Milton compares himself to two blind poets of the classic tradition – Thamyris and Maeonides. The latter is an epithet for Homer (III.35). Just like them, Milton would sightlessly sing not write, for by 1654 he was completely blind, dictating the entire poem to amanuenses including friends and family members (Campbell and Corns 271).

This relationship between song and epic could also be one of the reasons why Milton composed *Paradise Lost* in iambic pentameter, often referred to as among the closest of poetic approximations to the normal rhythm of human speech. At the time that Milton was writing, rhymed iambic pentameter was referred to as 'heroic verse': the appropriate metric line for the writing of epic. However, Milton does not adhere rigidly to the rhythm, but rather stretches its potential; varying it to describe, for example, Satan's chaotic fall from God's grace in the first book of *Paradise Lost* (I.44–49). While the reader encounters considerable variation in the use of pentameter at this point, it emerges in its purest form only when Satan's final plummet is echoed in five full iambs. Otherwise, the frantic nature of his fall is related through a subtle alteration of the rhythm and use of alliteration. Therefore, while we are conscious of the fact that Milton is writing for a newly literate public, his verse begs to be read aloud and heard, and as such sits comfortably within the oral tradition of the epic.

Having considered the way *Paradise Lost* is imbued with the sound of the human voice and of song, it is now worth directing the reader's attention to another aspect of its location within the epic tradition. In what way, it might be asked, can the poem possibly be regarded as a receptacle for the founding myths of the English nation given its biblical subject matter? In this respect, it could be argued that Milton appears to be shaping that Judaeo-Christian heritage to suit an exclusively Protestant audience.

Despite the apparent hubris of Milton's claim to be a personal envoy to the Godly (I.22–26), we can understand *Paradise Lost* as part of a wider appeal to the origins of Protestantism. As previously mentioned, one of the original aims of epic is the dissemination of foundational myths. Thus, *Paradise Lost* might be seen as the ultimate legitimation of a Puritan future with the fall of man the only suitable subject matter for a reinvented epic tradition. This would be a classic justification of the Puritan project, just as the victory over Troy or the myth of Aeneas' arrival in Italy signalled similar justifications for Greek and Latin cultures. Furthermore, the knowledge that the poem was first published seven years after the collapse of Cromwell's Puritan Commonwealth and the Restoration of the Stuart Monarchy in 1660 adds extra pathos to this reading of *Paradise Lost*. Never, it would seem, had Protestants been in greater need of reinforcing their sense of identity. *Paradise Lost* would therefore appear to take on a double meaning – not just as the tale of man's fall from God's grace, but of the loss of a society designed to restore people to His grace.

As previously mentioned, epic tends towards nostalgia in its yearning for a golden age from which a culture appears to have fallen or become disconnected. Genesis, with its notion of a pre-existent harmony on the verge of corruption, is one of the ultimate depictions of this type of fall. It is a harmony which also entails that much loved Protestant craving for order and hierarchy, as evinced in Book IV in which Adam urges Eve to rest in order to have the strength to tend Eden. She agrees, acknowledging Adam as her authority under God, and perceiving in this arrangement her own fulfilment as a woman (IV.634–638). The concept of order wrought through a defined hierarchy is therefore clearly apparent. The present age, Milton seems to suggest, has fallen from the Elysian ideal not because it is less heroic, but rather because of the disintegration of that orderly Eden which Adam and Eve inhabited. This is also another example of the way the values of a given culture or community are embedded in epic, for again Milton's paradise reveals itself to be very much a Puritan one. After all, Adam professes a clearly pronounced work ethic (IV.610–633). For Puritans, propensity for hard work revealed one's worthiness in the face of divine authority: a recognition of one's place within that cosmic hierarchy, with man acting as steward of the earth and of his wife. As long as that structure remains unchallenged, peace and harmony may be maintained. Rebellion is always and of necessity a rejection of what Milton regards as a natural and spiritual order, the ultimate example being Satan's refusal to acknowledge his role in the sacred plan.

III

It might well be argued that Milton, through embedding his text in Christian theology and tradition, is dragging the epic too far away from the form as it originates in classical literature. Yet, we might also refer to the idea – as previously stated – that epic has always proved palimpsestic in terms of the way each fresh iteration rewrites what has gone before it. A closer look at *Paradise Lost* reveals the extent to which it is clearly indebted to its classical predecessors.

We now read it, for example, in accordance with the revised edition published in 1674 with twelve books echoing the structure of Virgil's *Aeneid*. The poem itself is also an intertextual web of allusion, its classical references resting brazenly alongside its biblical root narrative, as when

The Epic   147

Satan's fallen army set out to explore their vast prison and encounter the rivers of Styx and Lethe (II.570–586). Far from being a dull dungeon of despair, Hell has a very clearly defined geography, derived from the Greek underworld rather than a Judaeo-Christian vision of eternal punishment. Furthermore, Milton's iconography has a surprisingly Greek or Roman cast, with winged messengers such as the angel Raphael reminiscent of Hermes or Mercury.

Milton's Christian re-inscription of classical imagery serves more than a purely aesthetic purpose. As Maggie Kilgour writes, his entire project was based around respect for and interrogation of those earlier traditions: "*Paradise Lost* … does not merely summarize the traditions of the ancients but also subjects them to scrutiny. Milton considers what it means to write an epic in the late seventeenth century and to use pagan forms for a Christian subject" (Kilgour 59). This last point also holds true when we consider the martial aspect of epic – its emphasis on battles, stirring speeches and acts of heroism. *Paradise Lost* both revisits and interrogates this tradition. In Book VI, for example, Raphael stirringly relates the apocalyptic battle between Satan and his rebel angels against the guardians of Heaven led by Gabriel and Michael. Yet three books later, the narrator questions the very need for epic to be defined through a focus on war and armed struggle. His narration of the fall of man, he claims, is every bit as heroic as the scenes of conflict we encounter in *The Iliad* (IX.13–16). Acts of heroism on the battlefield might have sufficed for our heathen ancestors, Milton suggests, but we now have more important issues to consider in poetry – namely, man's fall, and the grace of God. In fact, Milton claims, he intends to improve the status of poetry (IX.41–44), questioning our expectations of epic form and thereby breathing new life into an ancient genre. As previously mentioned, epic has always survived because of its capacity for transformation. Milton's rejection of convention here is a prime example of that interrogation of the form in terms of the way it can be moulded to fit the perspectives of a whole new age.

What Milton does not really alter, however, is the encyclopaedic scope of epic. This is evident in the cosmic reach of the poem, the interlacing of classical, medieval and renaissance timeframes, and the presence of an omniscient narrator who carries us from the gates of Heaven to the depths of Hell. Again, however, Milton alters the concept of the epic narrator in unexpected ways. Occasionally, for example, he makes intrusions into the poem – almost becoming an actor in its drama. Far from such digressions offering a mere comment on the action, they are surprisingly personal in flavour. The poet, for example, gives clear voice to the pain, frustration and loneliness he has experienced due to his loss of sight (III.40–50). It is in many ways a surprise to have the authoritative voice of the narrator suddenly diverge from the main subject matter of his poem and offer this level of personal insight. Yet this is just one example of *Paradise Lost* opening up its poetic terrain, inviting us to engage with epic in new and profound ways. In drawing attention to his own personal loss, the poet attracts our empathy by intruding on his own story.

We have seen, then, that *Paradise Lost* at once reiterates and challenges the epic ideal through its foregrounding of foundational narrative and values, the blending of classical allusion with the Judaeo-Christian tradition and the complicating of the omniscient narrator. We are left, however, with an outstanding question: if this is an epic, who is its hero? Is it Adam, the first man bearing the responsibility of God's law upon his shoulders, or even the tragic figure of Eve? Is it Jesus Christ, already preparing for his role as the saviour of humanity? Or could it be that the real hero is in fact Satan himself: an overreaching, charismatic and profoundly tragic figure who, in surveying the ruined landscape of Hell, declares: "The mind is its own place, and in itself/Can make a Heav'n of Hell, a Hell of Heav'n" (I.254–255).

These are lines which clearly valorise subjectivity and the mind's capacity to interpret and navigate experience. For twenty-first-century readers, it might in fact be far easier to side with Satan's privileging of agency than Adam's slavish appeal to divine order. This reading is further complicated by Milton's own role in one of the greatest anti-monarchical rebellions ever witnessed on English soil. Surely, then, there is an inherent contradiction here between the message Milton wants us to take from his poem and our inevitable reaction to Satan who is, to all intents and purposes, its epic hero.

IV

As stated at the beginning of this chapter, epic refuses to be consigned to the archives of literary history as some kind of record of the values of bygone ages. It survives through its ability to seep into other literary forms; to morph and remould itself into genres as diverse as the mock-heroic mode in the eighteenth century and even the novel, with Modernist writers paying tribute to the epic in prose form, perhaps most famously in James Joyce's *Ulysses* (1922). As late as 1990, it was reinvented as a work of postcolonial literature which deliberately locates the epic at the very centre of cultural narratives stemming not just from European traditions, but from Caribbean and African forms of storytelling. *Omeros*, by the Nobel laureate Derek Walcott, resituates *The Iliad* on St Lucia with its characters unwittingly taking on the roles of Achilles, Hector and Helen, a deliberate writing back to the European traditions which had left their cultural imprint on former colonies.

Foregrounding his epic as the product of diverse, intercontinental cultural traditions, Walcott broke and reinvented the form just as Milton had done some three centuries earlier. Epic is and always has been an act of appropriation – a writing back to poets from the past – a form of ancestral dialogue, carrying the ability to explain to us who we are and from where we have come. It consumes and recycles geography and history in its attempt to make sense of the world, and has done so for the past 4,000 years. There is no reason to imagine that it will not continue to do so in the future.

The Epic   149

> **NOW READ ON...**
>
> - The chapter references ⟋ mock-heroic poetry as Alexander Pope's jaded version of the epic.
> - The ⟋ heroic couplet is the form most commonly chosen for epics written in early modern English. The chapter on that particular form will let you find out more about its development.
> - Milton wrote *Paradise Lost* in ⟋ blank verse, and a more elaborate discussion of his prosodic technique can be found in the chapter on that particular form.
> - Some critics occasionally note significant overlaps between the epic, the ⟋ long poem and the ⟋ dramatic monologue. Look up those forms to discover how they differ from the epic, particularly in terms of their relationship to time: the epic with its dual relationship between events reported and the age they are reported in; the dramatic monologue with its (faux) historical characters; and the long poem with its social concerns in its contemporary period.

References

Beowulf, trans. Seamus Heaney. Faber and Faber, 1999.

Campbell, Gordon, and Thomas N. Corns. *John Milton: Life, Work and Thought.* Oxford UP, 2008.

Kilgour, Maggie. "Classical Models". *The Cambridge Companion to Paradise Lost*, ed. Louis Schwartz. Cambridge UP, 2014, pp. 57–67.

Merchant, Paul. "Epic Poetry in Translation". *The Cambridge Companion to the Epic*, ed. Catherine Bates. Cambridge UP, 2010, pp. 246–263.

Milton, John. *Paradise Lost*, ed. John Leonard. Penguin Classics, 2000.

Reichl, Karl. "Heroic Epic Poetry in the Middle Ages". *The Cambridge Companion to the Epic*, ed. Catherine Bates. Cambridge UP, 2010, pp. 55–75.

15 Free Verse

Andrew Rowcroft

I

From the French 'vers libre', free verse has no regular metre or line length and depends on the natural speech rhythms of stressed and unstressed syllables. But approach free verse with caution. It is anything but free. Unlike many other forms discussed in this book, free verse has no discernible set of rules. It does not use a consistent metre or rhyme and sometimes avoids metre and rhyme altogether. But the idea that poets can write whatever they wish – and are liberated from strict formal constraints – is a common misconception when encountering free verse for the first time. Free-verse poetry may not be burdened by the metical requirements of more traditional poetic forms, but it still requires craft and a degree of constraint in its composition. In the hands of talented poets, free verse can acquire melody and rhythm, and is no less demanding to write.

It is difficult to date the emergence of free verse, with some poets claiming that it stretches back to antiquity and the practice of common speech. In claiming the likes of Euripides and Homer as writers of free verse, poets are doing two things. They claim that their chosen form, and by extension their own work, captures the musicality of ancient literature – which is pretty high praise – and that free verse is a kind of pure poetry, not corrupted by the artificiality of later poetic forms which impose strict borders and boundaries on language. Even the most judicious comments carry a promotional edge. What is clear is that free verse came to dominate in the twentieth century, particularly in British and American poetry, and this hold shows no sign of weakening in the contemporary.

Before we have a look at a number of free-verse poems and their salient features, it is worth stating that amongst all the poetic forms, free verse stimulates most debate. It is, and still continues to be, subjected to questions about its quality ('lazy poets write free verse'), and even its existence ('good poetry has metre and rhyme'). The American poet Robert Frost said that composing free verse is like playing tennis without a net. For Frost, structure was more important than poetic freedom. These are questions that are seldom asked about other poetic forms. But as will become clear over the course of this chapter, free-verse poems often have a planned

DOI: 10.4324/9781003244004-17

Free Verse   151

and intricate organisation, and can be credited with audacity, vision, and a commitment to innovation. There are of course any number of bad free-verse poems, but this is true of all poetic forms.

II

The American poet Walt Whitman (1819–1892) remains a major figure in free-verse poetry. Whitman did not invent the form but unleashed a free-verse movement with the publication of *Leaves of Grass* (1855). Whitman actually self-published the book and spent most of his life expanding and revising the poems inside many times across successive editions. In the preface to the first edition, Whitman claimed that the "rhyme and uniformity of perfect poems show a free growth of metrical laws and bud from them as unerringly and loosely as lilacs or roses on a bush" (11). The movement towards free verse, thought Whitman, was as natural as strong flowers in full bloom. But free verse was also a determined, conscious choice. Whitman wanted to liberate poetry from the dusty, musty world of Victorian sentimentality, by penning poetry of vigour, with an idiosyncratic point of view.

Whitman's vision differed from many other poets. While others were engaged in the careful crafting of a ⊘ sonnet, ⊘ elegy, or ⊘ ode, Whitman thought the United States – the people, the land, and language – was itself the poem. This is an important distinction: such a position entailed capture, not creation. One of the most prominent features of Whitman's free verse is the list, sometimes referred to as the Whitman catalogue. In these extended lists, of names, objects, places, and things, in poems like "Pioneers! O Pioneers!" (1865) and "Song of Myself" (1855), Whitman expresses his belief in the expansiveness and all-inclusiveness of the United States. For Whitman, the poem becomes a place to pack in as much of the American experience as possible. Reading Whitman, one feels that the world he is trying to capture   the nineteenth-century United States – often bursts out of the formal limitations of the text itself. For Whitman, there was simply no way a sonnet could adequately capture the immense scope, diversity, and ambition of America. Free verse, then, was more adequate to this endeavour, as it did not require fitting the world as Whitman saw it into a metrical form. But it is also a form seemingly overwhelmed by what Whitman can see, hear, taste, and touch.

"Song of Myself" is Whitman's epic free-verse poem (unsurprisingly, free-verse poetry does not follow a prescribed length, and in a moment, we shall look at an immensely short free-verse poem). The poem favours a simple style and common language that could be read by many nineteenth-century Americans. But it also included unsavoury elements, such as slavery, prostitution, and sexuality, and was denounced by social conservatives and some prominent thinkers, even other poets. Not only was the content of the poem offensive to some sensibilities, but the verses themselves were unlike anything seen at the time. Free verse, we must

152 *Andrew Rowcroft*

remember, was not always commonplace but once scandalous, perplexing, and new.

In one section of the poem, Whitman records a child asking, "What is the grass?". This seemingly simple question quickly fractures into a multiplicity of metaphors. Whitman considers whether the grass is a gift, flag, handkerchief, or the "beautiful uncut hair of graves" (l. 110). These metaphors juxtapose as much as they unite, bringing people, places, and images together within a greater inclusiveness, and democratic spirit. Whitman can only achieve this through the long, unstructured line. Looking at the poem, as it appears on the page, is to see astonishing diversity, difference, and irregularity. Such long line poetics, at least in Whitman, encourage a kind of earthiness and enthusiasm. It is if Whitman's chosen subject – the United States, everything, and all of it – demands a form without ornament or decoration. There was very little that was conventional about Whitman, and free verse allowed him to voice a new kind of plain-spoken language and a radical democratic vision counter to the prevailing one in Europe.[1]

It is worth mentioning the work of the American essayist and poet Henry David Thoreau (1817–1862), who met Whitman in 1856. Some years before, Thoreau had undertaken a boat trip and written about his experience in a book, *A Week on the Concord and Merrimack Rivers* (1849). In one section, Thoreau is trading some goods with another man he has met on the banks of the river and writes in his journal: "The very names of the commodities were poetic, and as suggestive as if they had been inserted in a pleasing poem – Lumber, Cotton, Sugar, Hides, Guano, Logwood" (151). For Thoreau, the words of commonplace, everyday items were themselves the sources of poetic inspiration. Structure, it seems, was out.

III

Whitman's experiments in free verse proved immensely influential to future generations of British and American poets. The twentieth-century poet Allen Ginsberg (1926–1997) was a particularly close and avid reader of Whitman's work and chose to write almost exclusively in free verse. In "A Supermarket in California" (1956), Ginsberg imagines Whitman, still alive, but now a "childless, lonely old grubber" (l. 11). As the narrator wanders through the supermarket aisles, filled with bright, lurid fruit, a powerful indictment of the strangeness of American consumerism, he stumbles upon the figure of Whitman, and follows him around the store. Importantly, the speaker is always at a distance from Whitman, and never talks to him directly. He imagines a series of questions he could ask the great poet – none of which are answered in the poem – about where they will go, and what America once looked like. In imagining Whitman as a frail, old man, Ginsberg's poem addresses the legacy of Whitman's work, and the dreams Whitman once had for America. Ginsberg's poem is lacking the optimism we so often find in Whitman. Indeed, Ginsberg's poetics

Free Verse   153

is all about the failure of the American project, for the once great poet of the United States is now stuck buying food in a supermarket.

Similar to Whitman's style of free verse, Ginsberg's poem also features long unstructured lines, lists of items and commodities, and no rhyme or repetition. In this pitiable image of Whitman, making his way around the supermarket, lonely, confused, and lacking his poetic genius, Ginsberg asks the reader to reflect on the condition of the United States, but also draws important parallels between his poetry and Whitman's style of modern free verse. As much as Ginsberg wants to critique the United States, he is also drawing upon a poetic tradition founded by Whitman.

Some critics may argue that Ginsberg's work is actually a prose poem, that is, a poem written in prose rather than verse form, while still displaying poetic devices. Prose poetry is more 'free' than free verse because it has no metred line, where free verse can employ metre, if it so chooses. But there are enough similarities between the two to make the distinction more difficult than is often assumed.

Defining free verse has been a persistent theoretical occupation of the twentieth century. In this sense, the work of the American poet T.S. Eliot (1888–1965) is central. Eliot not only wrote extensively in free verse, but he also reflected on definitional questions, the form's abilities, and its limitations. It is important to remember that Eliot was likely the most influential modernist poet, and his views on literature, criticism, philosophy, and theology still remain immensely important today. In a now famous essay "Reflections on *Vers Libre*", written in 1917, Eliot argued, perhaps strangely, that free verse does not actually exist. Rather, he thought that free verse is a constant movement back and forth between rhyme and regular metre, or what he called fixity and flux. It can only be defined, Eliot wrote, in negatives. Free verse is, he thought, the absence of pattern, absence of rhyme, and absence of metre (Eliot, "Reflections" 32). Importantly, such descriptions – and there are many of them similar to Eliot's initial pronouncements – do not state what free verse is. They say only what the speaker thinks it lacks. It is of course problematic to think of free verse as a poetry of lack, but this still remains one of the best ways to identify free verse. As such, in your own readings, you may consider undertaking a process of accumulating negative facts: you may seek an established rhyme scheme, and find none, or you may try and find a specific metre, and notice that the poem actually has lines of different lengths.

I mentioned at the beginning of the chapter that free verse – that is, good free verse – requires craft, precision, and hard work in the process of its composition. Eliot goes on to make a series of further pronouncements about the worth of free verse. Firstly, he addresses any niggling concerns about poetry that does not use rhyme, stating emphatically that "there is no campaign against rhyme" (Eliot, *Prose* 36). For Eliot, free verse is not a coordinated offensive on traditional poetic sensibilities (for some poets it certainly was) but simply poets choosing to write differently. Secondly,

154 *Andrew Rowcroft*

Eliot wants to propose that free verse is modern (Eliot, *Prose* 32). The rejection of rhyme, he thought, imposes a greater depth to language because free-verse poetry has nothing to fall back on, no scaffolding to support its contents, other than the poem's own internal logic. For Eliot, free verse cannot be held to an objective standard; the worth of the poem can only be discerned through individual reading because each free-verse poem will be radically different, even purposely unique.

Eliot's "The Love Song of J. Alfred Prufrock" (1915) is a free-verse poem in which lines occasionally end in rhyme, but there is no pattern or consistent rhyme scheme. This gives the poem an often abrupt tone, where lines can come to a sudden and dramatic halt, or other times the rhyme acts as a cohesive device. The poem is the interior monologue of a middle-aged man, stricken with feelings of isolation, loneliness, and lacking the capacity for decisive action. Dissatisfied with his life – much of the poem is given over to a sense of existential crisis – the speaker laments his physical and mental decline, the ever-diminishing space that make up a series of ever-narrowing choices.

One of the most stunning and arresting images occurs early on, with Prufrock inviting the reader to accompany him as he makes his visit, presumably to the house of a friend. The evening is spread back against the sky "[l]ike a patient etherised upon a table" (l. 3). Eliot would return to this image again and again in his later works. If we were unsure of the impotence of the individual, and the crisis between self and society, this medical metaphor makes it clear. The pain of social interaction is made manifest, while we, as readers, will undoubtedly be examining the character Prufrock in our own readings, much like a patient under examination. The fact that there is no rhyme here makes the image particularly stark, but Eliot is certainly comfortable deploying rhyme elsewhere in the poem.

I want to consider one further modernist poem here, if only because it proves to be one of the most stunning, yet modestly elegant texts I have ever encountered. "In a Station of the Metro" (1913) is a two-line poem (or possibly a three-line poem, including the title) by Ezra Pound (1885–1972).[2] In this immensely short poem, Pound juxtaposes two powerful images: the speed of urban existence (think of catching the Tube in London or a train in the New York City subway) and the relative stillness of nature. The critical force of the poem comes from its oscillation between the two images, between fixity and flux, to use Eliot's observations on free verse mentioned above. The serene image of nature may act as compensation for the packed-in condition, the crush, jam, and rush of modern city life, familiar to anyone who has travelled in major cities. Alternatively, it is the pace, energy, and dynamism of city life that generates much of the appeal of that kind of social existence. In many ways the poem mimics the forms of accommodation all of us adopt as ways of living in the world. When the space of the city feels too much, we can turn to the serene, isolated images of nature. But, of course, as the poem suggests, these two are connected and symbiotic.

Free Verse   155

There are two further points to be made: the first regarding perception, or the act of looking. The apparition of a mass of people suggests an assault on the senses. Pound does not describe their faces; indeed, he cannot because there are simply too many. They appear and suddenly disappear. In contrast, observations on nature feel cleaner and more exact, much calmer, serene, and even peaceful. Nature is not static, but the image feels tranquil in contrast to the mass of human subjects that make up the crowd. Of course, in a crowd, individual identity is lost. While the crowd feels fractured – made up of different elements – its equivalent in nature feels whole. This is a deceptively simple free-verse poem that, like a magnet, exerts a field of force that ripples invisibly across the rest of the twentieth century.

IV

Most of the poems considered above are well known, so the chapter now moves to consider two other free-verse poems that do not have a similar status but are still deeply important for our discussion of the form. Robert Hayden's (1919–1980) "Those Winter Sundays" (1962) is a short and intensely beautiful poem about boyhood, parental love, and silence. Looking back at his youth, the speaker notes that on Sundays his father rose early in the cold to make the fire (l. 5). The "too" of the first line is immensely heavy and does a great deal of work in this poem. It captures the labour, exhaustion, and sacrifice the father must have made, for which he is never thanked by the boy, but which will be detailed in the rest of the poem. The boy hears the sounds of the father preparing the fire and is then called to the warmer room. The boy speaks indifferently to the father who has driven out the cold and polished his shoes (l. 12). Importantly, we never hear what is said between the father and son – indeed, the poem draws much of its power from the lack of dialogue between them – only the tone is important here, which is unconcerned and uncaring. There is even a suggestion of marital discord, as the poem references the angers of the house, although the mother is never mentioned. The anger may simply be in the relationship between the father and son, but perhaps it is a cold anger, shown through a failure of conversation and emotional distance or inexpression rather than cruelty. The father's love for the son comes through physical acts and domestic duties rather than linguistic acts, such as the building of the fire and the polishing of the shoes.

The final stanza of the poem is the moment of the boy's recognition of the father's labour. An important moment but one that arrives very late. Through the lighting of the fire, the father has driven out the harsh elements of the world – notably the cold and dark – and made a home for the boy. The son admits that he knew nothing of this, that he did not recognise the kind of love his father had for him, and, in the final astonishing line, he did not realise how lonely love's office is.

In keeping with our discussion of free verse thus far, this poem uses no rhyme scheme, although there are rhymes and half-rhymes, and the line

156 *Andrew Rowcroft*

length is fairly regular. The first and last stanza are each five lines, while the middle stanza is four. This means there are fourteen lines in total, so it is, loosely, a sonnet, but also a definitive departure from that form in its use of free verse, and not a poem we would recognise or immediately align with the sonnet. Also, while this examination of the text has used terms like son and boy, there is actually nothing in the poem to suggest this. If we pursue a reading based on a daughter, the poem might change quite dramatically.

Another important free-verse poem is by the American poet Muriel Rukeyser, (1913–1980) "Boy with His Hair Cut Short" (1938). It is a poem about poverty, hope, and the search for work. Like the poem above, it too takes place on a Sunday. But while "Those Winter Sundays" could refer to a multiplicity of places and spaces – and indeed attempts to capture the relationship between fathers and sons/daughters rather than a moment in time – this poem is more locatable: it refers to the L line, placing the action in Chicago, or possibly New York City. It is evening and the boy's older sister is cutting his hair with inexpensive shears, while all around those in the buildings nearby relax and listen to music. Clearly, the poem is demonstrating that while Sunday is traditionally a moment of tranquillity and respite, here, the two characters of the poem have their evenings taken up with anxiety, work, and worry. The sister is full of frustrated optimism, attempting to instil in the boy the confidence that he will find employment somewhere (l. 18). It becomes clear that he has been turned down for a job a number of times. Indeed, it is said that the sister is attempting to erase "the failure of weeks with level fingers" (l. 16). Behind her, the boy's one decent suit is laid out, with money for the commute. The poem is about the difficulties and hardships of the working poor, or put differently, the hunger and desperation that accompany the search for work in America and elsewhere. The poem has no rhyme scheme, which has traditionally been read by critics as a form of protest against a society that often pushes people into regimented, structured, back-breaking labour. The final stanza is particularly important, with each line ending with a series of ironic active terms ("splitting", "motion", "beating"). All this energy and movement in the poem, and yet the brother and sister have little to show for it.

This chapter has explored a number of engaging free-verse poems. Some, like the works of Whitman, are well established and among the most influential poetic works ever produced. Others, like the poem by Hayden, and the poem by Rukeyser, have a less popular status. Free-verse poetry is simply too large a subject to cover extensively here. What this chapter has achieved, however, is to impart a short critical selection that reveals the astonishing diversity, subjects, and formal experimentation of free-verse poetry. While free verse does not have set rules or requirements, it is not a lesser form. It is regarded by many of its most proficient practitioners as intensely difficult. It became the most prominent poetic form in the twentieth century and remains so today.

Free Verse 157

NOW READ ON…

- Free verse is often employed in more extensive poems and can be frequently found in the ⟋ long poem. That chapter features additional discussions of Whitman's and Eliot's poetry.
- You will also find "The Love Song of J. Alfred Prufrock" discussed in the chapter on the ⟋ dramatic monologue.
- Since neither uses rhyme, free verse is sometimes confused with ⟋ blank verse, despite the fact that blank verse is a much more traditional, much more regular form.
- If free verse is used in contexts where poets feel the need not to be boxed in by an artificial form, in projects entailing "capture, not creation", consider what that says about the use of highly restrictive forms such as the ⟋ sestina, the ⟋ villanelle, or the ⟋ sonnet.

Notes

1 As much as Whitman's project was counter to established European forms, the growth and development of American Transcendentalism was also guided by the initial work of European figures. See Samantha C. Harvey, *Transatlantic Transcendentalism: Coleridge, Emerson, and Nature*, Edinburgh University Press, 2013).
2 While the poem is considered a free-verse poem in the present context since it features no rhyme scheme nor a recognisable metre, some critics have argued that it was written in imitation of the Japanese form of the haiku.

References

Eliot, T.S. "The Love Song of J. Alfred Prufrock". *The Complete Poems and Plays of TS Eliot*. Guild Publishing, 1969, pp. 13–17.
———. "Reflections on 'Vers Libre'". *Selected Prose of T. S. Eliot*, ed. Frank Kermode. Faber and Faber, 1975, pp. 31–36.
Ginsberg, Allen. "A Supermarket in America". *Howl and Other Poems*. City Lights, 1956, pp. 23–24.
Harvey, Samantha C. *Transatlantic Transcendentalism: Coleridge, Emerson, and Nature*. Edinburgh UP, 2013.
Hayden, Robert. "Those Winter Sundays". *Collected Poems*, ed. Frederick Glaysher. Liveright, 1985, p. 41.
Pound, Ezra. "In a Station of the Metro". *New Selected Poems and Translations*, ed. Richard Sieburth. New Directions, 2010, p. 39.
Rukeyser, Muriel. "Boy with His Hair Cut Short". *Collected Poems*. McGraw-Hill, 1982, pp. 114–115.
Thoreau, Henry David. *A Week on the Concord and Merrimack Rivers, Walden; or, Life in the Woods, The Maine Woods, Cape Cod*. Library of America, 1985.
Whitman, Walt. "Song of Myself". *Leaves of Grass (1855)*. Library of America, 2011, pp. 1–146.

16 The Heroic Couplet

Alex Streim

I

The heroic couplet is a historical form. This is true in three ways. In the first, it is 'historical' simply because it is old – an artefact of the eighteenth century that has long since gone out of style. In this sense, the form is as historical, say, as St Paul's Cathedral in London. Both were constructed over a specific period of time in the past, and if you go out of your way now, you can still see them. The heroic couplet is also historical because it *incorporates* the past. St Paul's Cathedral is also historical in this way, insofar as it was reconstructed in the seventeenth century using ancient Greek and Roman elements of design. Like the cathedral, the heroic couplet is often engaged with ancient history and characterised by seeming older than it really is. The final sense in which the heroic couplet is historical is shared by all poetic forms. The 'heroic couplet', that is, is not simply another element – like hydrogen, or boron, or titanium – on some periodic table of poetry, a specimen discovered once and for all at a specific point in time. It is an idea. An idea that, for a number of reasons, some readers of poetry have found to be a useful way of thinking about how certain poems are constructed.

The phrase 'heroic couplet' has, of course, two component parts. The 'couplet' is a formal category and refers to a group of two lines, often rhymed.[1] What makes such a pair of lines 'heroic', however, has historically depended on criteria both formal and thematic. John Dennis was one of the first critics to stipulate *how* heroic couplets should be written. For Dennis, couplets could only be classified as heroic if they conformed to his "Principle of Pauses". According to that principle, "the Pause at the End of a Verse ought to be greater than any Pause that may precede it in the same Verse, and the Pause at the End of a Couplet ought to be greater than that which is at the End of the first Verse" (qtd. in Piper 6).[2] More recently, twentieth-century poets Mark Strand and Eavan Boland have offered a looser set of formal characteristics, suggesting that heroic couplets generally rhyme, are usually composed in iambic pentameter, and tend to include a caesura after the fifth or sixth syllable (121). But Strand

DOI: 10.4324/9781003244004-18

and Boland also remind us that such couplets only become conventionally heroic if they are also *about* certain things. According to them, the heroic couplet developed as a form in which "a high subject matter could be written. This was the form often used for translation of epic poetry from the classical Latin and Greek" (121).[3] In order to be conventionally heroic, that is, the poem's theme must be important, and will likely include an actual hero (such as Achilles, Odysseus, or Aeneas).

Critics date the ascendance of the heroic couplet in various ways, but most recognise that it remained popular throughout the eighteenth century. What the 25-minute sitcom episode was to television in the 1980s and 1990s, the heroic couplet was to poetry for over a century. Philip Hobsbaum dates the pre-eminence of the heroic couplet from 1640 to 1750; William Bowman Piper from 1660 to 1785; and Wallace Cable Brown from 1620 to 1819. The historical life of the heroic couplet is perhaps unique relative to other poetic forms in that the form was immensely popular for a particular stretch of time and then fell precipitously into disuse. Why the form became popular just when it did is a matter of some contention, although most critics would agree with Strand and Boland's suggestion that "in the Augustan Age when order was the dream, and decorum a necessity, the couplet seemed a micro-model of the age's intentions: closed-in, certain, attractive to the reason, and finally, reassuring to the limits of that elegant world" (122–123). But if the Augustan Age was marked by an aesthetic attempt to maintain "order", "decorum", and "limits", it also corresponded to a specific period of political economic history. Specifically, the Augustan Age witnessed the height of the transatlantic slave trade and the associated accumulation of capital in Europe and the United States. It is beyond the task of this chapter to show how the aesthetic urge towards order, decorum, and limitation may have been related to the slave economy, or why a generalised anxiety about slave uprisings might have reappeared in a poetic style predicated on hierarchy, recurrence, and predictability. But it is not beyond the task of this chapter to explore how certain practitioners of the heroic couplet have made such connections themselves.

For poets writing both during and after the so-called Augustan Age, the form of the heroic couplet invoked the history of the period in which it was popular. To state it boldly: the rhymed, pentameter couplet on classical themes comes stained with the blood of the enslaved. But since the fall of the heroic couplet was as precipitous as its rise (it began to fall out of favour around 1800), later poets pick up this history of obsolescence, too.[4] To write in heroic couplets is to invoke at once a highly decorous, stylish form, and one that now seems woefully out of fashion. Why poets might choose to saddle their poems with such complicated historical baggage is the question to which I will dedicate the rest of this chapter.[5]

160   *Alex Streim*

II

Alexander Pope is the most recognised practitioner of the heroic couplet. He used it, famously, to translate Homer, rendering the first lines of *The Iliad* as: "The Wrath of *Peleus'* son, the direful Spring / Of all the *Grecian* Woes, O Goddess, sing!" (ll. 1–2). Rhymed pentameter couplets complete with a hero (Achilles) and a high theme – these translations helped imbue the form with its characteristic gravity. He also used the form for two didactic poems, *An Essay on Criticism* and *An Essay on Man*. These poems were not about Greek and Trojan heroes, but about, respectively, reading poetry, and the relationships between humans, God, society, and the natural world. Here, Pope used the form to teach his readers specific lessons about art and moral life: "Hope humbly then; with trembling pinions soar; / Wait the great teacher, Death; and God adore" (ll. 87–88). Elsewhere, Pope used the form to lend undue ⬀ epic significance to a "trivial" theme – the cutting of a woman's hair at a game of cards: "The Peer now spreads the glitt'ring Forfex wide, / T'inclose the Lock: now joins it, to divide" (ll. 147–148). This poem, *The Rape of the Lock*, was primarily an exercise in comedic irony, as the poet described a minor incident in a verse form that seemed too important for its subject. Readers often trace later ironic uses of the heroic couplet to this poem (⬀ mock-heroic poetry).

Not long after Pope's comedic exercise, another poet also used rhymed, pentameter couplets to treat a theme supposedly inappropriate for such a refined form. When Phillis Wheatley published her *Poems on Various Subjects, Religious and Moral* in London in 1773, she became the first African American author to publish a book of poetry. The collection included the short, eight-line poem "On Being Brought from Africa to America". It begins by describing her own enslavement, which she recasts, from the perspective of her eventual conversion to Christianity, as a "mercy" (ll. 1–3). We might read this beginning as, in part, a subterfuge – a way of appealing to white readers unaccustomed to reading poetry written by a Black woman. It sets up the poem's final lines, which address those readers directly, this time with a more uncomfortable lesson: "Remember, *Christians, Negros*, black as *Cain*, / May be refin'd, and join th' angelic train" (ll. 7–8). It's not incidental that Wheatley gives this last reminder in a heroic couplet. That she is able to craft such verse – the standard of high poetic art at the time – provides a formal proof that "Negros, black as *Cain*, / May be refin'd", be it into artists, or into Christians.[6] This poem uses irony – although not, as with Pope's, to provoke a laugh. Instead, she repurposes a refined form to slyly critique (or, effectively, allow *us* to critique) how refinement itself acts as a kind of test, a rubric with which to grade someone's humanity. Although the poem is ostensibly an apology for enslavement and an argument for assimilation, it uses the reputation of the form in which it is written to begin to erode the dehumanising logic on which racism is built.[7]

III

Twentieth-century poets picked up where Wheatley left off. "Thoughts in a Zoo" (1927), a poem by Countee Cullen, for instance, uses heroic couplets to draw an analogy between literally caged animals and figuratively caged humans. The poem begins by staging an encounter between the two: "They in their cruel traps, and we in ours, / Survey each other's rage, and pass the hours" (ll. 1–2). While it's possible to read a twentieth-century sonnet without at first recognising that it is indeed a ⟨⟩ sonnet, it's harder to miss the fact of being inside a poem made of heroic couplets. As suggested above, modern heroic couplets tend to be quite conscious of the history of their own form. Cullen's opening two lines, in fact, allude to two different eighteenth-century poems. With the word "rage" he invokes Pope's Achilles, and with the word "survey" at the beginning of the second line, he recalls Samuel Johnson's *The Vanity of Human Wishes*, which begins with a directive to "Let observation with extensive view, / Survey mankind, from China to Peru" (ll. 1–2). But Cullen's heroic couplets do not only invoke the history of the form. They also invoke the history in which that form first developed. In one of her poems, Wheatley describes how "I, young in life, by seeming cruel fate / Was snatch'd from *Afric's* fancy'd happy seat" (ll. 24–25). Although Cullen's poem is in the first place a reflection on existential human imprisonment, it also doubles as a reflection on the way particular groups of humans (in this case, Black Americans) are actually subject to the "cruel[ty]" of others (l. 1). To write a poem in heroic couplets about animals in traps in the Jim Crow-era United States, that is, can evoke – if only distantly – the European "snatching" of Africans from their native lands.

Eighteen years after Cullen, Gwendolyn Brooks leverages the historical weight of the heroic couplet for a somewhat different effect. "The Sundays of Satin-Legs Smith" is a long poem about a young Black American man's typical Sunday in Chicago. It opens with a single heroic couplet about where the hero got his nickname: "Inamoratas, with an approbation, / Bestowed his title. Blessed his inclination" (ll. 1–2). That Brooks rhymes two long words with a Latinate ending while using an uncommon word ("inamoratas") where a more usual one (say, "lovers" or "girlfriends") would do invests the poem with a conscious irony. Like Wheatley, Brooks is putting on a show. Unlike Wheatley, Brooks means to mock her educated readers for taking that show too seriously. These first two lines are set off in their own stanza. Although the rest of the poem does not maintain the formal pattern, Brooks does continue to dip in and out of heroic couplets, reminding the reader that the poem is meant to feel important, classical. Over time, it becomes clear that this use of the form is meant to satirise the pedantic expectations of any readers who overvalue such decorum. After describing her protagonist's "sarcastic" and "cocky" Zoot suit, for instance, Brooks rebukes her readers for tacitly assuming that Satin Legs

162   *Alex Streim*

should share their same reverence for restraint and order (ll. 70–73). Here and elsewhere, Brooks teaches her twentieth-century readers that their tastes are in fact a product of certain historical conditions. By the time Satin Legs walks through a poor neighbourhood, past men unable to take pleasure in music because they are hungry, Brooks has invited her readers to begin to contemplate the historical reasons for that hunger (15). Wheatley's story is once again on the air.

Brooks' poem implies that developing a taste for the heroic couplet depends on the possession of a certain amount of wealth. Other twentieth-century poets also use the form to think about what it means to have a lot of money. Philip Larkin, for instance, in a poem called "Money", uses heroic couplets to ponder the pile of cash he keeps "upstairs": "Quarterly, is it, money reproaches me: / 'Why do you let me lie here wastefully? …'" (ll. 1–2). Larkin is less concerned with how money is made unfairly and distributed unequally than he is with how to spend the money he already has. His use of the heroic couplet to elaborate this concern aptly leverages the association he and his readers may feel exists between the heroic couplet and accumulated wealth. Stevie Smith, meanwhile, uses the heroic couplet to launch a scathing critique of "The Suburban Classes". Her poem of that name begins: "There is far too much of the suburban classes / Spiritually not geographically speaking. They're asses" (ll. 1–2). Here, Smith uses the rhymed couplet to mock a class of people with newfound access to personal wealth. At the end of that opening couplet, we experience the comedic dissonance of encountering a curse word that simultaneously stitches together a form noted for its good breeding.

There's a history, then, of twentieth-century poets using heroic couplets to allegorise human entrapment, teach readers about the connections between aesthetics and racial capitalism, and satirise the middle class. In each of these cases, the form itself lends the poem a whiff of the darker side of Augustan decorum. In most of these cases, the use of the form is meant to feel antiquated, a bit mis-matched to the subject at hand. I'll close this chapter by describing how poets have leveraged this sort of mismatch not so much for critique, as for pathos. In this tradition – dating back to Pope's rendition of the death of Patroclus – poets use heroic couplets to compose ☞ elegies for the dead. Wheatley herself wrote several and had a particular habit of using the form to eulogise dead infants and children. Gwendolyn Brooks continues this legacy all but directly in her 1945 poem, "the mother", an elegy in the voice of a woman for a group of aborted children. Once again, the poem slides in and out of heroic couplets, alighting briefly on the traditional form only to then break the pentameter or neglect the rhyme. Even these occasional 'heroic' moments, however, are able to lend a deserved gravity to the mother's experience of loss. One couplet near the end of the poem, for instance, ennobles the imaginary "giggling" of which it speaks (ll. 29–30). This use of the form isn't so much ironic as it is determined to afford this mother's complicated grief an expression adequate to its lived severity.

The Heroic Couplet 163

More recently, Thom Gunn's "Lament" (1992) uses the heroic couplet to eulogise a friend lost to AIDS. In this case, the effects of the form are multiple. For one, the couplets march down the page with a regularity that enacts the steadiness and equanimity with which the poet's friend lives his final weeks. After "two weeks of an abominable constraint", Gunn writes, "you faced [death] equably, without complaint" (ll. 73–74). Here, the regular couplets perform at once the "abominable constraint" of being confined to a hospital bed, and the controlled self-possession this heroic friend manages in the face of his ravaging illness. Just as the poet takes pains to hold his poem together, he and his friend attempt to hold their emotional selves together through a difficult end. But in the twentieth century, the long satirical and critical histories of the heroic couplet are never far afield. Insofar as no modern hero could ever be quite as heroic as, say, Achilles, to use the heroic couplet now is to deliberately risk a kind of overstatement. As courageous as this dying man is, then, Gunn's use of heroics to describe his bravery nonetheless places him into shoes too big to fill. The effect is a wryness that falls just short of humour. As tragic as the poem is, we might even feel the beginnings of a laugh. At one point, Gunn describes his friend as smiling at his own "silliness" (l. 86), and in this way the poem's form can heighten the image. But in addition to rinsing the poem with a kind of heartbreaking levity, the awkwardly fitting heroic couplets also call up the long history of poems – partially recounted above – that use polished heroic couplets only to remind us of the human life beneath that polish. In the case of "Lament", the heroic couplets almost seem to inject the poem with a feeling that this death was not entirely inevitable – that somewhere, at some point, off the page of the poem, the AIDS crisis was a product of human malice and neglect that might have been otherwise. Gunn, like Brooks, like Cullen, and like Wheatley, uses the history baked into the surface of the form to grieve not only accidental death, but purposeful wrongdoing. In these poets' hands, the heroic couplet, simple as it seems, expresses at once the possession, deprivation, and reclamation of human agency.

NOW READ ON…

- A number of forms discussed in this book make frequent use of the heroic couplet, so it might be worth looking up the chapters on the ⟳ epic, on ⟳ mock-heroic poetry, and on the ⟳ sonnet, which – in English at least – frequently closes on a heroic couplet.
- Pope's *Rape of the Lock* that is briefly touched upon in this chapter features more prominently in the chapter on ⟳ mock-heroic poetry.

164   *Alex Streim*

- The chapter on the ⏴ sonnet also features a consideration of Claude McKay's use of the oppressor's valued form to express resistance on the part of the oppressed.
- While Gunn's "Lament" is indeed noticeable for its use of heroic couplets, it can be further discussed in the context of the form of the ⏴ elegy.
- Gwendolyn Brooks' poem "In the Mecca" features prominently in the chapter on ⏴ blank verse.

Notes

1 Some critics distinguish between different kinds of couplets, according to whether or not their lines are end-stopped. Richard Haswell, for instance, differentiates the "closed couplet" from the "run-on couplet" and the "jammed couplet" (3–4).
2 Dennis uses the term "verse" to refer to an individual line and the term "couplet" to refer to a group of two lines.
3 The form is still being used for classical translations. See, for instance, Aaron Poochigian's 2010 translation of Aratus' *Phaenomena*.
4 The transatlantic slave trade was abolished in the English House of Commons in 1807.
5 See Caplan (1999) for another answer to this question.
6 In a way, the poem also has its own hero. Whereas Pope appeals to the muse to sing Achilles' wrath, Wheatley appeals to her Christian readers to sing Cain's Blackness.
7 Thomas Jefferson referred to Wheatley in his *Notes on the State of Virginia*: "Among the black is misery enough, God knows, but no poetry … . Religion has produced a Phyllis Whately [sic]; but it could not produce a poet. The compositions published under her name are below the dignity of criticism" (140).

References

Brooks, Gwendolyn. "The Mother". *Selected Poems*. Harper Perennial Modern Classics, 2006, pp. 4–5.
———. "The Sundays of Satin-Legs Smith". *Selected Poems*. Harper Perennial Modern Classics, 2006, pp. 12–18.
Brown, Wallace Cable. *The Triumph of Form: A Study of the Later Masters of the Heroic Couplet*. U of North Carolina P, 1948.
Caplan, David. "Why Not the Heroic Couplet?" *New Literary History* 30.1 (1999), pp. 221–238. https://www.jstor.org/stable/20057532.
Cullen, Countee. "Thoughts in a Zoo". *Collected Poems*, ed. Major Jackson. American Poets Project. The Library of America, 2013, p. 86.
Gunn, Thom. "Lament". *The Man with Night Sweats*. Farrar, Straus and Giroux, 1992, pp. 61–64.
Haswell, Richard. *The Heroic Couplet Before Dryden (1550–1675)*. 1931. U of Illinois, PhD dissertation.

Hobsbaum, Philip. *Meter, Rhythm and Verse Form*. Routledge, 1996.

Jefferson, Thomas. "Query XIV. Laws". *Notes on the State of Virginia*, ed. William Peden. U of North Carolina P, 1996.

Johnson, Samuel. "The Vanity of Human Wishes". *The Major Works*, ed. Donald Greene. Oxford UP, 2000, pp. 12–21.

Larkin, Philip. "Money". *Collected Poems*. Farrar, Straus and Giroux, 1989, p. 198.

Piper, William Bowman. *The Heroic Couplet*. Case Western Reserve U, 1969.

Poochigian, Aaron, trans. *Aratus: Phaenomena*. Johns Hopkins UP, 2010.

Pope, Alexander. *An Essay on Man: In Epistles to a Friend. Epistle I. Corrected by the Author*. 2nd ed., printed for J. Wilford, at the Three Flower-de-Luces, Behind the Chapter-House, St. Paul's, MDCCXXXV. [1735]. *Eighteenth Century Collections Online*, link.gale.com/apps/doc/CW0117245481/ECCO?u=balt85423&sid=bookmark-ECCO&xid=052138ad&pg=10. Accessed 4 March 2022.

———. *The Rape of the Lock: An Heroic-comical Poem*, ed. Alexander Pope, Esq. Printed and sold by W. Sergent, [1790?]. *Eighteenth Century Collections Online*. link.gale.com/apps/doc/CW0111409459/ECCO?u=balt85423&sid=bookmark-ECCO&xid=bcdc4a57&pg=27. Accessed 4 March 2022.

———, and Homer. *The Iliad of Homer*, trans. Mr. Pope, London, 1715. *ProQuest*. https://www.proquest.com/books/iliad-homer/docview/2148122348/se-2?accountid=11752.

Smith, Stevie. "The Suburban Classes". *New Selected Poems of Stevie Smith*. New Directions, 1988, p. 4.

Strand, Mark, and Eavan Boland, eds. *The Making of a Poem: A Norton Anthology of Poetic Forms*. Norton, 2000.

Wheatley, Phillis. "On Being Brought from Africa to America". *Poems on Various Subjects, Religious and Moral*. A. Bell, 1773. p. 18. Nineteenth Century Collections Online. link.gale.com/apps/doc/AMZBXJ429065912/NCCO?u=balt85423&sid=bookmark-NCCO&xid=e56b14cc&pg=19. Accessed 4 March 2022.

———. "To the Right Honourable William, Earl of Dartmouth, His Majesty's Principal Secretary of State for North America, &c". *Poems on Various Subjects, Religious and Moral*. A. Bell, 1773, pp. 73–75. Nineteenth Century Collections Online. link.gale.com/apps/doc/AMZBXJ429065912/NCCO?u=balt85423&sid=bookmark-NCCO&xid=e56b14cc&pg=75. Accessed 4 March 2022.

17 The Long Poem

Patrick Gill and Miguel Juan Gronow Smith

I

The term 'long poem' may of course broadly be taken to refer to any poem of significant length, and thus many of the poems discussed in this book could legitimately be described as such. The description and definition of types of poems based solely on the basis of the number of their lines, though, is of very limited usefulness, and while there is a purpose in categorising poems as 'short' (i.e. shorter than other relatively short forms such as the sonnet), describing both a 200-line ⬀ prospect poem and a 2,000-line ⬀ epic as simply 'long' tells us little of their respective qualities, which is why these poems are discussed in the present volume under those other headings. A more focused approach is required to speak of the 'long poem' in a fruitful way, and so when the term is used in this chapter, it refers primarily to a form of poetry associated with more recent periods of the history of English literature of the past one hundred years or so. The term could thus very well be amended to 'the modernist and postmodern long poem' or 'the twentieth-century long poem'. As will be outlined below, when the term is seen in this more narrowly defined sense, it helps us avoid "all its inadequacies as a designation" (Dickie 6). Seen in those terms, a long poem is usually defined by an abandonment of a cohesive narrative in favour of more fragmentary strategies bringing together aspects of its contemporary culture. But before we go any further into the characteristics of the long poem, we might want to start by looking at what it is *not*. The following paragraphs will thus be concerned with a few other forms that usually produce poems of indubitable length and with which the long poem enjoys a relation of both similarity and difference.

Sometimes compared to the ⬀ epic, the long poem usually features a very different outlook on the world. In contrast to the epic, which attempts to offer an omniscient view of how things were in a distant golden age and how perhaps they will – in some way – always (or never) be, the long poem is painfully aware that societies and cultures are not stable, and offers readers a snapshot of a culture at a stage of uncertainty – a snapshot of the present that includes snippets of the past to explain how we got to where we are today. So its relationship to the culture that produced it and

DOI: 10.4324/9781003244004-19

that culture's history is in most cases radically different from the project of the epic. This also finds expression in a very basic formal distinction: whereas the epic is a poem with an underlying narrative unity, a story of cause and effect, the sequential telling of events across a clearly defined story arc, the long poem is characterised by "its adherence to a ban on narrative in poetry" (McHale 3). Based on this "ban on narrative", the long poem has a tendency to appear to readers as a collection of fragments, which sometimes invites comparison with the poetic cycle or sequence of poems. But because of their very nature as sequences of individual poems, cycles tend to work quite hard at establishing a unifying theme. What is more, their constituent poems tend to be more uniform, featuring a certain number of ⌒ sonnets, for instance, whereas the long poem may appear to be put together out of individual portions of vastly varying forms and lengths. Furthermore, the long poem tends to feature speakers as witnesses of their respective culture, a fact that sometimes leads to comparisons with the ⌒ dramatic monologue. But again, the contrasts are obvious: most dramatic monologues are written from the point of view of an identifiable (if fictional or fictionalised) persona. They tread familiar ground, introducing the reader to historical events not for their own sake but in the form of a re-evaluation of the ostensibly familiar.

What characterises the long poem in negative terms, then, is its lack of narrative or formal coherence as well as the absence of an identifiable narrator figure. The impression that the entire genre sounds like an attempt at avoiding something rather than an attempt at constructively establishing something has sometimes led to the verdict that the twentieth-century long poem is:

> a desperate solution to the problem the high modernists ... set for themselves of achieving poetry commensurate with their ambitious designs on literary history and the culture at large, but without violating the doctrine of the image, which held that the individual image was the foundation of poetic value, and without relapsing into overtly narrative modes. (McHale 2)

What modernist poets are looking for, then, is a form that is extensive and complex on the one hand, but relies on individual images on the other – a long form of individual, isolated moments of affect. To find out where the roots of this form might be found, the following section will consider two examples from earlier centuries.

II

While some critics locate the roots of the modern long poem in the first half of the eighteenth century (see Jung 55), a fruitful starting point in the present context would appear the Romantic movement of the late

168 *Patrick Gill and Miguel Juan Gronow Smith*

eighteenth and early nineteenth century. William Wordsworth's *The Prelude* (1850), though originally intended as an introduction to an even more substantial work, can easily be classified as a long poem, and, ironically, this classification is aided by the fact that when the 1850 edition was published, the poem "would not fit into any one genre as neatly as [the Victorians] desired, for it is missing both sustained narrative interest, and the sustained passion of lyric poetry" (Morgan 71). This incompatibility with established nineteenth-century forms gives us the freedom not to consider *The Prelude* as primarily belonging to this or that genre. Instead, we can look at the poem as through a telescope, with the ancient epic at one end of the equation and the modern long poem at the other. As its subtitle says, *The Prelude* is concerned with the "Growth of a Poet's Mind", so that if we want to consider it within the framework of the ∅ epic, it has to be read as an epic of the individual: reviewing his life and childhood, *The Prelude*'s speaker remembers individual "spots of time" (l. 208), meaningful occurrences in his childhood and youth that have shaped his personality over the years. These individual episodes are variously recounted excitedly as if experienced afresh; or contemplated philosophically, their full meaning only gradually teased out by the speaker; or looked at nostalgically, with a bitter-sweet glance back at childhood happiness and innocence. What all of these techniques do, however, is to establish a meaningful relation between the speaker's past and present. "The Child is father of the Man", as Wordsworth writes in his short lyric "My heart leaps up" (l. 7), and *The Prelude* attempts to trace the development of the man, the poet, back to isolated childhood episodes. In pursuit of this project, Wordsworth seems intent on eschewing obvious formal models: his language is relatively straightforward, he writes in blank verse, and there is little if any stanzaic organisation.[1] It is because in terms of its formal features and outlook the poem refuses to be identified with any precursor genres that *The Prelude* is such a useful antecedent to consider when it comes to the twentieth-century long poem. Other Romantic long poems, such as George Gordon, Lord Byron's *Don Juan*, or John Keats' "Hyperion", are more easily identified with precursor genres and are thus less obvious candidates for inclusion in the grouping that is here called 'the long poem'. In contrast, *The Prelude*, as Herbert Lindenberger famously remarks, is "a poem in search of a genre" (15), and in search of that genre, it presents us with perhaps the first recognisable instance of an accumulation of the negative generic markers given above: a poem of considerable length that is neither a cycle of shorter poems; nor represents the musings of a fictionalised historical figure; nor makes a chronological narrative its main focus. So if it fits our criteria in those ways, how does it differ from what we would expect a modern long poem to be? Well, for one thing, even though the poem's "I" is not a figure from history or mythology, *The Prelude* is even more self-centred than the dramatic monologue. It has one subject, and one subject alone: the growth of one individual's mind. The typical long

The Long Poem   169

poem, though, is interested in society rather than individual personalities. In line with this championing of the social over the individual, the long poem also tends to prefer urban settings where Wordsworth's prevalent interest in the lonely individual out in nature is more than obvious.

That championing of the individual also features in the next poem that might be considered a stepping stone on the way to the modernist and postmodern long poem, Walt Whitman's "Song of Myself".[2] But whereas Wordsworth's "I" in *The Prelude* is solipsistically concerned with selfhood, Whitman's "I" – obviously foregrounded by the poem's title – identifies with a "you" (ll. 2–3) representative of all of contemporary American society. As important a stepping stone as Whitman's famous poem is in the evolution of the modern long poem, a more thorough discussion of his writing is provided in the chapter on ⟁ free verse, so that some few observations ought to suffice: "Song of Myself" takes Romanticism's obsession with the individual and turns it into an obsession with society and the world expressed in an individual voice. The free verse, the element of lists, the sudden turning from people's housing conditions to sights, sounds, smells, these sudden shifts all pave the way for the modernist long poem emerging in the 1910s.

III

Perhaps the most famous of modernist long poems is T.S. Eliot's *The Waste Land* (1922). In this 434-line poem, divided into five sections, we can see the principles of the modernist long poem at work: its fragmentary nature, its fusion of disjointed elements, its use of multiple speakers, different languages, barely identifiable 'I's and 'you's. The poem contains quotations from or allusions to medieval legends, Ovid, *The Divine Comedy*, Shakespeare, contemporary popular culture, and the Hindu Upanishads. What Eliot tries to do in the wake of the First World War is to capture the essence of society and culture within but also beyond the Anglosphere. The way he goes about doing so is not by fashioning a master narrative, some heroic foundational myth, but by collecting what cultural fragments he can find in a kind of textual museum: "*The Waste Land* is essentially a collection of fragments, many of which owe their existence directly to other texts, appropriated by Eliot in such a way as to form a new whole" (Dobson 91).

The first puzzling aspect of *The Waste Land* typical of the genre of the long poem is that of the identity of its speakers. Whereas in the ⟁ dramatic monologue, the speaker has to be identified early on (ideally in the title of the poem) so that readers can fully embark on the experience through their eyes; and in ⟁ epic, the narrator steps back to let the story unfold, providing an omniscient account largely de-coupled from ideas of voice and personality, only rarely imposing themselves on the story, *The Waste Land* falls awkwardly between those two positions, featuring a series of speakers well-nigh impossible to identify while at the same time leaving the reader with an overbearing *desire* to identify them. Whereas identifiable speakers or an anonymous authoritative voice would lend a semblance of coherence to the text, switching from speaker to speaker while not knowing who these speakers are provides a structural basis of instability and unknowability.

What further adds to the disorienting features of the poem is its fragmentary nature. The purpose of this collection of fragmentary intertexts is the documentation of contemporary culture without the narrativisation of it: as in a museum, the individual fragments are there on display. Be it snippets of song, isolated lines of everyday conversation, allusions to classical mythology or to medieval romances, *The Waste Land* collects them all. But their meaning is established not just by themselves individually, but by virtue of the fact that they have all been gathered together and united in a shared context. As such, *The Waste Land* employs the long poem's expansiveness to turn itself into a cultural landmark, a receptacle of all the fragments of culture left at the end of the Great War.

The notion of scope or expansiveness is a third major generic marker of the twentieth-century long poem, besides its collage-like fragmentation and the indeterminacy of its speakers. Of course, the very term 'long poem' already suggests a certain scope, but the long poem's ambition goes far beyond the mere accumulation of lines: "Long in the time of composition, in the initial intention, and in the final form, the Modernist long poem is concerned first and last with its own length" (Dickie 6). What may sound like an uncharitable verdict does contain an important truth: long poems are major works. They take a long time to compose, may be less certain of publication than a brief lyric, and are by definition less accessible to a potential audience. From this it follows that they must be written with a certain degree of ambition, an ambition to produce a major work. That ambition, though, is not limited to the physical dimensions of the poem in print. It extends beyond mere length to the number of aspects and examples that can be combined into the long poem's collage, as well as the universality of the meaning that can be contained within the lines of the poem. If modernist long poems are like collections or museums, gathering together remnants of a culture, then the more aspects of that culture they contain, the more important they are. By dint of their technique of collecting cultural artefacts and collating them into new constructs, long poems become major works of a melting-pot-like function, where the remnants of the old can be forged into the new. As major works, they stand out of the literary landscape like lighthouses: while they themselves "survey[] and judge[]" (Dickie 6) the surrounding culture under the gaze of their beacon, everyone else can look to them for guidance.

In its overall meaning, *The Waste Land* is ambiguous, even its opening section containing simultaneously the idea of fertility and death (ll. 1–2). The entire project of long poems such as *The Waste Land* – fragmentary,

The Long Poem   171

collage-based, encyclopaedic – can be seen in one of two possible ways, as MacGowan explains:

> [I]n [*The Waste Land*] and many collage poems in which fragmentation is a central feature, there remains the issue of what status to give to the poem's continuities – its motifs, symbols, myths, recurring figures and voices. Are they ironic echoes of a form that can no longer bring coherence? Or do they reflect a foundational potential that has some possibility of recovery[?]. (288)

As a receptacle for the various snippets of song, disjointed voices, chants, and quotations, what is the function of *The Waste Land*, what is its attitude towards the fragments contained within it? Does it look at them mournfully as the dead remnants of a past irretrievably lost? Or does it look on them full of hope as cultural fragments out of which a new culture will emerge? The text itself gives us indications of both, the eponymous waste land as a place of terminal decay and as fertile ground for a rebirth.

IV

Having seen what effects the withholding of identifiable speakers, the collage-like fusion of divergent materials, and the ambition and scope of the twentieth-century long poem have in *The Waste Land*, we can turn to a somewhat less famous work to see how those aspects characterise a poem equally capacious and ambitious but not as universally known as Eliot's classic. *Perduta Gente* is a 1989 long poem by English poet Peter Reading. The "unofficial laureate of a decaying nation", Reading "writes with a journalistic commitment to the present social moment" (Paulin 204). *Perduta Gente* ('the lost people' or 'the forgotten people') offers a collage of artefacts documenting life in London. Each of its pages[3] "contains a complete item", making "the page ... the integral unit" (Barry 84). What the pages constituting *Perduta Gente* contain varies tremendously: descriptive prose paragraphs, newspaper clippings, handwritten notes, health warnings, and real-estate advertisements all go into the making of the poem. As in *The Waste Land*, the poem is characterised by undisclosed speakers, the fragmentary nature of the eclectic mixture of texts collected within it, and its scope, taking in many aspects of London life.

The speakers of *Perduta Gente* seem to change depending on the context of each passage, though in the case of supposedly 'found' material such as adverts or newspaper articles, a supposed speaker's voice disappears altogether, replaced by the documentary evidence. The mixture of voices and documents thus establishes patterns of juxtaposition as when a letter to the editor demanding harsher sentences for benefits cheats and a cutting of benefits altogether on one page (166) is preceded by an anecdote of a homeless couple involved in an accident on the underground (165).

172   *Patrick Gill and Miguel Juan Gronow Smith*

The gradual accruement of these documents, their common fate in having been collected in the poem, allows the reader to establish a picture of a divided society. In this world, the affluent may have luxury flats with "river views" advertised to them (161) while the homeless light fires outside the city limits (171); the rich may enjoy a classical concert while the poor are serenaded by the sounds of human excretions (both 160).

What Reading uses his own version of the literary museum for, then, is to document and contrast two very different modes of existence in contemporary London:

> The force of the juxtaposition is evident: ... two cities are contrasted, an ideal and an actual, but ... both concerts are here and now, the musical masterpiece with its Romantic transcendence, and the subterranean nightmare in which people are treated with less care than material goods, like animals at best. (Barry 85–86)

In terms of the messaging, there is little ambiguity here. Reading relinquishes any attempts to aestheticise his journalistic impressions into anything tame and pleasing, instead employing his documentary evidence to demonstrate that for a forgotten and discarded underclass like the homeless of London to come into being, the state must have wilfully neglected them, eradicating jobs and stripping away safety nets. That is the univocal conclusion Reading draws from his observation of the reality of England after ten years under Margaret Thatcher. If that sounds unusually blunt for a twentieth-century long poem, that's because it is. But Reading sees no point in making use of his "'imaginative power' which is usually the driving force in poetry, and feels that this 'antipoetic' stance is the only response which does not trivialise or in some way belittle that reality" (Barry 84). The great achievement of *Perduta Gente*, though, is not that it takes the side of the weak and disadvantaged but that it constructs its two parallel worlds in such a way as to make them permeable: "Don't think it couldn't be you" (173). For all their separateness, then, the world of the affluent and that of the homeless are shown as intimately connected, everyone constantly living at one remove from addiction and abject poverty.

V

The twentieth-century long poem is a form characterised by scope, eclecticism, and indeterminacy. In terms of its scope, the long poem has the ambition to be a major work encapsulating the spirit or culture of its age. In terms of its building blocks, it is eclectic, taking its sources where it can find them, from previous periods, other linguistic traditions, and/ or contemporaneous popular culture. In terms of the coherence it might establish either through the arrangement of its eclectic mix of ingredients or through its use of speakers, the long poem has a tendency to remain elusive and leave the joining of dots to its readers. What has clearly distinguished the twentieth-century long poem from its eighteenth- and indeed most nineteenth-century predecessors is its rejection of narrative elements in favour of a collage-like intertextual eclecticism. Rather than offering a plot, a story, such long poems have tended to fuse together fragments of different genres and text types.

As far as the current state of the long poem is concerned, some have argued that the past decades have seen a gradual return of narrative to the genre. McHale points out that some contemporary writers of long poems also work as novelists, and that others avail themselves of borrowings from earlier narrative genres than the novel to equip their long poems with story arcs (3–4). That contemporary long poems seem to be making a return to narrative may mark an important change in and of itself. The fact that it is seen as noteworthy simply confirms the basic orthodoxy that for the past one hundred years, the long poem has striven to get by without sequentiality, plot, and narrative thrust.

NOW READ ON...

- As this chapter suggests, there are productive comparisons to be drawn between the long poem, the ⬀ dramatic monologue, and the ⬀ epic.
- Many long poems are composed in ⬀ free verse, so a look at that particular chapter may prove useful.
- In contrast to the modernists' use of free verse, Wordsworth's *Prelude* is written in ⬀ blank verse, another form worth investigating.

Notes

1 There are allusions to other works, however, foremost among them Milton's *Paradise Lost*, a fact that further supports the idea of *The Prelude* as an epic of selfhood. The fact that there are these intertextual allusions at all hints at the long poem's capacity to unite different texts and text types within its boundaries.
2 The vagaries of publication histories might give the impression that *The Prelude* and "Song of Myself" are near-contemporaneous, the former having first been published posthumously in 1850 and the latter having first been printed in an early version in 1855. A comparison of the vocabulary, styles, and formal features of these poems, however, will remind us that the first version of *The Prelude* was drafted by Wordsworth in 1799, whereas Whitman kept expanding, redrafting, and even renaming his poem until shortly before his death in 1892.
3 Unpaginated in the original edition but with pagination added for easier reference in the *Collected Poems*.

References

Barry, Peter. *Contemporary British Poetry and the City*. Manchester UP, 2000.

Dickie, Margaret. *On the Modernist Long Poem*. Iowa City: U of Iowa P, 1986.

Dobson, Timothy. "Eliot, T(homas) S(tearns) (1888–1965)". *Encyclopedia of Literary Modernism*, ed. Paul Poplawski. Greenwood P, 2003, pp. 88–94.

Eliot, T.S. "The Waste Land". *The Complete Poems and Plays of T.S. Eliot*. Faber and Faber, 1969, pp. 59–80.

Jung, Sandro. "Generic Hybridity and Structural Technique in James Thomson's *Spring* (1728)". *AAA: Arbeiten aus Anglistik und Amerikanistik* 32.1 (2007), pp. 55–68.

Lindenberger, Herbert. *On Wordsworth's Prelude*. Princeton UP, 1963.

MacGowan, Christopher. *Twentieth-century American Poetry*. Blackwell, 2004.

McHale, Brian. *The Obligation toward the Difficult Whole: Postmodernist Long Poems*. U of Alabama P, 2004.

Morgan, Monique R. *Narrative Means, Lyric Ends: Temporality in the Nineteenth-century British Long Poem*. Ohio State UP, 2009.

Paulin, Tom. "Peter Reading". *Grand Street* 7.4 (Summer 1988), pp. 202–211.

Reading, Peter. "Perduta Gente". *Collected Poems 2: Poems 1985–1996*. Bloodaxe Books, 1996, pp. 159–214.

Whitman, Walt. "Song of Myself". *Whitman: Poetry and Prose*. The Library of America, 1982, pp. 188–247.

Wordsworth, William. "From The Prelude: Book Twelfth". *The Norton Anthology of English Literature*, ed. Meyer Howard Abrams et al., vol. 2., 6th ed. W.W. Norton, 1993, pp. 267–274.

———. "My Heart Leaps Up". *The Norton Anthology of English Literature*, ed. Meyer Howard Abrams et al., Vol. 2, 6th ed. W.W. Norton, 1993, p. 187.

18 Mock-Heroic Poetry

Purificación Ribes Traver

I

The *Oxford Companion to English Literature* defines "mock epic (mock-heroic)" as "a satirical form that generates humour through the presentation of low characters or trivial subjects in the lofty style of classical epic or heroic poems" ("mock epic"). This genre flourished in England between 1682 – when John Dryden's *Mac Flecknoe* was published – and 1743, when Alexander Pope completed *The Dunciad in Four Books*. Other outstanding works of the genre are Sir Samuel Garth's *The Dispensary* (1699), and, above all, Pope's *The Rape of the Lock* (1712/1714/1717). Unlike travesties such as Charles Cotton's *Virgile Travestie* (1664) – an adaptation of Paul Scarron's *Virgile Travesti* (1642–1653) – mock-heroic poems do not parody a single work – in this case, Virgil's *Aeneid* – but a whole genre, and their characters – unlike those in the travesties – do not use a low, but an elevated language. The tone of their satire, moreover, can range from the light irony we find in *The Rape of the Lock* to the harsh satire of *The Dunciad*. The epic poems whose conventions they parody belong to the classical Graeco-Roman and the vernacular traditions, and include Homer's *Iliad* and *Odyssey,* as well as Virgil's *Aeneid* and Milton's *Paradise Lost.* The theoretical foundations of the mock-heroic were established by Le Bossu in his *Traité du poème épique* (1675).

The mock-heroic flourished in England during the Augustan Age, an age that takes its name from the admiration it felt for the Roman Emperor Augustus, who ruled from 27 BC to AD 14. This period was renowned for its political stability, economic growth and artistic excellence. It is therefore not surprising that Augustus himself wished to have his age immortalised by means of a national epic, the *Aeneid*, written in imitation of its great Greek precedents, Homer's *Iliad* and *Odyssey*. Virgil's *Aeneid* successfully met his expectations, and furnished the Roman emperor with a mythical forefather, the descendant of a goddess and a hero, who landed in Latium after a long and eventful journey, comparable to that of Ulysses in the *Odyssey*, and, after prolonged warfare, akin to that of *The Iliad*, brought about peace and prosperity to what would eventually become the Roman Empire.

DOI: 10.4324/9781003244004-20

176 *Purificación Ribes Traver*

Starting in the late seventeenth century, and, especially during the first half of the eighteenth century, England enjoyed unprecedented political stability, together with rapid economic growth and a revival of the arts which, during the early decades of the eighteenth century, would be profoundly influenced by the classical past. This included admiration for the Graeco-Roman epic poems, which were translated by the most outstanding writers of the period, meeting with great success. Dryden's translation of Virgil's *Aeneid* as well as Pope's translations of Homer's *Iliad* and *Odyssey* enjoyed wide circulation, not just because of the age's reverence for these classical authors, but also because of the translators' careful updating of their source texts, where the goriest passages were sanitised in line with the taste of the times. Comic epic poems such as the pseudo-Homeric *Margites* or *Batrachomyomachia* (*The Battle of the Frogs and Mice*) were almost as popular as the epic poems themselves. This must have paved the path for the genre best suited to the Neoclassical period, the mock-heroic, especially if we take into account that Aristotle, whose *Poetics* was revered by the Neoclassical theorists, acknowledged the importance of comic epics.

Although the mock-heroic genre would experience its greatest development in England, it first flourished in France. Nicolas Boileau's *Le Lutrin* (1674–1683) is regarded as its first Neoclassical example. Like the pseudo-Homeric *Batrachomyomachia,* which parodies *The Iliad*, it revolves around the idea of a bloodless conflict, in this case over the position of a lectern in a French church. Unlike its Greek precedent, however, the characters in *Le Lutrin* are human, though their actions are similarly influenced by supernatural forces such as Discorde or Pieté. The weapons employed by the conflicting parties are books whose effectiveness does not depend on their size as much as on their contents, being most effective when most boring, as they may put those they hit to sleep. In spite of its comic tone, however, the poem is not without a moral, as the worldly behaviour of the priests in the poem is the object of ridicule. Its ending, moreover, echoes the patriotic tone of the classical epics by praising the French king, Louis XIV.

A similar patriotic ending would be accorded by Sir Samuel Garth to his mock-heroic poem *The Dispensary* (1699), written in imitation of Boileau's *Le Lutrin*. Like him, Garth divided the poem into six books, which is exactly half the number of the books in the *Aeneid*, and a quarter of the books in *The Iliad*. Like Boileau's, the poem ended in a panegyric of the ruling king, William III, and like its French forerunner, it was not void of a moral, as its subject matter, the dispute over the construction of a dispensary of medicines for the poor, whose main obstacle was the prospective reduction of the apothecaries' profits, was of social significance. The nature of the weapons the conflicting parties hurled at each other – pill-bottles and vials – contributed, as in *Le Lutrin*, to the poem's amusing tone. Supernatural forces, such as the god Sloth or the goddess Health, similarly affected the course of the action, which was further influenced by delaying motifs, such as the visit to the Underworld, devised after Aeneas' visit to his father Anchises in search of advice on the future of his journey.

As prophesised by his father, Aeneas would become a powerful ruler over Latium, where his son Ascanius would eventually found Alba Longa. This significant episode in the history of Rome, which the *Aeneid* glorifies, would be parodied by John Dryden in his mock-heroic poem *Mac Flecknoe* (1682), where he ironically praises the accession of "Sh..." to the kingdom of Nonsense, a kingdom presided over by his father, Mac Flecknoe, who clearly stands for Dryden's contemporary Richard Flecknoe, a writer whose dullness, in Dryden's regard, could only be matched by that of his literary son, the playwright Thomas Shadwell, who, after the accession of William III and Mary II to the throne of England in 1689, would supersede Dryden as Poet Laureate and Historiographer Royal.

One year before Dryden's replacement by the Whig Thomas Shadwell as Poet Laureate, the birth of a son – James Francis Edward Stuart – to James II by his Catholic wife Mary of Modena, triggered the Glorious Revolution, which ended with the king's deposition and replacement by his Anglican daughter, Mary, and her Protestant husband, William of Orange. The *Bill of Rights*, which was passed in 1689, excluded Roman Catholics from the line of succession, and the *Toleration Act*, passed that same year, guaranteed religious toleration to Protestant nonconformists, but did not extend it to Roman Catholics, whose rights would be frequently curtailed, as the Catholic Alexander Pope, born in 1688, painfully discovered in the course of his life. His personal experience, as David Nokes points out (25–36), had its reflection on the increasingly harsh tone of his mock-heroic works, which reached its summit in 1743, a year before his death, when the enlarged version of his *Dunciad* was published. This date is often taken to mark the end of the Augustan period, and Pope's *Dunciad in Four Books* is looked upon as the literary farewell to the Humanistic values he had so deeply believed in throughout his life.

II

The tone of Pope's *The Rape of the Lock*, written in the poet's youth, although far from the vitriolic quality he would exhibit later in his life, already shows an awareness of the literary, political and sociological maladies of the day, which he nevertheless depicts with delicious irony. The irony is so subtle that critics often have difficulties in determining to what extent the poem praises or condemns the society it depicts, an ambivalence that, as Jones highlights, lies at the root of the poem's currency. Another reason for its sustained popularity is the accessibility of its contents, which do not require copious footnotes or detailed explanations, such as those included in *The Dunciad Variorum* of 1729. The action, characters and incidents of *The Rape of the Lock* can be understood even by those who are unacquainted with the specific context which gave rise to it.

178 *Purificación Ribes Traver*

Following the epic pattern which the poem consistently parodies, *The Rape of the Lock* opens with a proposition where the narrator announces the poem's subject matter, the "dire offence" that springs from "amorous causes" and leads to "mighty contests" that, as he surprisingly announces in the second line of his first ♪ heroic couplet, arise from "trivial things" (Canto 1, ll. 1–2). The first couplet sets the tone of the poem, and anticipates the contrast between the elevation of the epic motif it echoes – the Trojan war ensuing from Helen's abduction – and the triviality of the poem's subject matter – the rape of a lock of hair from the head of a contemporary belle. The poem next follows the customary steps of epic poems, which include the invocation to the muses, the warnings about impending dangers, detailed description of the hero's armour, an epic journey, epic games, an injury to honour that must be revenged, a visit to the Underworld, open warfare where a military engine plays a key role, the conflict's ending, brought about by the *deus ex machina*, the celebration of the hero's immortal fame and a final moral message. It also includes the supernatural beings usually found in epic poems, and is written in heroic couplets, the metrical form chosen by Pope for his translation of *The Iliad* that consists of rhyming pairs of iambic pentameters which, in *The Rape of the Lock*, have a deflating effect often associated with the second line of the couplet, which reverses the elevated tone of the first. All these epic devices are related to the poem's contemporary context, the reign of Queen Anne, which saw the union of England and Scotland through the Act of Union 1707, and enjoyed great economic growth, favoured by its overseas trade. The Queen and her entourage, however, are not cast in as positive a light as the monarchs and high dignitaries in *Le Lutrin* or *The Dispensary*, but are depicted as members of a fashionable society obsessed with expensive miniature objects, who devote greater attention to their acquisition and display than to serious matters of state. This affects the Queen herself, whose superficiality the narrator highlights by means of a zeugma where he tells her that she "sometimes takes counsel" and "sometimes tea" (Canto 3, l. 8), implying, through the semantic distance of the two direct objects of 'take', that both activities are interchangeable in her regard. The male members of this coterie, moreover, far from protecting the honour of the ladies attending those social gatherings, do their best to 'conquer' them and exhibit the prize that attests to their conquests, thereby ruining the ladies' reputation, the most valuable of jewels, whose loss may render them unsuitable for the marriage market. In *The Rape of the Lock*, that prize is precisely the lock of hair that the Baron cuts off from Belinda's head without her consent, and which he intends to display as the proof of her surrender to him. As Thalestris makes clear, that could entail the end of her chances of marrying well. That was the greatest of priorities to any lady of quality, as Clarissa lets the reader know in the speech she delivers in the poem's last canto, where she equates the world's decay with dying unmarried, and lets Belinda know that rejecting a man is the surest way to that dreadful end (Canto 5, l. 28). Accordingly, she advises the heroine to use her powers well and keep good humour regardless of her losses (Canto 5, ll. 29–30). Clarissa's piece of advice is ambiguous, as she does not explain what using her powers 'well' may entail, or what may go lost in the process. Somewhat earlier, Thalestris had gone as far as to suggest that ladies were paradoxically ready to resign all they had, even virtue, at Honour's shrine. This implies a further twist of the concept of honour, and reveals the ladies' vulnerability, as they could be forced to forego their honour in order not to lose their reputation, should a despicable rake press them to do so. The poem features the same stereotypes the comedy of wit had taken to the stage over the previous fifty years, and whose value was closely related to the kind and extent of their wit, which was highest in the *truewit* – *The Rape of the Lock*'s Baron – and lowest in the *witwoud* or fop – the poem's Sir Plume. There was, however, a substantial difference, that, whereas in Restoration comedies witty women played an active role, *The Rape of the Lock* had no room for them. Besides, the 'gay couple' of the Restoration comedies of the first decades ended up in happy marriage, even though the rules regarding the sexual behaviour of the two members of the couple were not the same, as pre-marital chastity was a prerequisite for marriageable ladies, whereas experience in the field was not regarded as inappropriate for male wits. It must be borne in mind in this regard that a large number of aristocrats regularly attended the comedies of manners of the first decades, and it was of utmost importance for them that the women they married had not had any previous extra-marital affair that might cast a doubt on the legitimacy of their issue. Although the moral climate had substantially changed by the time *The Rape of the Lock* was published, and the behaviour and dialogues of the characters in the comedies was more moderate – and dull – the readership of *The Rape of the Lock* was educated and shared the importance attached to the virtue of marriageable ladies. *The Rape of the Lock*, moreover, exhibits an admirable command of witty language and ambiguity that had disappeared from the comedies of manners contemporary with it, as they had to cater for a larger audience with an increasing number of middle-class spectators that required a more direct language. There is no doubt that *The Rape of the Lock* is an elitist work, full of subtle irony. It shows both the glittering surface and the darkest side of the society it depicts, whose affective disorders may negatively affect the emotional and mental balance of women, and, to a lesser extent, of men, as the grotesque figures Pope draws in the Cave of Spleen evidence. The machinery in the poem, which parodies pagan gods and Miltonic angels, highlights the tensions of fashionable ladies, whom their tiny aerial sylphs transform – with the aid of make-up and jewels – into irresistible goddesses. These goddesses, however, require their ineffective protection from predatory men, the same men that could become their husbands, and whom the ill-willed gnomes advise to reject, with the gloomy prospect of ending up in the Cave of Spleen.

180   *Purificación Ribes Traver*

The epic motifs and devices the poem parodies are closely connected with contemporary issues, a feature that Broich highlights as essential to mock-heroic poetry (27–37), and which many definitions of the genre ignore. The invocation to the Muse that follows the poem's proposition replaces the customary pagan gods of the classical epics, and the Christian Holy Spirit of *Paradise Lost,* with John Caryll, a friend of Pope that had asked him to write the poem in order to reconcile the Fermors and the Petres in shared laughter. The impending danger Belinda is warned about in a dream brought about by her sylph Ariel is no other than a gallant. The weapons she is provided with for the encounter with that gallant are the beautiful attire, make-up, perfume and jewels the sylphs adorn her with. Special attention is paid to an item whose description is modelled on Achilles's shield, her seven-fold fence petticoat – echoing the shield's seven layers of leather – that is protected by fifty sylphs on the epic journey Belinda takes to Hampton Court up the river Thames. There she engages with the Baron in the card game called *ombre,* which is described in military terms, symbolic of the battle of the sexes. Belinda's triumph is celebrated by drinking coffee in the company of the scheming Baron, who cuts off her treasured lock of hair without her consent despite the effort of a 1,000 sylphs to prevent the catastrophe from taking place. The nymph's lament follows, in the dire tones of Achilles's own over his dead friend Patroclus. The battle for the recovery of the stolen lock is further sparked off by the bag of adverse winds that the gnome Umbriel casts over the assembled company. He has been given it by the goddess of Spleen in a scene reminiscent both of the Underworld visited by Aeneas in search of advice and of Aeolus's gift to Ulysses while on his island. Open warfare ensues, with Belinda's triumph over the Baron, who loses the lock thanks to the heroine's military engine, a pinch of snuff that stops the Baron's 'vitals', in the same way as the Trojan horse secured the Greek epic victory. The lock goes lost as a result, and it is suggested that it has mounted to the lunar sphere, that place below the moon where the courtier's promises, the lovers' hearts, the sick man's prayers, deathbed alms, the tears of heirs, the smile of harlots and the beaux's wits can be found. The poem reaches its end with the metamorphosis of the lost lock into a star that – like Berenice's own – ascends to the heavens, and, as the poem's narrator explains, ensures the heroine's literary immortality in a way comparable to that of epic poems, even though it does not celebrate heroic deeds, but beauty. The poem lacks the sixth canto that both *Le Lutrin* and *The Dispensary* have, where their moral teaching is expressed. Instead, the third edition of *The Rape of the Lock,* published in 1717, includes Clarissa's speech, which ambiguously reflects on the battle of the sexes the poem deals with in a mock-heroic style.

John Gay's *The Fan* (1714) mimicked parts of *The Rape of the Lock,* and highlighted the importance that fashionable items had for young ladies. Here, the fan, made by Venus's cupids, and decorated by Minerva, removes Corinna's resistance to Strephon's advances, the moment he presents her with it.

Mock-Heroic Poetry 181

III

The Augustan Age's next outstanding mock-heroic poem was Pope's *The Dunciad*, which, like Dryden's *Mac Flecknoe*, was modelled on Aeneas's journey to Latium. It focuses on the transfer of the Kingdom of Dullness from the popular district of Smithfield – where the cattle market was located – to the refined area of the West End, the dwelling place of the king and the rich elite. In Pope's first version (1728), the epic 'hero', Tibbald, stands for the scholar Lewis Theobald, the son of Goddess Dulness (Dullness), and, in Pope's opinion, the epitome of pedantry. Pope's 1743 *Dunciad in Four Books* replaced its hero with the new Poet Laureate, Colley Cibber, and transformed what was initially conceived as a largely personal attack on a scholarly rival, with scathing criticism that went beyond the personal and into the universal. The poem's biting satire is directed against a large gallery of poets, journalists, critics and politicians, who no longer share the values of Humanism. It includes an apocalyptic note that parodies *Paradise Lost* by presenting Cibber as the "Antichrist of wit" (Book 2, l. 16), and regrets that "Morality expires" (Book 4, l. 650), and "universal Darkness buries all" (Book 4, l. 656). The universal nature of Pope's satire would be reduced to personal invectives by his imitators, with the epic reference progressively lost. One example of this tendency is Christopher Smart's *Hilliad* (1753), a direct attack on the botanist Dr Hills.

The "universal Darkness" Pope decries at the end of *The Dunciad in Four Books* (1743) was prefigured by the "Gothic library" of Book 1 which had no room for the Classics (ll. 145–146). With the passage of time, the popularity of classical epic poems faded away, which brought about the eventual demise of the mock-heroic, as its comic effect could no longer depend on the contrast between the heroic style and the unheroic society it depicted. The 1740s saw increased attention to the psychology of characters, something the genre of the novel could satisfy better than mock-heroic poetry, due, among other things, to its greater length. That is why the function previously fulfilled by mock-heroic poems was transferred to the novel, as can be seen in Henry Fielding's novels, which he defined as 'comic epics in prose'. The technique of the paradoxical encomium, which is inherent to the mock-heroic, was employed in *Jonathan Wild*, for example, where crime is the object of praise. As the century progressed, the outward expression of feelings was increasingly appreciated. It influenced sentimental novels such as Henry Mackenzie's *The Man of Feeling* (1771), published ten years before William Hayley's mock-heroic poem *The Triumphs of Temper*, where Serena's benevolence is rewarded with an irreproachable middle-class husband, and where the heroine's 'struggle' to make herself worthy of that prize has nothing left of the intensity of the epic battle.

Some poems of the 1780s which place nature at their centre, such as William Cowper's *The Task* (1785), occasionally include mock-heroic set pieces where trivial objects or animals are aggrandised. Cowper's frequent

182 *Purificación Ribes Traver*

identification with some of the insignificant animals of his poems, moreover, helps him show God's condescension, and, simultaneously, his sinning soul's ascension to the Almighty, an ascending movement that, in Terry's view, can be associated with the mock-heroic (153–171).

The American Declaration of Independence and the events leading to the French Revolution also left their mark on English literature, as one of the last mock-heroic poems of the eighteenth century, Peter Pindar's (John Wolcot) *Luisiad* (1785–1795), shows. The poem breaks both social and stylistic decorum by placing the country's ruler, King George III (1760–1820), at the centre of a comic poem, and having him lose a rhetorical battle against his cooks, whose command of English exceeds that of the king himself and his German-speaking entourage. Although the king asks his cooks to shave their heads so as to prevent further lice from falling on his plate, he loses the rhetorical battle against a persuasive cook who sparks a rebellion in the style of Milton's Satan. The comic tone of the poem, however, is never lost, and the louse, which, after all, had fallen from the king's own head, is metamorphosed – in the manner of Berenice's or Belinda's locks – into a star.

Later offshoots of the mock-heroic would include Byron's *Don Juan* (1819–1824), which, unlike Augustan translations and parodies of the classical epics, does not shun the depiction of bloody warfare. The gloomy atmosphere of Eliot's *The Waste Land* (1922), moreover, would partially echo the apocalyptic ending of Pope's *Dunciad,* even though Eliot, as Claude Rawson points out, seems to have felt closer to Shakespeare's approach than to the classical or vernacular epics that gave rise to the mock-heroic.

NOW READ ON...

- Since mock-heroic poetry mimics and satirises the ⏎ epic in style and substance, it will be worth looking at that chapter.
- Milton's *Paradise Lost* in particular seems to have been a consistent source of inspiration in the eyes of writers of mock-heroic poems – even though most of them disagreed vehemently with his politics and theology, The poem is discussed in greater detail in the chapter on the ⏎ epic.
- Mock-heroic poetry frequently employs the ⏎ heroic couplet.
- T.S. Eliot's *The Waste Land* with its (possibly) ironising style is discussed in the chapter on the ⏎ long poem.

References

Broich, Ulrich. *The Eighteenth-Century Mock-Heroic Poem*. Cambridge UP, 1990.

Jones, Emrys D. "An Appetite for Ambivalence: Pope Studies in the Twenty-first Century". *Literature Compass* 15.12 (2018), p. e12502.

"Mock epic". *The Oxford Companion to English Literature*, ed. Dinah Birch. Oxford UP, 2009. https://www.oxfordreference.com/view/10.1093/acref/9780192806871.001.0001/acref-9780192806871-e-5135.

Nokes, David. "Pope's Friends and Enemies". *The Cambridge Companion to Alexander Pope*, ed. Pat Rogers. Cambridge UP, 2007, pp. 25–36.

Pope, Alexander. *The Dunciad (1728) and The Dunciad Variorum (1729)*, ed. Valerie Rumbold. Longman, 2007. Vol. 3 of *The Poems of Alexander Pope*.

———. *The Dunciad in Four Books*, ed. Valerie Rumbold, 2nd ed. Routledge, 2014 (1999, 2009).

———. *The Rape of the Lock*, ed. Elizabeth Gurr. Oxford UP, 2007 (1990).

Rawson, Claude. "Mock-Heroic and English Poetry". *The Cambridge Companion to the Epic*, ed. Catherine Bates. Cambridge UP, 2010. *ProQuest*. https://www.proquest.com/books/mock-heroic-english-poetry/docview/2137992727/se-2?accountid=14777, http://dx.doi.org/10.1017/CCOL9780521880947.010.

Terry, Richard. *Mock-Heroic from Butler to Cowper: An English Genre and Discourse*. Ashgate, 2005.

19 The Ode

Florian Klaeger

I

The ode is one of those forms, like tragedy or ⟋ elegy, that have acquired an extended, non-technical meaning in everyday use. When a recipe is described as an 'ode to my homeland', or a dress made of lost and found zipper pulls as a 'wearable ode to luggage', the term simply describes one thing celebrating the value of another. The more specific, technical meaning is hardly less general in its origins: Greek *odé* [ᾠδή] simply means 'song'. However, as the *OED* points out (s.v. 'ode, *n*'), this term derives from the verb ἀείδειν (to sing/to chant), cognate with αὐδή (human voice) and ὑδεῖν (to call, name) – thus, the form's very name already suggests a complex union between ode, music, odic voice or subject, and odic object. During the sixteenth century, mainly through the poets of the French Pléiade, the term acquired the connotation of lyric poetry in the elevated style. This became the basis for the modern technical meaning of the term in English: an ode is a lyric poem meditating on some worthy object – such as a person, place, event, idea, feeling, etc. – that is apostrophised and/or praised in a serious, exalted style, reflected in lofty diction and elaborate prosodic, stanzaic, and/or metrical form. Such meditation and celebration may be explicitly directed at a wider public, or framed as private and intimate.

To complicate things further, the term has had another, more comprehensive meaning from antiquity into the modern period. At the end of the eighteenth century, Dr Johnson's *Dictionary* identified the form with "a lyrick poem" (s.v. 'ode, *n*.'), and into the nineteenth century, the term continued to stand synecdochically for what we today call lyric poetry, and 'poetic speech' in general. Given this identification, the ode has long had a meta-poetic dimension: odic apostrophe and praise posit that poetry is the adequate medium for contemplating greatness and bestowing prestige, and thus, that it enjoys a certain greatness and prestige itself. The same is true of the odist: the form tends to identify the speaker rather closely with the poet, and thus, *its* praise is *theirs*. They are the source of whatever capital the ode bestows on its object, and hence, the ode constitutes a self-conscious performance of authorship (see Fry and Jackson). If poetic

DOI: 10.4324/9781003244004-21

The Ode   185

forms are seen as answers to specific questions arising from historically contingent social and aesthetic circumstances, the long history of the ode's transformations and applications may thus be seen as an index of the public estimation and function of poetry in each particular historical moment.

Johnson distinguished between the 'greater ode' marked by "sublimity, rapture, and quickness of transition", and the 'lesser ode' "characterized by sweetness and ease" (s.v. 'ode, *n.*'). To some extent, these 'secondary' attributes follow from the ode's pre-history. Its ancient models derive, for the most part, from poets whose place in the canon was firmly secured: the Greek poet Pindar's structurally complex and stylistically sublime odes (fifth century BC) in paid celebration of victors at various athletic competitions, written for public choric performance, and the Roman poet Horace's more private, genial, and isometrical odes (first century BC). Third, the psalms ascribed to King David (tenth century BC, many now thought to have been composed over later centuries) commanded both religious and aesthetic authority. From these fountain-heads, modern ode-writing derives various currents: following Pindar, some English odes employ a passionate and inspired voice, striking and allusive imagery, and as their basic building block a triadic sequence of two verse groups in identical metre (*strophe* and *antistrophe*), and an *epode* of related, but different metre.[1] Some, following Abraham Cowley's seventeenth-century 'Pindaric' example, use irregular stanzas; some employ uniform stanzas of variable or regular line lengths. This latter controlled form looks back to Horace, who also bequeathed on the ode tradition a mood of tranquil, detached contemplation, at once smoothly urbane and sympathetic to rustic simplicity. During the later eighteenth century, these distinctions began to lose their purchase, and the ode form was emancipated from its classical traditions to some extent. But these developments are the subject of the next section.

II

In view of the great historical variability in the form, the development of the ode in English will be traced here by reference to a small number of landmark texts (for wider surveys, see Shafer; Shuster; Jump; Fry; and, more recently but less comprehensively, Hass 209-291). Following the above suggestion about the form's meta-poetic function, a secondary aim is to explore the extent to which the ode can be seen as an indicator of the public place of poetry, and poets, over time. As you read the poems discussed here, I encourage you to consider (1) which objects are deemed 'worthy' of odic address; (2) how the poems bestow prestige on their object; (3) what this entails regarding the poets' self-perception as agents of praise, and of poetry as a medium; in particular in (4) the relation to the sister art of music. In Pindar, the answers are relatively straightforward, as may be illustrated by the example of his earliest extant ode, *Pythian* 10. In

186 *Florian Klaeger*

four thematically separate triads (each consisting of strophe, antistrophe, and epode) composed on the occasion of celebrating a racer victorious at the Pythian games, young Hippocleas, and his Thessalian home, Pindar extols the virtues of the athlete and his family. At the same time, he reminds them of their limitations as mortals by linking, and contrasting, them with mythical gods and ancestors. Pindar's confidence in his own skill and suitability for the task – even at this early point in his career – is reflected in his complex and challenging style, his daring imagery, and abrupt mental leaps. At the beginning of the final triad, the poet posits that his song, repeated in Hippocleas' hometown (stressing the 'portability' of the form), will make the athlete respected among men and desired among women. This hyperbole is deflated slightly by the reminder that fortune is fickle, and no one knows what the future holds. A similar theme is also treated in an example of the other major strand in early ode tradition, Horace's ode iv.7. It can be usefully examined in A.E. Housman's translation, posthumously published in 1936. As a classicist and a poet in his own right, Housman grasped the full implications of Horace's stylistic choices. Significantly, he chose to regularise Horace's dactylic alternating hexameters and dimeters into pentametric quatrains, replacing the metrical and structural contrasts of the original with a more solemn, elegiac tone (⬀ elegy) recalling that of Housman's own poetry. Housman's version thus constitutes both a translation and a self-conscious revision acknowledging the changed circumstances for both poetry and poet: interwar Britain is no Augustan Rome, and the bookish Cambridge don no poet to princes, like Horace. The topic of Horace's ode is mortality. On the occasion of spring returning to the world, the speaker addresses his friend Torquatus and contemplates that while nature is subject to cyclical renewal, human existence is linear and finite. Observing the reawakening to life of nature after winter, he is reminded that human death is inescapable and final, as illustrated in mythical figures such as Hippolytus and Pirithous. His advice to Torquatus, hence, is to seize the day (the famous phrase, 'carpe diem', is from ode i.11). The topic, then, is of an indisputably universal relevance – it is literally a matter of life and death. The poem opens with an idyllic survey of blooming nature, but soon intimations of mortality intrude upon the speaker. In the poem's pivotal central line (l. 14), we (*nos*) and our own hopelessness are juxtaposed to the moon's eternal cycle. From here on, the focus is on the human – or indeed, on mythical humans. Consider that a poem on human frailty and marginality, which derives this very theme from the contrast with perennial nature, places 'us' dead (pardon the pun) in its centre. It references mythology to illustrate how final death is – and yet, what is myth, if not an illustration that human ideas can transcend individual death? That is small consolation for the individual, it is true, and the ode registers this in its very concession that 'we' are central to ourselves. The only possible advice is then to enjoy the present – the present, it is suggested, in which this ode is written to a friend, or spoken, read, or sung. Thus, both odic objects, the specific human and the abstract notion of mortality, are celebrated poetically. This celebration becomes an instance of just what the ode advises – and the reference to myth corroborates that poetry transcends death, and that 'universal' truths of life transcend the individual case. To translate this poem, and to adapt it to a much-changed modern world – one in which the role of poetry, and of poets, had declined, and total warfare had ostensibly cheapened the value of individual lives – is then to offer a nostalgic comment on what has been lost. Housman's circumlocutional diction, more convoluted and indirect than Horace's original, suggests that the undeniable fact of mortality cannot be addressed as simply and as pithily any longer. Poetry is more self-involved, and the poet less assured about his role as adviser, even (or especially) where a commonplace like 'seize the day' is concerned.

III

During the sixteenth and early seventeenth century, Ben Jonson and others had written odes in imitation of the classical models, but the young John Milton transformed these models in a spectacular manner. The poem he chose to open his first collection, "On the Morning of Christ's Nativity" (1629, pub. 1645), is now usually called "The Nativity Ode", and it offers us an idea of how the classical ode was transposed into a Christian context. Four introductory stanzas in regular iambic pentameters establish the poem's occasion, Christmas morning (Milton maintained that it came to him on the day specified in the title, in 1629). The speaker appeals to his muse to greet the infant Christ with a gift and lay his "humble ode" before the manger (l. 24). It is this ode that follows, titled "The Hymn" (linking it to the third ancient source of the tradition) and divided into 27 stanzas that fall broadly into three parts: the first sets the scene at the time of the birth of Christ, with Nature paying homage and universal peace suspending all dissension. The second part rapturously renders the music of the spheres merging with the angelical choirs in celebration of the Incarnation; the third offers a vision of the old pagan deities noisily fleeing the world, before the final stanza returns to the tranquil stable. Milton thus appropriately shapes his nativity gift on the occasion of God becoming not only man, but child, of the divine entering the mundane, through a number of contrasts, including that between silence, music, and noise. The angels' song in the holy night also recalls their music at the very creation of the world (stanza 12), although in a parenthesis (l. 117), the speaker defers authority for this parallel, conceding that his epiphanic present *recalls* the grandeur of the Incarnation, but still he can only intuit Creation itself. The poet remains unassuming, as he appeals to the heavens to sound (l. 125) but, in a second parenthesis, allows that the celestial music may not be audible to human ears (l. 127). He prays to heaven, however, that this might be so in some future moment of bliss (l. 126),

188 *Florian Klaeger*

framing his description in terms of an as-yet unfulfilled, perhaps even un-fulfillable desire. The hymn continues in the conditional mode (stanza 14), before the sublime vision is shattered bluntly by the reminder that be-fore future bliss, superhuman suffering awaits. Consider stanza 16 to see how Milton makes use of the stanzaic form he created specifically for this poem. Just as the harsh, largely monosyllabic trimeters jar with the me-lodious first pentameter, the bitterness of the crucifixion intrudes on the serene nativity scene: the smiling infant is transformed into the anguished man of sorrows in the space of two lines; "infancy" and "glorify" refuse to rhyme properly (ll. 151, 154). The ecstatic music is banished as this piv-otal stanza rushes into the next, initiating the hymn's final movement on the banishment of the pagan powers. When the cacophony of idols dies away, the final stanza returns to the manger, where Mary puts her child to rest. The scene is silent, except for the poet's voice, offering a self-effacing conclusion (l. 239). The object of this ode is utterly hyperbolic: it is the greatest moment in the history of salvation, from the creation of the world to the Incarnation and crucifixion and the end of time. Understandably, then, the poem is framed in modest terms – indeed, in the conditional, presenting itself as a vision and an appeal, rather than a statement of fact. Still, its sublime thematic range and powerful musical language suggest the advent of a major poet, and we encounter here precisely the mutual ennoblement of Christian subject and classical form that Milton will later effect, on a much grander scale, in *Paradise Lost* (⌁ epic). In a 'Christian-ised' ode on the greatest story ever told, the poet must be self-consciously humble, while at the same time he can be supremely assured that his work could have no worthier subject.

Abraham Cowley initiated a fashion for irregular odes in imitation of Pindar in the mid-seventeenth century, with his *Pindarique Odes* (pub. 1656). John Dryden's "Alexander's Feast" (1697) illustrates the neoclassical adaptation of the form rather well. It was composed on the occasion, as the subtitle tells us, of St Cecilia's Day. This early Christian martyr was associated with spiritual music, and in Restoration England, the church service on her annual feast day was followed by the public performance of an ode written and composed for the purpose. Dryden's poem celebrates the power of music both through its own musical form and through its subject, a victory celebration in Persepolis after Alexander the Great's de-feat of the Persians. Court musician Timotheus manipulates the conqueror by the music he plays, taking Alexander through the emotional extremes of mythical and public apotheosis, inebriated pride, abject pity for the fallen enemy, sentimental love, and finally, lust for revenge for the fallen companions. The rapid shifts between these states of mind, alongside the sublime subject and language, render the ode a specimen of the Cowleyan Pindaric, as does the irregular stanza form. Exploiting an even wider met-rical range than Milton's ode to full dramatic effect, Dryden lends poetic shape to the affective power of music, emphasising the close connection

The Ode   189

between the two arts. In his conclusion, he arrives at a similarly Christianising gesture as Milton had: Timotheus' musical skill on the lyre, praised so extravagantly before, turns out to be only the foil for the real object of praise, Cecilia, and the instrument she was thought to have invented, the organ – while the ancient musician is said to have elevated mortal Alexander to the heavens (in deifying him), Cecilia "drew an angel down" (ll. 169–170). Once again, the contrast between pagan antiquity – revered for its aesthetic achievements, but suspect for its morals – and the new Christian age is central. Dryden milks the classical references for all their pomp and pathos, and he uses them to illustrate a 'higher truth' about the power of music – but ultimately, the hyperbolic excess of the past feast is contained by the spiritual sublime of the present holiday. The ode, then, follows the same principle of appropriating the ancient form while also ennobling it with a Christian subject – or conversely, it spices up the solemn Christian holiday with pagan revelry, as expressed through the 'excess' of the Pindaric.

IV

During the eighteenth century, the ode remained a highly popular form, but it was emancipated further from emulating the classics. Recent bibliographical research has unearthed a large number of eighteenth-century odes by poets lacking a university education, suggesting that their use of the form may have been determined more by imitation of immediate predecessors than of classical models (see Jung 514 and passim). The association with the spiritual we have seen in Milton and Dryden remains intact, supplied by the element of meditation. The same is true of the theme of music as a sister art and of the praise of some external object. William Collins' influential odes add to this an allegorical dimension (in praise of abstract notions, rather than particular persons or occasions) and a descriptive method (with natural objects stirring reflection on some great idea or concept inherent in them), and, hence, an emphasis on poetic inspiration and a celebration of native poetic tradition, a theme also encountered in Thomas Gray. Next to a number of widely admired specimens of the form, Gray also produced the "Ode on the Death of a Favourite Cat, Drowned in a Tub of Goldfishes" (1747), which exemplifies a departure from tradition in two ways: first, like many other odes of the time, it abandons the Pindaric triad in favour of a stanza repeated uniformly throughout the poem, and, second, it assumes a ♪ mock-heroic tone, suggesting that the obligation towards serious topics had collapsed and the form had become prone to parody. The basis for such parody, however, was the commonly understood identification of the 'Great Ode' with the lofty and sublime. From the neoclassical period onwards, the ode had been associated with irregularity, vehemence, and liberty in the expression of genius, standing in contrast to the controlled measure and artifice of supposedly

190 *Florian Klaeger*

less poetical forms – Norman Maclean describes it as "'the free verse' of the neoclassical period" (424).

These eighteenth-century developments clearly align the form with key concerns of the Romantics. M.H. Abrams has written influentially of "the greater Romantic lyric" that came to replace, during the Romantic period, both odes on the elevated Pindaric model and those of the 'lesser' Horatian type. The ode is not the only, but the paradigmatic form of this "greater Romantic lyric", and Abrams finds in it the basic structure of an encounter with some (usually particularised) external object that prompts a meditative inward turn in the speaker, who at the end of the poem returns to the outward scene in a changed manner (527–528). You will note a shift in the formal relationship between poetic subject and object: whereas in earlier odes, an event or idea offered a mere prompt or occasion for the poet to display their skill, now it elicits a reflection that will change the poet and the way they see the world. The significant change, then, is in the ode's function: whereas before it was primarily concerned with representing the outside world, and/or with affecting the addressee/audience, it is now about expressing the sentiments of the poet (cp. Abrams 539). This signals a watershed in the perceived purpose and potential of the form and, by extension, of poetry at large. It can be observed in all the major Romantic odes, including Wordsworth's "Intimations of Immortality", Coleridge's "Dejection", Keats' great odes of 1819, and Shelley's "Ode to the West Wind", to name only a few. All of them have elicited extensive critical discussion, which the present chapter cannot begin to summarise. Given the emphasis placed here so far on the role of music and song for the definition of the form, reference may briefly be made to John Keats' "Ode to a Nightingale" (1819). Formally, it is closer to the Horatian model in its homostrophic uniformity (although Keats' stanzaic form more immediately derives from his experiments with the ♪ sonnet, and within the stanza, the metre is varied). Like many Romantic odes, it captures a moment of crisis for the poet: the occasion is the experience of hearing a nightingale's song; the speaker's meditation leads him from wishing for a union with the un-self-conscious bird to mentally attaining this union for a brief moment and losing it again; at the conclusion, he is left with the wish for the permanency of such an experience. Thus, the ode illustrates the almost-but-not-quite circular pattern also evident in the examples from Pindar, Horace, and Milton: an external occasion – the athlete, spring, Christmas morning – triggers a meditation (an inward journey of the mind), which ends with a return to the outward occasion, but with a changed attitude. Keats' ode already differs, however, in its very opening, which does not apostrophise or celebrate the object, but instead describes the speaker's mental disposition, only directly addressing the nightingale in a subordinate clause (l. 7). It becomes clear that the encomiastic is subordinated to the expressive function. The bird's song, and the associations it raises in the speaker, are described in a highly allusive, indirect fashion – although all the senses are addressed, experience is mediated verbally first

The Ode 191

and foremost. Contrast the ecstatic, but natural music of stanzas 6 and 7 in particular with the ceremonious pomp of Dryden's ode, rendered memorably in G.F. Händel's setting (HWV 75), and with the sonorous rhythm of Milton's "Nativity Ode": the song Keats celebrates is not instrumental or choral music, but birdsong in all its mythical overdetermination, transgressing the boundaries of the secular and the sacred, of time, space, and the arts. The resigned conclusion, in its baffled disorientation between wakefulness and dream (l. 80), leaves speaker and reader suspended between the world of poetry (this ode) and external reality. Not dissimilar to the "Nativity Ode", the "Nightingale" holds up the sublime experience and denies it at the same time. The central aim seems here less spiritual, however, than aesthetic and vocational, as the ode explores the relationship between mind and body, imagination and brute fact, art and life.

V

While the later nineteenth century produced a number of great specimens (such as Tennyson's "Ode on the Death of the Duke of Wellington"), the twentieth and twenty-first century have seen a decline in the ode form. The implicit argument in the preceding pages has been, of course, that this may be related to the changed public place of poetry and poets. Where it is felt – as we have seen in Housman's translation of Horace – that the poet, and poetry, hold little authority of their own, they have little prestige to bestow on another. The ode does remain, however, a medium for the poet whose task it is to celebrate. The current Poet Laureate, Simon Armitage, in "Ode to a Clothes Peg" (2019), handles the form in a self-consciously post-Romantic way, referencing the long shadow of Keats. The clothes peg's transformation comes to stand for the ode itself, changing its material but not its purpose. It is intractably bound up with the memory of those who used it before, and the final Keatsian association with "death masks and shrouds" (l. 22) may suggest that the form seems stale at present, but the change in the peg's user – for the first time, a man – suggests that times do change, and the future is not foreclosed. For a supremely mundane object to spark meditations on the purpose of poetry is to argue for the latter's continued relevance, even in 'un-poetic' times.

All poems discussed here as milestones in the history of the ode form were written by white men who, on account of their gender and race, spoke from a position of privilege. To pretend that this is irrelevant for the development of the form would be naïve at best. As has been described here, 'odic voice' assumes a liberty of address that is not easily available for the disenfranchised (see Jackson 309 and passim). For powerful recent examples of how the form can be reclaimed, consider American poet Anaïs Duplan's "Ode to the Happy Negro Hugging the Flag in Robert Colescott's 'George Washington Carver Crossing the Delaware'" (2018), joining Pindaric daringness of vision and complexity of style with great

192   *Florian Klaeger*

intimacy, and Sharon Olds' collection, *Odes* (2016), which celebrates female physicality in poems such as "Ode to the Hymen", "Ode to Stretch Marks", or "O of Multiple O's". Examples such as these suggest that for all the weight of tradition, and because of it, the ode form may counter the unspoken hierarchies it has been predicated on.

NOW READ ON...

- In its use of the progress of ideas rather than any external markers as a structuring device, the ode has quite a few aspects in common with both ⟋ sonnet and ⟋ elegy.
- The project undertaken in Milton's "Nativity Ode" features significant overlaps with his *Paradise Lost*, which is discussed in more detail in the chapter on ⟋ epic poetry; and also with "Lycidas", which features prominently in the chapter on the ⟋ elegy.
- When its lofty style is parodied in the eighteenth century, the ode moves tonally towards ⟋ mock-heroic poetry.
- The use of a form favoured by the (erstwhile) oppressor with which the present chapter ends also features in the chapters on the ⟋ heroic couplet and on the ⟋ sonnet.

Note

1 Ben Jonson's translation of these terms as 'turn', 'counter-turn', and 'stand' reflects their origin in Greek choral dance performance.

References

Abrams, Meyer H. "Structure and Style in the Greater Romantic Lyric". *From Sensibility to Romanticism: Essays Presented to Frederick A. Pottle*, eds. Frederick W. Hilles and Harold Bloom. Oxford UP, 1965, pp. 527–560.

Armitage, Simon. "Ode to a Clothes Peg". 2019. www.simonarmitage.com/wp-content/uploads/Ode-to-a-Clothes-Peg-by-Simon-Armitage.pdf.

Dryden, John. "Alexander's Feast". *The Norton Anthology of English Literature. Digital Edition*, eds. Stephen Greenblatt and Meyer H. Abrams, 9th ed. Norton, 2012, pp. 2246–2250.

Duplan, Anaïs. "Ode to the Happy Negro Hugging the Flag in Robert Colescott's 'George Washington Carver Crossing the Delaware'". 2017. www.poets.org/poem/ode-happy-negro-hugging-flag-robert-colescotts-george-washington-carver-crossing-delaware.

Fry, Paul H. *The Poet's Calling in the English Ode*. Yale UP, 1980.

Gray, Thomas. "Ode on the Death of a Favourite Cat". *The Norton Anthology of English Literature. Digital Edition*, eds. Stephen Greenblatt and Meyer H. Abrams, 9th ed. Norton, 2012, pp. 3050–3051.

Hass, Robert. *A Little Book on Form: An Exploration into the Formal Imagination of Poetry*. Ecco, 2017.

Horatius Flaccus, Quintus. "Ode iv.7". *Odes and Epodes*. Harvard UP, 1978, pp. 310–313.

Housman, Alfred Edward. "Diffugere Nives: Horace: Odes iv 7". *The Collected Poems of A.E. Housman*. Jonathan Cape, 1939, pp. 163–164.

Jackson, Virginia. "Historical Poetics and the Dream of Interpretation: A Response to Paul Fry". *Modern Language Quarterly* 81.3 (2020), pp. 289–318.

Johnson, Samuel. *A Dictionary of the English Language*, 8th ed. Printed for J. Johnson […], 1799.

Jump, John Davies. *The Ode*. Methuen, 1974. The Critical Idiom 30.

Jung, Sandro. "Ode". *The Oxford Handbook of British Poetry: 1660–1800*, ed. Jack Lynch. Oxford UP, 2016, pp. 510–527.

Keats, John. "Ode to a Nightingale". *The Norton Anthology of English Literature*, eds. Stephen Greenblatt and Meyer H. Abrams, 8th ed. W.W. Norton, 2006, pp. 903–905.

Maclean, Norman. "From Action to Image: Theories of the Lyric in the Eighteenth Century". *Critics and Criticism: Ancient and Modern*, ed. Ronald S. Crane. U of Chicago P, 1952, pp. 408–460.

Milton, John. "On the Morning of Christ's Nativity". *The Norton Anthology of English Literature. Digital Edition*, eds. Stephen Greenblatt and Meyer H. Abrams, 9th ed. Norton, 2012, pp. 1901–1909.

OED Online. "ode, n." March 2022. www.oed.com/view/Entry/130418. Accessed 23 March 2022.

Olds, Sharon. *Odes*. Jonathan Cape, 2016.

Pindar. "Pythian 10". *The Complete Odes*, trans. Anthony Verity, introd. Stephen Instone. Oxford UP, 2007, pp. 80–83.

Shafer, Robert. *The English Ode to 1660. An Essay in Literary History*. 1918, Gordian P, 1966.

Shuster, George N. *The English Ode from Milton to Keats*. Columbia UP, 1940.

20 The Prospect Poem

Roslyn Irving

I

In his study of William Wordsworth's "Tintern Abbey", Henry Weinfield defines the prospect form as "a poem that in describing a place from a distance gains perspective both on space and time" (257). Prospect poetry uses a vantage point, often from a bridge, mountain, or hill, to observe society and comment on futurity. This explanation emphasises the sense of 'place', which is central to prospect poetry and retained throughout the development of the form. However, is it possible to consider a prospect poem distinct from other topographical writing, and can the presence of a viewpoint constitute a poetic form? A large body of research exists on Renaissance and eighteenth-century examples of prospect poetry. For instance, John Foster suggests that in John Denham's *Cooper's Hill* (1642), which is one of the first prospect poems, "perspective became physically credible instead of ideal and unrealistic, and ... the poet became an observer instead of an omnipresent witness" (233). More recently, Ingrid Horrocks has investigated eighteenth-century transformations in prospect poetry, positing that the onlooker, originally a "disinterested gentleman" as found in Alexander Pope's *Windsor Forest* (1713) and James Thomson's *The Seasons* (1726–1730), gives way to the voice(s) of itinerant figures (665). This chapter will address concerns around prospect poetry as a distinct tradition using Wordsworth's ⌀ sonnet "Composed after a Journey across the Hamilton Hills, Yorkshire" (1807) (hereafter referred to as "Hamilton Hills") and Norman Nicholson's "Scafell Pike" (1981). These poems demonstrate how prospect continued to resonate in the nineteenth and twentieth centuries. This chapter considers articulations of change and journeying in the form, beginning with Wordsworth's prospect sonnet. Subsequently, the discussion will move on to Nicholson's response to Romantic poets such as Wordsworth as he captured the national landscape and interactions between the Lake District and local communities (Cooper 172). Interestingly, it appears that Nicholson returned to the rhetorical position of an aloof observer, akin to early examples of prospect poetry from the seventeenth and eighteenth centuries.

DOI: 10.4324/9781003244004-22

II

It is necessary to preface engagement with Wordsworth's sonnet on the Hambleton Hills[1] by considering other well-known examples of his prospect poetry. Through panoramic vistas of the Lake District, Yorkshire, the Wye Valley, and London, the poet raised questions around faith, permanence, and change. Comparing Wordsworth's and Elizabeth Tollet's sonnets on the view from Westminster Bridge, John Sitter makes a case for the sociological impulses in the prospect form. He finds that Wordsworth's curation of the city is "autobiographical" and privileges the natural world in the urban space, whereas Tollet recollects centuries of the Thames's history and celebrates industrial transformations (Sitter 183–184). Tollet calls on the Roman Emperor Caesar to examine the capital and revere the architecture which seems to "ascend" into the sky (qtd. in Sitter 182, ll. 1–3). Differing preoccupations inspired by the same vantage point contribute to the sense of ambiguity around the form. Wordsworth's "Composed upon Westminster Bridge" was written just over a month prior to "Hamilton Hills" (Gill 710–711). The autobiographical quality of these poems is crucial considering that the latter was not merely "Composed after a Journey", but shortly after the poet's wedding (Regan 96). Regardless of the setting, the prospect form allowed Wordsworth to reflect on and adjust to change. Included in his 1807 collection, *Poems, in Two Volumes*, "Hamilton Hills" demonstrates the emotive force of prospects while encountering the physical and philosophical challenges of journeying. In "Hamilton Hills", the promised view of the Yorkshire landscape, "whereof many thousands tell", never manifests (l. 4). A template that perhaps builds on his earlier prospect poem, "Tintern Abbey", in which Wordsworth's engagement with the sensory experience and recollections of the pastoral landscape, topographic features, and inhabitants, does not refer to the ruinous abbey (Levinson 24–25). Wordsworth finds "deep seclusion" in the Wye Valley and the opportunity to consider both his early vigour and the insight he has gained after a five-year absence ("Tintern Abbey" l. 7; Weinfield 280–281). The poet suggests that his thoughts have frequently revisited the scene for "tranquil restoration" ("Tintern Abbey" l. 31). It is a historically, politically, and personally informed poem, as Marjorie Levinson puts it, "the landscape figures as a repository for outgrown ego-stages, themselves enshrining certain social values Wordsworth was, throughout his life, keen to preserve" (23). In "Hamilton Hills", the poet appears to be searching for a picturesque landscape, perhaps to facilitate reflections on his bachelorhood and consider how marriage may change his life. However, the first four lines of the poem describe the disappointment of the travelling party, arriving just after nightfall, thus unable to experience the "power / Of prospect" they had anticipated (ll. 3–4). Having missed the daylight by a brief window, dusk precludes their examination of the hilltops. Stephen Regan notes that the sonnet is unusual in its "immediate denial of the

196 *Roslyn Irving*

anticipated pleasures of the prospect, and its robust refusal to settle for any substitute conjured up in the clouds" (95). Therefore the poem does not fit the prospect form in a traditional sense, as Wordsworth does not systematically review the surroundings, itemise sites, or categorise the geography (Foster 255–256). Most of the topographical observations are the effect of the company's imagination on the clouds, but they conjure ruins that could be found embedded in the hills of Yorkshire. As the sublime skyline lacks materiality, Wordsworth turns away from the nightscape, and his priority becomes the feeling of the space and his uncertain place in the darkness. The poem sits in harmony with the sentiments of Wordsworth's "Ode: Intimations of Immortality", which featured in the same collection of poems. It also foreshadows the fears he describes in *The Prelude*, published decades later.

The sonnet is retrospective, written in the past tense, seemingly after the travellers have departed. Therefore, the "space and time" that Weinfield suggests are critical to the prospect form seem to be unfixed in the sonnet (257). As previously mentioned, Horrocks uses eighteenth-century prospect poetry to demonstrate how the figure of the poet was transformed from a profoundly exclusive and geographically fixed surveyor, articulating the perspective of aristocratic men, to "the wanderer" (665). This change was anticipated by the itinerant figures, which expose the dangers of an obscured perspective, distinct from the orderliness of the poet and his benefactor in "Autumn" and "Winter" of Thomson's *The Seasons* (Horrocks 671). Such wanderers represent "a kind of nightmare, inverted, version of prospective boundlessness, and demonstrate[] what the prospect might become were it to lose its center and elevation" (673). According to Horrocks, thirty years later, Oliver Goldsmith reinvented the poet as a discontented mobile voice in "The Traveller, or a Prospect of Society" (1760) (680). "Hamilton Hills" seems to follow this tradition, as Wordsworth sought a single "center and elevation" in the daylight, which eluded him. Out of time in the impenetrable valleys, the companions are forced to look upwards and accept a very different prospect to the vista they had hoped for.

Employing plural pronouns "we", "us", and "our" throughout the sonnet, Wordsworth attempts to record the collective thoughts and feelings of the chagrined travelling party. In fact, "we" appears six times across the fourteen lines, producing a sense of community while making it unclear whom the journey serves. While the wedding party might be small, by the closing lines of the poem, "we" comes to mean all with a faulty memory. This encounter is, in many ways, universal. Notably, the sonnet only speaks of feelings shared, not how the travellers differ. Stephen Gill offers an extract from Dorothy Wordsworth's diary in his explanatory notes: "Before we had crossed the Hambledon hills and reached the point overlooking Yorkshire it was quite dark. We had not wanted, however, fair prospects before us as we drove along the flat plain of the high hill" (qtd. in Gill 711). Dorothy also employed plural pronouns to describe the carriage ride and cloud-formed architecture. However, she does not share in her brother's disappointment or regret when faced with "Castles, Ruins among groves … forms of a sober grey" in the sky (qtd. in Gill 711). In the absence of conventional picturesque constructions, the scene remained captivating and memorable for both Wordsworth siblings, despite William's concern over memory loss. Hence "we" in the sonnet continues to represent the poet's singular vision and version of the prospect. From line five, the travellers turn westward in unison, the direction in which the sun perhaps continued to set. While the intended prospect never appears, Wordsworth observes a strange and rewarding nightscape. The bell tower in the spectacle of silhouettes evoking tolling and time-keeping.

Despite the darkness, the prospect functions as an emotive force, as Wordsworth curates his physical experience of the Hambleton Hills into a commentary on memory loss, where the modal verbs "might" and "should" in the final passage stress his uncertainty ("Hamilton Hills" ll. 12–14). The topographical features of the prospect, only accessible from his hilltop vantage, are secondary to Wordsworth's reconciliation with the limitations of the human mind. As Wordsworth cannot survey the countryside and suggests that he will forget his vision of the evening in due course, the poem is structured around frustration and imagination. These emotions are provoked by the (lack of) panorama atop the hills. Given Wordsworth's recent marriage, the silhouette of a church or cathedral and reflections on "earth-bound actuality" speak to changing phases of life (Regan 96). The final two lines rearticulate the spatial and temporal distance of the travellers on the journey through Yorkshire, acknowledge Wordsworth's growing distance from his youth and bachelor days, as well as the expectations of his future married life.

For Romantic writers such as Wordsworth, prospect poetry was the outcome of being moved by an elevated vantage point. Foster posits that such emotional engagements were the result of a rather more empirical tradition, as "the expert handling of perspective, configuration, and point of view upon which the Romantic poets could call when they wished originated with the topographical poets" (256). Denham's *Cooper's Hill* and Richard Jago's *Edge-Hill* (1767) exemplify the meticulous and systematic origin of the prospect form. Foster marks the triangulation of sites which allows the reader to locate the positions of the poets (243, 254). For example, Denham carefully specifies the turn of his head from St Paul's Cathedral to "Windsor the next (where Mars with Venus dwells, / Beauty with strength) above the Valley swells" (qtd. in Foster 240). The sites viewed from Cooper's Hill near the Thames are deliberately named and ordered. However, Foster does not apply his "eye-as-visual-instrument" model to poetry after the early nineteenth century and seems to suggest that Romanticism may have brought empiricism in the topographical genre to an end (256):

198   *Roslyn Irving*

Apart from the fact that the genre was growing increasingly regionalist and local in appeal, the attitude toward landscape that informed it was falling out of fashion with progressive poets. Romantic poets reacted against a methodical observation of nature that was at base scientific and informative and which made of the poet at best an aggressive observer of something external to him.

(Foster 253–255).

According to Foster, topographical poetry was outward-facing and, in the case of Denham's work, " a kind of allegory, with the English nation" (237). This thought is echoed in Levinson's comparison of "Cooper's Hill" and "Tintern Abbey", as she suggests that the poets employed prospects to allude to broader political interactions and histories (17). As "Hamilton Hills" is spatially and temporally specific, Wordsworth accounts for the conditions under which his observations were made. However, the poet is introspective, more concerned with articulating memory and interpretation as a consequence of engaging with the prospect than the topography of rural Yorkshire. While Romantic poets may have broken with the tradition of "aggressive" examination of the landscape, this analytical style was not completely lost to the topographical genre. It is a tone and technique that resonated with later poets.

III

Having addressed Wordsworth's private ruminations on a prospect, the discussion which follows considers "Scafell Pike", a "regionalist" and "scientific" encounter with the Lake District and the industrialised towns of Cumbria in the twentieth century (Foster 255). Composed centuries after *Cooper's Hill* and *The Seasons* and following the significant changes to the topographical genre realised by the Romantic movement, Nicholson returns to the role of a surveyor in his poem. This resonates with contemporaries such as W.H. Auden (Cooper 172–173). Paola Marchetti states that Auden used topography to explore "the fugitive beauty of life which must be enjoyed while it lasts" (208). His landscapes are dynamic because they attend to and parallel human experiences. For example, "In Praise of Limestone" (1948) celebrates a substance that symbolises stability yet attests to gradual change (Auden ll. 3–15). The stone is full of plains and crevices that parents, children, water, light, animals, and emperors move across, beneath and within over centuries. Similarly, "Scafell Pike" is "a revisionist, post-Romantic representation of his [Nicholson's] native region" (Cooper 172). The poet overlays a distant mountain with the trappings of industry and the trepidations of a community experiencing vast change.

In the first two stanzas, Nicholson guides the eye through the streets of a town, likely Millom, towards the peak of Scafell Pike, "On the plate-glass window of the sky!" (l. 16). By the third stanza, the symbolic force

The Prospect Poem   199

of the mountain, which initially seems a trifling mark, becomes apparent. Re-visiting the scene centuries in the future, Nicholson imagines what of the town and its surroundings might withstand a test of permanence. He foreshadows the collapse of human activities, as places of work and worship become debris, quite unlike the distant crag (Nicholson ll. 24–36). Only grey skies and Scafell Pike remain unchanged for millennia. According to Cooper, Nicholson's late poetry offers a "retrospective reconstruction of a way of life that ceased to exist" after de-industrialisation in the 1950s, and the poet's oeuvre is "geographically rooted and theologically informed" (185). In "Scafell Pike", Nicholson connects his Christian faith with topographical musings by paralleling the chapel's roof and mountain's peak (Nicholson ll. 5–11). Furthermore, life itself "ceased to exist" in the desolate closing lines, which echoes the uncertainty of industrial-mining towns after the mid-century. Scafell Pike becomes a hopeful emblem, as the site will endure profound changes to human life and society. This explains why the mountain remains fixed at the centre of the poet's sightline, even after centuries. As mentioned throughout this chapter, similar reflections on national identity, organised religion, faith, and change can be found in Denham's, Wordsworth's, and Auden's topographical commentaries (Foster 237–238; Levinson 17; Marchetti 208).

In his poem, Nicholson directs the gaze towards the mountain, transitioning across the three stanzas from industrial and domestic spaces to intangible, imaginary ruins in millennia to come. Wordsworth frequently employed a high vantage point to distance his reflections from the urban "din" ("Tintern Abbey" ll. 26–27). However, human elements are inescapable in "Hamilton Hills" through the track, carriage, and unmet expectations of the vista. Nicholson continues such explorations by examining the effects of heavy industry on the Lake District. However, he pays no attention to the cloud and falling light by pushing natural phenomena to the background, including the titular mountain. His observations in the first two stanzas attend to the smog of the town and the ramshackle buildings, where Scafell is an ever-present and unassuming part of daily life. The poem is striking in its irregular structure and fluid narration. The line length varies from the opening single-syllable to complex phrases. Nicholson boldly begins by inviting or even instructing the reader to look at the scene not yet described, building expectations (Nicholson l. 1).

The undeviating sightline of the poet creates a sense of tunnel vision in "Scafell Pike", as Nicholson attends only to the prospect before him and the years ahead. He describes nothing on the periphery. Like early examples of the form, the poet occupies a "single, stable position" but does not represent the interests of aristocrats and landowners (Horrocks 665). Nicholson offers the voice of a local man with a local interest. The solitary narrator is unaccompanied, and although he hints at the community in the town, perhaps cooking meals, attending the chapel, or finding employment at the power station, no one appears in the streets.

Using the third person allows him to remain an onlooker, like the fell on the opposite horizon. The report-like quality of the description is instantly accessible. Nicholson writes for an audience who need not be familiar with the Lake District or even imagine a pastoral idyll. His prospect is that of industry set against the countryside. As mentioned, the distant view of Scafell is an opportunity to think critically about the future of the town, a practice in keeping with Wordsworth's "Tintern Abbey", which Levinson convincingly argues "originates in a will to preserve something Wordsworth knows is already lost" (37). "Scafell Pike" also accords with "Hamilton Hills" by conjuring a somewhat frustrated sense of expectation. Nicholson's description has a photographic quality, like a series of mental pictures taken with "the click of an eye" (l. 23). In the poem, Scafell Pike does not appear as an indomitable body but a scientific fact, the distant outcome of volcanic activities, simply the ancient ridge of a magma flow.

IV

This chapter has drawn on late examples of prospect poetry to identify distinct features of the form. Wordsworth's and Nicholson's vantage points differ, the structure of their poems is dissimilar, and they consider different durations of time. On the other hand, both use their spatial position to explore beyond their surroundings. Perhaps then the most crucial element of Weinfield's definition is the idea of "gaining perspective" (257). Horrocks' study of the changing narrator's voice and position in eighteenth-century examples of the form is reflected in Wordsworth's "Hamilton Hills", which problematises journeying in the literal sense through delay and darkness, and figuratively through life phases and memory loss. Despite the collective pronouns, there is a sense of loneliness in the prospect and the poet's reflections on the limits of human memory. Very little of the landscape is featured in Wordsworth's descriptions. As the light fails, the dales are no longer accessible and no longer of concern for the poet. Such isolation is even more apparent in Nicholson's work though created through intense specificity and representing a return to some original elements of the prospect form, namely the use of survey and a relatively fixed viewpoint. "Scafell Pike", though visually irregular, is "methodical" in its approach (Foster 255). Just as Denham fixed his position on the Thames, Nicholson stands directly opposite the mountain and scans the landscape from the proximate lanes and rooftops out towards the peak on the horizon. By the end, the view of the mountain affords critical engagement with de-industrialisation and the effects of time on the Lake District. While nature endures, the town, at least in Nicholson's imagination, will decay, which in many ways resonates with Wordsworth's thoughts on his fleeting memories of the Yorkshire hills.

The traditional prospect poem tends to be quite long and often
The Prospect Poem 201

> ### NOW READ ON...
>
> - As you will have noticed, this chapter references several poems
>   besides those discussed in more detail, so do feel free to look at
>   Pope's _Windsor Forest_ or Denham's _Cooper's Hill_ if you are inter-
>   ested in earlier forms of prospect poetry; or turn to Auden's "In
>   Praise of Limestone" if you would like to see how the form is
>   handled in the mid-twentieth century.
> - The traditional prospect poem tends to be quite long and often
>   makes use of formal elements typical of the ⌁ long poem, e.g.
>   ⌁ blank verse or ⌁ heroic couplets.
> - Unusually, Wordsworth's "Hamilton Hills" is a ⌁ sonnet fea-
>   turing (or frustrating) some of the characteristics of prospect
>   poetry. If you would like to investigate the poem's relation to
>   that form, turn to the chapter on sonnets.

Note

1 Hambleton Hills is the correct spelling of the region of Yorkshire that Word-
   sworth visited. It is referred to by William Wordsworth as "Hamilton" and
   by Dorothy Wordsworth as "Hambledon" (Gill 711).

References

Auden, Wystan Hugh. "In Praise of Limestone". _Auden: Everyman's Library
   Pocket Guide_, selected by Edward Mendelson. Penguin Random House, 1995,
   pp. 136–140.
Cooper, David. "'Matter Matters': Topographical and Theological Space in the
   Poetry of Norman Nicholson". _The Yearbook of English Studies_, vol. 39, no. 1/2.
   Modern Humanities Research Association, 2009, pp. 169–185. www.jstor.org/
   stable/25679868.
Foster, John Wilson. "The Measure of Paradise: Topography in Eighteenth-
   Century Poetry". _Eighteenth-Century Studies_ 9.2 (1975), pp. 232–256. https://
   doi.org/10.2307/2737599.
Gill, Stephen. "Introduction and Notes". _The Major Works Including The Prelude
   by William Wordsworth_, ed. Stephen Gill. Oxford UP, 2008, pp. xiii–xxxii and
   682–740.
Horrocks, Ingrid. "'Circling Eye' and 'Houseless Stranger': The New Eigh-
   teenth-Century Wanderer (Thomson to Goldsmith)". _ELH_ 77.3 (2010),
   pp. 665–687. www.jstor.org/stable/40963182.
Levinson, Marjorie. "Insight and Oversight: Reading 'Tintern Abbey'". _Word-
   sworth's Great Period Poems: Four Essays_. Cambridge UP, 1986, pp. 14–57.
Marchetti, Paola. "Auden's Landscapes". _The Cambridge Companion to W. H.
   Auden_, ed. Stan Smith. Cambridge UP, 2005, pp. 200–211.

202   *Roslyn Irving*

Nicholson, Norman. "Scafell Pike". *Selected Poems 1940–1982*. Faber and Faber, 1982, pp. 59–60.

Regan, Stephen. *The Sonnet*. Oxford UP, 2019.

Sitter, John. "Prophecy and Prospects of Society". *The Cambridge Introduction to Eighteenth-Century Poetry*. Cambridge UP, 2011, pp. 178–197. https://doi.org/10.1017/CBO9781139029186.016.

Weinfield, Henry. "'These Beauteous Forms': 'Tintern Abbey' and the Post-Enlightenment Religious Crisis". *Religion & the Arts* 6.3 (2002), pp. 257–290. https://doi.org/10.1163/15685290260384416.

Wordsworth, William. "Lines Written a Few Miles above Tintern Abbey". *The Major Works Including The Prelude*, ed. Stephen Gill. Oxford UP, 2008, pp. 131–135.

———. "Composed after a Journey across the Hamilton Hills, – Yorkshire". *The Major Works* Including The Prelude, ed. Stephen Gill. Oxford UP, 2008, p. 287.

21 The Sestina

Matthew Kilbane

I

What do wind-swept clouds, folk dancing, a slinky, a snake eating its own tale, scrambled eggs, wickerwork, ping-pong, and the sensation of "riding a bicycle downhill and letting the pedals push your feet" (Lehman 64) have in common? All these motley phenomena are handy metaphors for a particularly bewildering poetic form known as the sestina. If that seems confusing to you – if you're scratching your head and wondering what ping-pong could possibly have to do with scrambled eggs – then I'll suggest you're in precisely the right headspace for thinking about sestinas.

Since the form's invention more than 800 years ago, poets have composed sestinas on every conceivable sort of topic, from timeworn literary concerns like love, death, war, and the splendours of the natural world, to the bric-a-brac of modern life, including home movies and Popeye the Sailor Man (Whitlow and Krysl 29; Ashbery 47–48). And yet, despite its varied subject matter, the sestina is a linguistic contraption so distinctly built that many diverse examples of the form appear to share a common attitude towards their miscellaneous occasions and themes. In fact, it may sometimes seem as if all sestinas are really, at bottom, about just one thing: namely, *the limits of knowledge*. The poet Mary Leader has observed that the sestina is well-suited to dramatising situations in which a poetic speaker is at pains to make sense of something they can't quite fathom (Leader). Since in reading a sestina we too often feel ourselves in the dark, groping along with the speaker for a conceptual light switch, it's an excellent venue for simulating puzzlement. If you survey instances of the form across history, you'll see that the sestina has been especially popular as a means of complaint. What sestina-writing poets are lamenting most fundamentally, it seems to me, is the fact that human knowledge has limits.

First, the nuts and bolts. The classic sestina is a poem of 39 lines in seven stanzas. The first six stanzas each have six lines (hence the name 'sestina', from the Latin 'sextus' or 'sixth'), while the final stanza, sometimes called the 'tornado' or 'envoi', is half as long. A sestina's most conspicuous feature is its complex pattern of line endings. Run your eyes down the right margin of any sestina and you'll notice immediately that each line ends

DOI: 10.4324/9781003244004-23

204   *Matthew Kilbane*

with one of six repeated keywords, or 'teleutons'. These end-words are the teeth that turn the gears of the form. They shuffle throughout the poem according to a specific procedure called 'retrogradatio cruciata'. If you number the teleutons of the first stanza 1–2–3–4–5–6, you'll find those six words rearranged, at the end of the second stanza's lines, into the order 6–1–5–2–4–3. The third stanza's order – 3–6–4–1–2–5 – is a product of the very same pattern of repositioning. The point is not to memorise these numbers, but to grasp the procedure that allows a poet to generate the teleuton sequence of any new stanza from the previous one:

The end-word of line 1 moves to the end of line 2 in the new stanza

2 moves to	4
3 moves to	6
4 moves to	5
5 moves to	3
6 moves to	1

As these repeated end-words incessantly reorganise themselves throughout the poem, they bob and weave, migrate, surprise, and uncannily repeat, in complex permutations that can sometimes feel like messy scrambled eggs, sometimes like the overwhelmingly intricate designs of wickerwork (Zukofsky 69), and sometimes like a highly choreographed "dance of the intellect" (Pound, *Literary* 25; Shapiro 27). Typically, this dance draws to an elegant close in the three-line envoi, where the six words return for one more encore, now paired two-to-a-line, one in the middle and one at the end.

Given that each stanza picks up where the last left off, replying like a ping-pong shot or cascading like a slinky, there is something alluringly automatic or self-generative about the sestina. Poets use this demandingly elaborate form not only to show off, but also because its arbitrary constraints spur the imagination in directions it might not otherwise go. This is what John Ashbery means when he proposes that writing a sestina is like letting the pedals of a bike push your feet on a downhill ride (Lehman 64). You just let gravity take you. For the reader, however, the experience may be quite different. According to one nineteenth-century French proponent of the form, the Comte de Gramont, the reading of a sestina "is nothing other than a reverie, in which ... the same objects present themselves to the mind under successively different aspects, but retain a certain resemblance to each other, undulating and transforming like clouds in the air" (Gramont 33–34, my translation; Preminger 1297). The sestina daydreams at the very margins of sense, courting rich confusions. It's this aspect of the form I aspire to trace in these pages, following the sestina from its early use by Petrarch right up to the present. During much of this time, indeed for hundreds of years at a stretch, "the sestina remained an extremely minor form in English"

(Caplan 19). After stirring to life again in the nineteenth century, the form flourished in the twentieth, and it remains a staple of creative writing workshops today. We might ask why a poetic form so adept at figuring the limits of knowledge – at running the bewildered mind right up to what it just can't comprehend – should enjoy such an enthusiastic reception in the twentieth and twenty-first century. But to that question you probably already have an answer, if you, like me, feel that every day there is more we know we don't understand.

II

The single surviving sestina by the form's inventor, the twelfth-century troubadour Arnaut Daniel, recounts a speaker's extraordinary desire to enter their beloved's bedroom: "Now it hurts my heart worse than strokes of osiers, / That where she now is, her slave gets no ingress" (ll. 15–16). When Dante and Petrarch, inspired by Daniel, pick up the form one hundred years later, they too wield it as a fine-tuned instrument of courtly love. In other words, this form's first job was complaining about unfulfilled desire.

Petrarch's "The burdened air and unrelenting cloud" ("*L'aere gravato, e l'importuna nebbia*") sets into motion six teleutons drawn from the Provencal landscape: cloud ("nebbia"), winds ("venti"), rain ("pioggia"), rivers ("fiumi"), valleys ("valli"), and ice ("ghiacco") (ll. 1–6). As in many sestinas, these keywords shift dramatically in meaning and use throughout the poem. Petrarch opens with a description of seasonal change – clouds bandied by wind letting loose torrents of rain, overfilling rivers that just as quickly freeze over. In the second stanza, though, these end-words dilate in reference, detailing not only the external world but the speaker's inner life as well, their ice-cold heart and clouded thoughts (ll. 7–12). Comparing the two separate climates his form has yoked together, the speaker is pained by the sharp disparity. Whereas the natural world transforms – the hard rain clearing, the ice melting, the clouds dispersed by wind above the valleys – the speaker's emotional circumstances, indifferent to the greater world, admit of no such welcome change: "I weep when it's clear, I weep in the rain" (ll. 20, 13–21). Their heart is a snow-globe in summer; there's no hope for an inner spring.

Why does the speaker feel so affectively immobilised? Here Petrarch opens his teleutons to a third level of reference, hailing the true subject of this courtly lament. In the fourth and fifth stanzas we discover that the speaker's petrified misery is a direct response to their beloved's icy disregard and clouded inscrutability (ll. 19–30). We owe this bad weather, in other words, to a confrontation between two potent weather systems: the speaker's turbulent longing and the beloved's chilly indifference. "I don't know if my love loves me" – that's one way to summarise the limits of knowledge at stake for Petrarch's frustrated speaker.

206   *Matthew Kilbane*

This sestina's quicksilver movement between landscape, speaker, and beloved heightens the contrast between a changeful world and the maddening straitjacket of thwarted desire. But the form's rapidly turning endwords do not *only* mock the speaker; by the poem's end, they also deliver a provisional resolution. In the final stanzas, the teleutons shift in meaning once more to salute not the speaker's tortured state, nor the occlusion of their love, but their own happiest memory – a long-ago love-sealing encounter with the beloved in a landscape of green shade and "sweet ice" that now serves as a cherished place in the mind, a safe retreat in a world of storms (ll. 33, 31–45). We may surmise the speaker is emotionally stuck to the precise extent they remain fixated on the past, but the sestina itself operates like a little consolation machine, a whirring linguistic motor, for moving imaginatively past the grief that comes with just not knowing enough about those we desire.

III

The first English-language poets to use the sestina – Sir Philip Sidney and Edmund Spenser – helped to transpose the form from the rarefied spheres of courtly love to the woods and fields of the pastoral, from the introspective anguish of beseeching lovers to the cries of lamenting shepherds. In Agelastus, the poet-speaker of Sidney's "Since wailing is a bud of causeful sorrow", we find a particularly eloquent example of such a shepherd. This sestina is one of the lyric poems that Sidney scatters throughout *The Countess of Pembroke's Arcadia,* his long pastoral romance. It appears directly after the "universal mischief" of the Duke Bausilius' supposed death, when the mourning shepherds call upon Agelastus to epitomise their grief with a "universal complaint" (246). The task proves difficult, however, for the scale of this tragedy seems to exceed any individual's ability to properly grieve it. Agelastus' sestina must grapple with something definitively oxymoronic in the phrase "universal complaint". How can one set of weeping eyes, one keening mouth – or, for that matter, any number of individual sets of eyes and mouths – sufficiently bemoan a disaster so thoroughgoing that it threatens an entire nation's future?

As is often the case with sestinas, this poem's central problem can be gleaned from just its six teleutons: "sorrow", "fortune", "damage", "public", "Nature", "wailing" (ll. 1–6). When fortune and nature conspire to kill a beloved ruler, "Arcadia's gem", the damage is so *public* in kind that the sum total of all the mourners' wailing still fails to do justice to the enormity of the loss (l. 18). The fourth stanza reveals that only in the modes of fantasy and hyperbole can individual expressions of bereavement achieve the proper public magnitude – if shepherds could cry oceans, breathe flames, and think of absolutely nothing but damage, then Bausilius might be properly laid to rest (ll. 25–30). Barring these impossible feats, "furious inward griefs" bore into the soul, cultivating a "secret sense" of misfortune that grows ever more intensely poisonous (ll. 33, 35). Agelastus' chiastic image for this burrowing grief recalls the sestina's own recursive dynamic: "And sorrow feed, feeding our souls with sorrow" (l. 36).

The only escape, the only suitable expression of grief, is death (38). This is what Agelastus says, in any case. But the poem itself implies otherwise, for as soon as readers mark the resemblance between the sestina form and the inward-turning shape that sorrow takes, we suspect that by composing this wailing into a sestina – by letting sorrow ring out in the echo chamber of the form – the poem has managed public utterance after all. Living on as a literary work amongst the shepherds, Agelastus' poem will "breathe out in public" for as long as Bausilius' memory survives (l. 32). The idea that the sestina, by formally exercising the shepherds' tunnelling woe, wins a degree of 'universality' for this complaint helps explain an odd contradiction in Sidney's poem. Agelastus, in the third stanza, states his intention to fashion a "monument in public" to Bausilius, but two stanzas later, he insinuates the impossibility of such an enterprise (ll. 15, 25–30). Insofar as the sestina requires the recycling of words, it often leads poets (perhaps in attempts to avoid saying the same thing twice) to expressly contradictory statements. Sidney's poem complains about its limited access to a specific type of emotional know-how – how to grieve, as a community, an inestimable loss. And then, the very same poem just goes ahead and finds a way.

IV

After the Renaissance, the sestina went into a period of literary-historical hibernation. It awakened briefly in the nineteenth century, under the skilful pens of poets like Algernon Charles Swinburne, Edmund Gosse, and Comte de Gramont. But it's not until the twentieth century – when the radical transformation of human limits seemed the inveterate norm, and their calamitous violation too frequently that norm's result – that this poetic form emerged as a fixture of English-language verse cultures. To some critics, in fact, the mid-twentieth century deserved to be called the "Age of the Sestina" (Breslin 38; Caplan 14–41). As David Caplan explains, the form was ripe for exploit because it was both rarely used but also celebrated by contemporary critics; it offered poets of the 1930s "a field both wide open and defended" (22). And if, as Caplan argues, the sestina gave certain poets a way to address social issues without recourse to the explicit political messages of "sloganeering" poetry, it also furnished a suitably puzzle-like tool for exploring those dark riddles of interior life which themselves resist direct statement (21).

Such is the case in Elizabeth Bishop's "Sestina". This masterful poem begins squarely in the everyday. A child and her grandmother are in the kitchen having tea on a rainy evening and reading from an almanac (ll. 1–6). In the final line of the first stanza, however, Bishop hints at a juggernaut of grief lying just on the other side of speech: enjoying the almanac's

208   *Matthew Kilbane*

jokes, the grandmother laughs "to hide her tears" (1. 6). Whereas the poem's other five end-words – "house", "grandmother", "child", "stove", and "almanac" – establish this quotidian scene, only "tears" – like a sharp nagging pain – returns in each stanza to index this unspoken discord, the reason for which the grandmother knows but the child evidently doesn't (ll. 1–5). The subject is not, in any case, up for discussion between them. How do you write a poem about something one party can't speak about, and the other party may not even know?

Well-adapted to limit cases and states of incomprehension, the sestina is just the right device for this challenging representational task. By virtue of the way the form leads Bishop to animate the scene, endowing its object with extraordinary powers, her readers become increasingly sensible throughout the poem of an extreme emotional crisis pressurising this household. As each teleuton returns it comes back stranger, figuratively transformed by the groping imagination of a speaker who seems to share the child's estrangement from whatever agonising truth lies unsaid.

Consider the case of the almanac. In the first stanza, it merely contains the jokes the grandmother is reading (1. 5). Soon we learn that the almanac foretells not only the rain presently falling but also the grandmother's "equinoctial tears" (ll. 7–8). The speaker tells us next that it's "clever" and "birdlike" (ll. 18, 19), hanging on a string above the kitchen where, now fully personified, it speaks in the oracular tones of a sybil (1. 26). Most audaciously, the almanac finally becomes not only the prophet of rain but its source, too, letting fall "little moons ... like tears" into the flower bed the child has sketched in their drawing of an "inscrutable house", where these moon/tears change, with one further metaphorical turn, into seeds (ll. 33, 39). And in this first line of the envoi Bishop draws tight the metaphorical threads thus far spun from the words "almanac" and "tears" (1. 37). We're meant to ask the obvious question: what grows from tears? In the silent wake of the poem, the child's uncertain future (a future bereft of the grandmother, and bereft of the man elegised in her drawing) rises up in answer (1. 29).

The sestina's incessant returns have driven the poet to re-invest the almanac, again and again, with the sort of childlike attention that freights an object with the emotional weight of what language itself cannot bear. In this way, the poem acts like an almanac miraculously capable of announcing, if not disclosing, its secrets. 'I know what I know', says the sestina. We can add "almanac", then, to the list of sestina-like things that open this chapter. We might also add "inscrutable house", for that matter, since it's the special prerogative of this form to let us to dwell in unknowing.

V

We can set Evie Shockley's "clare's song", our final exhibit, in a long and venerable line of sestinas that play innovatively with the form's constraints. As far back as Sidney, who composed a double sestina, poets have discovered that the sestina's ludic structure reliably solicits the invention of even more rules, even further degrees of "gamesmanship" (Beasley). In fact, Stephanie Burt has argued that the contemporary vogue for English-language sestinas can be attributed to their technical, arbitrary, game-like aspects, which poets find nicely suited to the task of lamenting their own "diminished or foreclosed hopes for their art" (220). For Burt, then, the last several decades have witnessed the sestina registering the ostensible limits of poetry itself. To the extent that Shockley departs from this reigning fashion, she does so with the aim of interrogating, I think, the impediments and the possibilities baked into poetry's raw material. We've now seen the sestina in action on the subject of erotic longing (Petrarch), public grief (Sidney), and private trauma (Bishop). In "clare's song", Shockley points this poetic form at the limits of language itself.

The poem's postscript identifies the "clare" of Shockley's title as Clare Kendry, the light-skinned African-American protagonist of Nella Larsen's 1929 novel *Passing*. Unlike her childhood friend Irene Redfield, with whom Clare attempts perilously to reconnect throughout the book, Clare has elected to "pass" for white, crossing the colour line to live in upper-middle-class white society with her racist husband Jack Bellew. The poem's six teleutons – "light", "clear", "form", "cast", "drop", "pass" – are key-words for Larsen, too, but rather than use these terms merely to retell Clare and Irene's story, Shockley rings their changes to set resonating the song we might imagine Larsen's characters would sing if someone asked them to share their thoughts on language's relationship to social being (ll. 1–6).

And yet a reader of this sestina will know immediately this is song of an odd sort, less an eloquent expression than a lexical experiment. We can imagine a sestina-writing poet searching the dictionary for fresh meanings of a particular end-word, and each time Shockley's teleutons appear they do indeed carry a wholly distinct definition. Light, for instance, refers variously to colour (light skin), a relative painlessness (light task), a diverting attitude (light verse), a lack of weight (feather-light), a perspective (in this light), an effulgent source (lighthouse), and the quality of brilliance (a lit window) (ll. 1, 8, 16, 23, 27, 36, 38). But Shockley's poem also operates like a mini-thesaurus, in that each line of the poem features six to nine synonyms for the teleuton, strung together paratactically without any punctuation. In all, then, this sestina contains 41 words for 'light'. Combined with similar lists for the other end-words, the result is a dense network of shifting acceptations and slippery equivalents that dazzles the imagination with shimmers of connotational difference between supposed synonyms. We might say the poem throws into relief the difference always secreted in identity – a fitting lesson in connection with Larsen's novel and the social experience of racial passing.

Shockley's programme pays off largest in the envoi, which stages a dramatic encounter between the demands of the sestina form and the lexical rules she has set for herself. Since the form requires her to employ two end-words in each line, she must either depart from her own protocol of filling each line with only synonyms, or else claim for two different teleutons a relation of equivalence. Because Shockley opts for the latter, the sestina folds in on itself, revealing that the poem's long chains of semantic similarity are in fact linked. Thus, its final line – "ebb fade wane depart drop end die decease pass" – doesn't only introduce a new definition for "pass" that resonates with Clare's tragic fate at the end of *Passing* (l. 39). It also specifies the narrative circumstances of that tragedy by encoding a gruesomely relevant meaning for "drop": readers familiar with the novel will remember that after her vicious husband discovers she has been passing as white, Clare dies by dropping from a sixth-story window to her death. With a breathtaking concision made all the more effective by its deadpan formality, this final line interfuses the meanings of "drop" introduced in previous stanzas: to fall, of course, but also to "disown" or "renounce", as well as "drop" in the sense of "bead" or "ounce" (l. 34, 9, 5). This last meaning recalls us directly to the infamous 'one-drop rule', that enforcer of the colour line codified by early-twentieth-century US law, according to which any evidence of African ancestry established a person's Blackness, regardless of their appearance (Caplan xvi).

While Larsen's novel is about visual codes of race, Shockley's sestina gestures at the way language, too, reflects and reinforces racialising systems of oppression. She shows how entire social orders appear springloaded inside single words (what does it mean to "pass" as white, if passing also implies "succeed[ing]" or "suffic[ing]" (l. 6); why does the word "drop" index both the circumstances of Clare's death and the exclusionary legal terms under which she lived?). And yet, in the act of adopting and adapting the sestina's constraints, Shockley also contends that language and its manifold possibilities for making meaning are indispensable tools for manoeuvring through unjust worlds. In its penultimate line, Shockley's procedure requires her to make similes of the nouns "cast" and "form", terms that to my ear connote differing degrees of agency (l. 37). I take this envoi to suggest that the roles into which a social order so violently casts its subjects are also opportunities for resistant form-making, and the sestina form asserts this is so even though, in Clare's case, the "clear … light" in which Shockley invites us to consider this later possibility ultimately passes in tragedy (l. 38). In other words, language sets limits on who and how we are in the world, and in so doing, casts us into confusion. Poetic form – and the sestina form in particular – is a means for exploring those limits, sounding them out, complaining about them, and renegotiating how to survive their strictures while never ceasing to imagine what it might take to live beyond them.

The Sestina 211

NOW READ ON…

- Petrach's use of the sestina to contemplate his love and her possible rejection of him ties in well with the beginning of the chapter on the ⟋ blazon.
- If you are fascinated by the complexity of the sestina and the idea that strictures of rhyme and metre actually encourage creativity rather than stifling it, a look at the chapter on the ⟋ villanelle might well be worth your while.
- Many of the earlier practitioners of the sestina mentioned in this chapter were also avid writers of ⟋ sonnets.
- In case you would like to explore more sestinas, particularly more modern ones, you could look up the following: Algernon Charles Swinburne, "The Complaint of Lisa"; Ezra Pound, "Sestina: Altaforte"; John Ashbery, "Farm Implements and Rutabagas in a Landscape"; Marilyn Hacker, "Untoward Occurrence at Embassy Poetry Reading".

References

Ashbery, John. *The Double Dream of Spring*. E. P. Dutton & Co., 1970.

Beasley, Sandra. "Flexing the Form: Contemporary Innovation in the Sestina". *Poets.org*, 30 September 2018. https://poets.org/text/flexing-form-contemporary-innovation-sestina. Accessed 27 December 2021.

Bishop, Elizabeth. "Sestina". *Poems*. Farrar, Straus and Giroux, 2011, pp. 121–122.

Breslin, James E. B. *From Modern to Contemporary: American Poetry, 1923–1964*. U of Chicago P, 1984.

Burt, Stephanie. "Sestina! or, The Fate of the Idea of Form". *Modern Philology* 105.1 (2007), pp. 218–241.

Daniel, Arnaut. "Lo Ferm Voler Qu'el Cor M'intra". *Poems & Translations*, trans. Ezra Pound. Library of America, 2003, p. 503.

Gramont, Ferdinand de Comte. *Sextines: précédées de l'histoire de la sextine dans les langues dérivées du latin*. Alphonse Lemerre, 1872.

Kaplan, Carla. "Introduction: Nella Larsen's Erotics of Race". *Passing*, trans. Nella Larsen and ed. Carla Kaplan. Norton, 2007, pp. ix–xxvii.

Larsen, Nella. *Passing*, ed. Carla Kaplan. Norton, 2007.

Leader, Mary. "Sestinas & Other Chances". *Friends of Writers: Fostering New and Vital Literary Voices*, July 2012. https://store.friendsofwriters.org/product/mary-leader-sestinas-other-chances/. Accessed 23 March 2022.

Lehman, David, and Angela Ball, eds. *Next Line, Please: Prompts to Inspire Poets and Writers*. Cornell UP, 2018.

Petrarch, "The Burdened Air and Unrelenting Cloud". *The Poetry of Petrarch*, trans. David Young. Farrar, Straus and Giroux, 2004, pp. 53–54.

212   *Matthew Kilbane*

Pound, Ezra. *Literary Essays of Ezra Pound*, ed. Thomas Stearns Eliot. New Directions, 1968.

Preminger, Alex, et al. "Sestina". *Princeton Encyclopedia of Poetry and Poetics.* 4th ed.

Sidney, Sir Philip. *Old Arcadia.* Oxford UP, 2008.

———. "Since Wailing Is a Bud of Causeful Sorrow". *Old Arcadia*, Oxford UP, 2008, pp. 246–247.

Shapiro, Marianne. *Hieroglyph of Time: The Petrarchan Sestina.* U of Minnesota P, 1980.

Shockley, Evie. "clare's song". *The New Black.* Wesleyan UP, 2011, pp. 15–16.

Whitlow, Carolyn Beard, and Marilyn Krysl, eds. *Obsession: Sestinas in the Twenty-First Century.* Dartmouth College P, 2014.

Zukofsky, Louis. *Anew: Complete Shorter Poetry.* New Directions, 2011.

22 The Sonnet

Patrick Gill

I

When discussing the sonnet, arguably "to this day the oldest poetic form still in wide popular use" (Oppenheimer 3), it is important to pay tribute to its tremendous variability. While it may occasionally seem as if this variability is something the sonnet form achieved over the course of the centuries, it is worth remembering that as early as the sixteenth century, "'the' sonnet was too malleable a concept to be captured by a single definition" (Müller-Wood 62). It thus follows that this discussion of the sonnet is not first and foremost concerned with precise prosodic aspects: the various permutations of rhyme schemes and metrical patterns the sonnet has undergone in its long history.[1] Before taking a closer look at what is at the heart of this chapter, though, it might be useful to look at some key ingredients of the sonnet form.

The sonnet is a fourteen-line poem, and, in its Italian form, those fourteen lines are divided into an octave and a sestet with a rhyme scheme of ABBAABBA CDECDE or ABBAABBA CDCDCD. Given that rhymes are more difficult to find in English than in Italian, upon arrival in England the sonnet gradually changed into a form that did not have to rely on a mere two rhymes for its first eight lines. Instead, the English sonnet divided its fourteen lines into three quatrains and one closing couplet with a rhyme scheme of ABAB CDCD EFEF GG. English sonneteers appreciated the greater variety of rhyme words, and they also loved the closing couplet, which lends the form a strong sense of closure.

There are two other important terms that need to be introduced before we proceed with our consideration of how the sonnet structure shapes the ideas expounded in its lines. The first of these is the *conceit*: based on the Italian word for 'concept', the conceit constitutes the basic recipe, the underlying comparison when it comes to a given sonnet's imagery. If my conceit is, for instance, that love is like a fever, then at other times in my poem I can identify additional parallels between words related to 'love' and words related to 'fever': My love is like a fever; the longer I suffer/ long for my beloved, the weaker I become/the less resolve I have; until my only cure is in my demise/complete submission to her. Ideally, a conceit

DOI: 10.4324/9781003244004-24

214   *Patrick Gill*

constitutes an extended metaphor spun out across the fourteen lines of a sonnet.

The final ingredient I want to draw your attention to is the *volta*, or 'turn'. This is a point in the poem upon which a sudden change in mood or outlook hinges, and it separates the sonnet into two distinct portions – the one before the *volta* and the one after. Given the function of the *volta*, it should be clear that the two portions of a sonnet enjoy a logical or argumentative relationship with one another. If the sonnet consists of one portion representing one opinion/mood/attitude and another one representing an altered opinion/mood/attitude, we can assume that sonnets follow a logical progression and constitute a "structured and argumentative form" (Müller-Wood 56). Oppenheimer, postulating that the sonnet is "the first lyric of self-consciousness, or of the self in conflict" (3), emphasises the nature of this dualistic conception. As Fuller explains: "The essence of the sonnet's form is the unequal relationship between octave and sestet … . This bipartite structure is one of observation and conclusion, or statement and counter-statement" (2).

In terms of its argumentative structure, the sonnet utilises these two systems in order to represent "either a logical or a psychological division of the topic" (Jost 228), but this division is far from unbridgeable. It is much rather aimed at achieving some form of resolution between conflicting ideas or emotions. This sense of closure offered by the sonnet is perhaps best summarised in the use of the closing couplet in English specimens of the form. The basic argumentative structure of the sonnet, then, consists of the representation of two distinct and separate systems of thought or argument and the capacity to offer however provisional a resolution of the conflict between them. Any poem that wants to make maximum use of the communicative efficacy of the sonnet form will have to employ these two basic tenets. That is not to say that it will of necessity have to adhere to them in the sense of a strict set of rules. In this regard, what Dubrow says about the Petrarchan tradition in English poetry when she calls Petrarchism "the basso continuo against which arias in different styles and genres are sung" (7) is true of the sonnet in much more general terms as well: its form is effective in communicating even if not all the traditional expectations are met. Or rather, it is particularly effective where it deviates from standard expectations.

Given the tremendous variety of topics and occasions sonnets have been produced on over the past 700 years, it makes little sense to focus our discussion on the one theme the sonnet form is most immediately associated with, i.e. that of love. Of course, love is the foremost concern of sonneteers producing poems in a courtly setting, be that in thirteenth-century Italy or in sixteenth-century England. But Spiller argues that love has hitherto been seen as the primary concern of the sonnet mainly because it is seen as the "supreme and inalienable individual experience" (125). Since the concept of love is "culturally contingent" (ibid.), it might be better to replace it with a more general notion of desire. And where there is desire, there must be a desideratum, which is why, in Spiller's argument, sonnets are traditionally informed by "the sense of an absence, or, more exactly, a need to abolish an absence" (125):

> It was Petrarch's extraordinary achievement to find in the sonnet a space where the movement between the desiring /I/ and its goal could be rhetorically mapped … . Thereafter, however desire might specifically be focused, the sonnet could express it, and Petrarchan love becomes the master analogy for all desire … . (Spiller 125–126)

In its further course, the present chapter will investigate how "the desiring /I/ and its goal" are represented in a small selection of poems. In doing so, particular attention will be given to the question of the respective speaker's agency. After all, the conflicting moods or propositions represented by a sonnet's two argumentative portions suggest that the speaker must have some (though not much) agency. Consider a speaker trapped in a situation that they cannot escape and will thus have to accept. That speaker will not really be experiencing a conflict as such. Then again, a speaker who is completely free to do as they wish would be equally free of conflict and not really caught up in any quandary at all. It thus follows that the sonnet has to present a situation in which a speaker feels they can or must act while at the same time their freedom to do so is constrained by circumstance.

II

As an initial approach the question of the agency afforded a sonnet persona, I would like to briefly consider three English Renaissance sonnets of different generations. The first of these is Sir Thomas Wyatt's "Who so list to hounte", a translation of a Petrarchan sonnet and one of the earlier specimens to be written in English. As such, it follows a mixed pattern, employing a traditional Italian octave (ABBA ABBA) in combination with a sestet contrived to end in a closing couplet (CDDC EE). Based on a conceit equating love for a woman with the hunting of a deer, the poem consists of the speaker's invitation to others to join the hunt for the desideratum, the deer/lady (l. 1), and his admission that he himself will have to admit defeat as trying to catch this particular deer is like trying to catch air in a net (l. 8). The next line ought to feature the turn, the *volta*, a new position or counterargument. What it introduces instead is the admission that everyone's endeavours will come to nought as the deer/lady has already been promised to the king.

The two logical propositions propounded by this sonnet, then, are that the speaker cannot hope to possess the woman he is in love with and, after the turn, that no one else can hope to possess her either. She is the king's

216 *Patrick Gill*

and thus is out of bounds. If that is the case, though, what is the conflict and what the resolution outlined in this sonnet? Wyatt's is a feudal stance: his desires (and those of everyone else) are curbed by a higher power, the monarch. His sonnet, then, offers very little choice or agency – the speaker is the "victim of coercive energies" (Spiller 89), meaning that he had no agency all along. The only avenue open to him is to submit to fate.

A somewhat different picture is offered in Edmund Spenser's "One day I wrote her name vpon the strand". In this sonnet of three quatrains and a couplet (ABAB BCBC CDCD EE), the speaker and his beloved are at the seaside where he proceeds to write her name into the sand, only to see it washed away by the waves (ll. 1–4). Unsurprised at this erasure of her name, she admonishes him for his naïve attempt at making her immortal (ll. 5–8), whereupon he promises to make her immortal in his poetry (ll. 9–12). The categorical difference between this sonnet and Wyatt's is the extent of the speaker's agency. In "Who so list to hounte", Wyatt's speaker can only capitulate: I love this woman but my pursuit of her is in vain. Lines one and nine are virtually identical – no discernible turn has occurred. Faced with the existential question of his beloved's death, Spenser's speaker in "One day I wrote her name vpon the strand" can introduce a new idea, that of her survival through his art. As powerless in the face of (biological) death and decay as Wyatt's speaker is in the face of the king's might, Spenser's speaker nonetheless finds an answer to the sonnet's implicit question of how mortals can gain immortality. His answer is, through art, and through *his* art at that! So is there a conflict in evidence in this sonnet, a real contrast between two distinct argumentative stances? Line nine, which is where the *volta* is usually to be found in sonnets of Italian provenance, begins "'Not so'", marking the clearest possible break with what has gone before.[2] Spenser's speaker, then, faces a real quandary and finds a way to exert his influence on the situation. While he is powerless in the face of death, he can promise his wife immortality of a different kind. The sonnet's resolution can thus be seen as an actual accommodation rather than the portrayal of utter helplessness we see in Wyatt's poem.

The final Renaissance sonnet to be discussed in this chapter is Philip Sidney's "I might, unhappie word, ô me, I might", which locates its conflict firmly within the person of the speaker himself. Where Wyatt's speaker faces the wrath of the king if he lays a finger on his beloved; and Spenser is faced with his and his beloved's inevitable mortality, Sidney's speaker is not constrained by powerful external forces but by his own decision-making. The sonnet's very first line with its repeated "I might" tells us that it is – or rather would have been – in the speaker's power to affect his own fate: he was offered his beloved's hand in marriage but turned her down, thinking the possible bride to be too young (l. 12). Now he finds that she has blossomed into the woman who could have brought him happiness (l. 2) if only he had chosen her at the time. The two portions of the sonnet are not separated as much as one might expect, and the sense of accommodation and acceptance is barely tangible, but there is a distinct bipartite structure: line 9 begins with the word "But", marking the logical distinction between the list of things the speaker cannot blame for his predicament (the first eight lines) and the one person he *can* blame, viz. himself. So while it is now too late to rectify his mistake, Sidney's speaker knows that he is solely responsible for the situation he now finds himself in, and knowing it would have been within his power to bring about a different state of affairs makes the entire situation even less bearable.

As we have seen, then, the sonnet tends to adopt different attitudes towards its speakers' agency. The kind of suffering (as well as the extent of that suffering) the speaker has to endure and their future outlook, the idea of accommodation or closure offered by the ending of the sonnet, are all intimately interwoven with the amount of control a given speaker has over their fate. Even within the short time span of the sixteenth century, there is already a tremendous variety of ways of portraying the speaker's fate in relation to their agency. I would argue that the most universally applicable approach to the sonnet is to be found in exactly this question: how do individual sonnets portray the conflict they outline and their protagonist's part in it? What is the balance between passive suffering and active response that they strike in their portrayal of their speaker's fate? The most fascinating sonnets will be those that create an exquisite balance between coercion and agency for their speakers.

III

While there are many famous names connected to the history of the sonnet in English, such as Shakespeare, Milton, and Wordsworth, one woman's contribution to the resurrection of the genre after it had gone out of fashion throughout the eighteenth century is often forgotten. In 1784, Charlotte Smith published *Elegiac Sonnets*, a book that was to prove very popular and go through a number of expanded editions in the wake of its initial success. *Elegiac Sonnets* captured the sentimental mood of the second half of the eighteenth century: a widespread belief that all humans were connected by bonds of shared emotions.

The opening sonnet, called Sonnet I in the collection but frequently referred to by its opening phrase, "The partial Muse", sets the tone for the entire collection. What the sonnet outlines is that its speaker is fated to endure suffering ("rugged path" in l. 2, "thorn" in l. 8). The greater power that has chosen this path for her is her "Muse", who also provides her with artistic inspiration (ll. 4, 7). Overall, then, her own suffering and her artistry are identified as stemming from the same source: "*those paint sorrow best – who feel it most*" (l. 14, emphasis in original). Clearly, this is an instance of a higher power (fate, the muse) identifying a hapless victim and singling them out for a seemingly undesirable and unavoidable fate. As an expression of the speaker's agency, then, "The partial Muse" may

218   *Patrick Gill*

seem closer to Wyatt than to Sidney or Spenser. That said, no attempt is made to repudiate the fate she has been singled out for. Perhaps that is the case because said fate is unavoidable. Perhaps it is also the case because said fate represents her "manifesto for the rest of the collection" (Fletcher 48). In fact, what may appear as an expression of the persona's passivity is part of a very deliberate act of establishing the persona's role and voice, a "self-dramatising and self-referential" act (Fletcher 48): she will experience and express suffering (her own and others') to which she, as an artist, is particularly sensitive. Her readers can then participate in these exchanges and experience both pain and pity vicariously through others. By putting her own suffering and empathetic powers on display in this way, Smith's persona very deliberately takes on the role of a conduit of sensibility. Given that this would be seen as a highly privileged role in Smith's contemporary culture, her speaker's helpless suffering distinguishes her from her readers or at least provides them with someone to emulate. To establish this type of persona in the first poem of a collection may be seen as the result of many things – a lack of agency, though, is not one of them.

Thanks in part to Smith's pioneering work, the English Romantics rediscovered the sonnet form for their writings of the early nineteenth century. Of the first generation of English Romantics, Wordsworth in particular showed an interest in the sonnet form. Of more immediate concern with the question of the speaker's agency, however, are the sonnets of the second generation of Romantic poets, in particular those of John Keats. In "Bright star, would I were steadfast as thou art", Keats' speaker wishes for the constancy of a star (perhaps the North Star) (l. 1) as he rests his head on his sleeping lover's "ripening breast" (l. 10). The poem proceeds like a funnel, making each successive wish on behalf of the speaker less ambitious and more likely to occur. The first two stages of this are (in the first two quatrains) that he wants to be like the star, though not in those ways most typical of the star: not in isolation (l. 2), not in its constant watchfulness (ll. 3–4). These are *not* the ways in which he envisions himself akin to the star. The third quatrain then argues that the quality of the star he covets for himself is only that of being "unchangeable" (l. 9) in his current resting position, enjoying his beloved's embrace.

Finally, since the star's properties are unlikely to become the speaker's, the only alternative he is left with to constancy and unchangeability is encapsulated in the poem's final word: "death" (l. 14). This seems to be the only outcome achievable from a human perspective. Again, as in Smith's poem, the speaker's agency seems limited: there isn't much he can do beyond first wishing (the operative verb in the sonnet's first line) and later giving in to his human limitations, the fact that steadfastness and constancy are out of reach as humans are mortal. But instead of considering the decreasing ambition of the successive portions of the sonnet mentioned above as limitations to the speaker's agency, there is also a way of reading the final "death" as in some way commensurate with the speaker's ambition: yes, constancy and mortality appear opposites, but by being introduced into the same conversation, they almost become substitutes for one another. Death, paradoxically perhaps, seems the only human means of achieving the desired state of constancy. As illogical as this may perhaps sound to modern ears, the younger Romantics would have recognised this kind of sentiment – that death is a way of transcending human limitations – as one of their major preoccupations. After all, other contemporary literary landmarks such as Mary Shelley's novel *Frankenstein* and her husband Percy Bysshe Shelley's closet drama *Prometheus Unbound* revolve around precisely the question of human limitations and their transcendence – for better or worse.

IV

As has been shown, the sonnet form is at its most affective where two competing ideas or arguments are held in balance and some form of resolution can be achieved. That that resolution does not always constitute happy endings and wonderful compromises has been amply demonstrated. After all, in representing a real quandary, an unsolvable problem from the outset, the sonnet offers little opportunity for pat finales and simplistic conclusions. Of course, it may be difficult in a short chapter such as this to see the quandaries presented by Smith and Keats in their respective cultural contexts, but the fact of the matter is that they both construct personae to whom the ostensibly negative outcomes of their sonnets are, if not a *positive* way of moving forward, then at least a way of moving forward. The following example will, I trust, illustrate this principle without the need for too much explanation of the historical context. Jamaican-born poet Claude McKay wrote a number of sonnets throughout his career, but the most famous of these is called "If we must die". Written in response to Red Summer, a series of attacks, lynchings, and other terrorist acts perpetrated on the black population of parts of the United States in 1919, the poem proceeds from the idea that the black victims of these attacks are just that: victims. As the incipit suggests, "If we must die" assumes that death is a likely outcome for the undisclosed group referred to by the personal pronoun "we". That would presumably mean that they do not have any agency in this. In the context of Red Summer, it is clear that the conflict was instigated by the white majority's racial hatred, and that the black minority stood very little chance against lynch mobs and other forms of violence.

McKay's sonnet takes the initial assumption of "[i]f we must die" and immediately moves to confirm it on the one hand but resist it on the other. What the poem's opening quatrain expresses is the resolve not to die as helpless victims. The second quatrain reiterates the incipit "If we must die" but continues it with something more positive than the first quatrain: death may be inevitable, but this community can choose an honourable death (l. 8). The option of not dying like hunted animals (ll. 1–4) and instead dying honourably (l. 8) is turned into an obligation by means of the

220 *Patrick Gill*

beginning of the third quatrain: With a direct address ("O kinsmen!"), the poem's speaker turns to his audience and admonishes them to fight back. However hopeless the situation may be, the sonnet's closing line assures listeners of the worth of "dying, but fighting back!".

The quandary McKay's speaker and his community find themselves in is obviously a hopeless one: Maliciously attacked by white supremacist mobs, they are outnumbered and cannot hope to survive. Their agency in this situation would appear to be minimal. The only options they are left with are to go like lambs to the slaughter or to die fighting. McKay's sonnet is designed to assure them of the value, the necessity even, of the latter path: to grasp what little agency they have and to resist, even though their resistance will inevitably fail. In their futile act of resistance, McKay's addressees will be able to wrest some kind of agency from events beyond their control, gaining strength and dignity from a hopeless situation.

The question in this instance is why a black Jamaican-born writer would choose such a traditional form representative of his oppressors' culture as a means of calling on other black Americans to resist. But it is the very fact that he uses his oppressors' language that makes McKay's poem especially powerful: to call for resistance against the white supremacist mob in a cultured language they ought to respect pits the cultured and civilised poet against a violent mob perpetrating senseless acts of cruelty.

V

As this discussion has illustrated, when it comes to its themes and arguments, the sonnet is a very versatile form. Far from being restricted to the topic of love, sonnets have been written on any number of topics, making 'the' sonnet an almost impossible proposition to discuss. What most sonnets have in common, though, is their bipartite structure, their division into two separate portions. These two portions can be used to represent conflicting ideas, or a problem and its solution, a conceptual cul-de-sac and the only way out of it. In its argumentative structure, the sonnet is designed to rehearse that particular conflict, and as we have seen, it does so with its speakers equipped with varying degrees of agency. Before you memorise the rhyme schemes of the English and Italian sonnets, before you read up on the lives of individual sonneteers, this is the one thing you should know about a sonnet, and the one thing you should ask yourself every time you approach a new sonnet: sonnets are argumentative structures, a representation of a logical conflict. What is the conflict on display here, and to what conclusion is it brought? And, finally, how much freedom or coercion is at play when it comes to the speaker's ability to influence outcomes. You will encounter cases where these questions cannot productively be asked of a specific sonnet. But those cases are then interesting in and of themselves for refusing to participate in the type of discourse we usually encounter in the sonnet.

The Sonnet 221

NOW READ ON...

- The chapter on the ⬦ blazon features additional information on the sonnet's earliest development as well as a closer look at the sonnet's Italian/Petrarchan and English/Shakespearean forms.
- The sonnet is a prescriptive form, meaning it consists of a set number of lines with a certain metre and rhyme scheme (like the ⬦ sestina or the ⬦ villanelle); but it also follows the logical structuring of certain non-prescriptive forms (like the ⬦ ode and the ⬦ elegy).
- While the foregrounding of an "I" is typical of the sonnet, there are sonnets that are not concerned with an amorous or existential conflict undergone by a subjective speaker. These sonnets, such as William Wordsworth, "Composed upon Westminster Bridge" or Percy Bysshe Shelley, "Ozymandias", seem more outward-looking. Do they still follow a discernible sonnet structure? What about a poem as innovative as Ralph Waldo Emerson's "Woods, A Prose Sonnet"?
- More of Keats' poetry is discussed in the chapter on the ⬦ ode as well as the chapter on ⬦ ekphrastic poetry
- Charlotte Smith's volume is called *Elegiac Sonnets*. See if that title makes any sense if you read up on the ⬦ elegy.
- McKay wrote quite a few sonnets, and many of them on the topic of oppression. Look up other sonnets such as "Enslaved" or "The Lynching" and try to work out what value they derive from being written in a verse form originally devised for thirteenth-century love poems.

Notes

1 The lack of prosodic uniformity in the long history of sonneteering is briefly outlined by Jost with regard to rhyme schemes and metres (227). Referring to Petrarch's sonnets in particular, Jost notes that he "did not recommend or prescribe a single, rigid form" (228).
2 If in doubt as to the location of a sonnet's *volta*, look out for conjunctions expressing dissent or a contrast, such as "but", "yet", "however".

References

Dubrow, Heather. *Echoes of Desire: English Petrarchism and Its Counter-Discourses.* Cornell UP, 1995.

Fletcher, Loraine. *Charlotte Smith: A Critical Biography.* Palgrave, 2001.

Fuller, John. *The Sonnet.* The Critical Idiom. Methuen, 1972.

222 *Patrick Gill*

Jost, François. "Anatomy of an Ode: Shelley and the Sonnet Tradition". *Comparative Literature* 34.3 (1982), pp. 223–246.

Keats, John. "Bright Star, Wish I Were Steadfast as Thou Art". *The Poems of John Keats*, ed. Jack Stillinger. Heinemann Educational Books, 1978, pp. 327–328.

McKay, Claude. "If We Must Die". *Complete Poems*, ed. William J. Maxwell. U of Illinois P, 2004, pp. 177–178.

Müller-Wood, Anja. "English Poetry in the Sixteenth Century: Sir Thomas Wyatt, Henry Howard, Earl of Surrey, Anne Locke and the Petrarchan Sonnet Tradition". *A History of British Poetry*, eds. Sibylle Baumbach, Birgit Neumann, Ansgar Nünning. WVT, 2015, pp. 55–65.

Oppenheimer, Paul. *The Birth of the Modern Mind: Self, Consciousness, and the Invention of the Sonnet.* Oxford UP, 1989.

Sidney, Philip. "I Might, Unhappie Word, ô me, I Might". *The Poems of Sir Philip Sidney*, ed. William A. Ringler, Jr. Oxford UP, 1962, p. 181.

Smith, Charlotte. "The Partial Muse Has From My Earliest Hour". *The Poems of Charlotte Smith*, ed. Stuart Curran. Oxford UP, 1993, p. 13.

Spenser, Edmund. "One Day I Wrote Her Name Upon the Strand". *Edmund Spenser's Amoretti and Epithalamion: A Critical Edition*, ed. Kenneth J. Larsen. Medieval and Renaissance Texts and Studies, 1997, p. 98.

Spiller, Michael R.G. *The Development of the Sonnet: An Introduction.* Routledge, 1992.

Wyatt, Thomas. "Who So List to Hounte". *Collected Poems of Sir Thomas Wyatt*, eds. Kenneth Muir and Patricia Thomson. Liverpool UP, 1969, p. 5.

23 The Villanelle

Patrick Gill

I

When the ⟳ sonnet arrived in England from Italy during the Renaissance, it quickly had to adapt to the dearth of rhymes in English – or the multiplicity of word-endings (relative to Italian) – by relinquishing the strictures of a rhyme scheme built around four rhymes (ABBAABBA, CDCDCD) and adopting instead the less rigid English form allowing a greater variety of line endings (ABAB, CDCD, EFEF, GG). Any poetic form imported from the Romance languages that was even more restrictive would surely undergo a similar process of assimilation, one would imagine. But this is the story of how a form with more lines but even fewer rhymes than the Italian sonnet prospered in, of all places, English literature.

The villanelle is a nineteen-line poem following an intricate pattern of rhyme schemes and refrains. As Kane elaborates, it consists of:

> five three-line stanzas followed by one four-line stanza in the scheme $A_1bA_2\ abA_1\ abA_2\ abA_1\ abA_2\ abA_1A_2$. The first and third lines, A_1 and A_2, are "refrain" lines that must be repeated three times and positioned precisely as shown. All of the $a/A_1/A_2$ lines rhyme with each other, as do all of the b lines. (427)

This might sound a little complicated, but it should be obvious that a nineteen-line poem based on only two rhymes (A and B) may present a challenge to any poet, let alone to those poets working in languages in which words do not predominantly end on vowels.

Etymologically, the term 'villanelle' is derived from the Italian 'villano', meaning a peasant or a farm hand. When the *Princeton Encyclopedia of Poetry and Poetics* writes that the form is actually "derived from an It[alian] folk song of the late 15th–early 17th c[entury] and first employed for pastoral subjects" (893), it is giving a view not necessarily shared by all critics.[1] For the purposes of the present chapter, the decisive question is not whether early villanelles were, in fact, shepherd's songs or whether they were written by courtiers in *imitation* of shepherd's songs – what is structurally most interesting about the villanelle is that of its nineteen lines, eight are made

DOI: 10.4324/9781003244004-25

224   *Patrick Gill*

up of the same two refrains, repeated in an alternating pattern at the end of each of its tercets. This insistence on the constant repetition of familiar lines can be thought of as a formal feature of a song, portions of which (the two refrain lines) are sung by a group, whereas other portions (the ever-changing first two lines in each tercet) are sung by a soloist. Structurally speaking, then, the villanelle strikes a fine balance between the new and the familiar, but the familiar is what it will always return to at the end of each tercet (and in its final couplet where *both* refrains are combined in closing the poem). The effect this produces on the part of the reader is one of double anticipation: of listening out for the new and looking forward to the familiar. A good example of this is W.E. Henley's "Villanelle" (1888),[2] where the two alternating refrains are "A dainty thing's the Villanelle" and "It serves its purpose passing well". Every time one of these lines closes a tercet beginning with two new and unfamiliar lines, the reader welcomes the return of the familiar while also acknowledging the poet's craft in making that self-same line fit a new and different context. The result is, as one would imagine, a rather playful experience in which the poet's dexterity is foregrounded, while simultaneously the reader can anticipate outcomes. Under these conditions the villanelle combines the key elements of repetition and variation to such a degree that it celebrates the artist's originality while simultaneously making portions of the poem predictable enough for the audience to participate in in an almost ritualistic manner.[3] Hence the call-and-response comparison with an (imagined) peasant song made earlier.

What the villanelle offers, then, with its two rhymes across nineteen lines and its exact repetition of two alternating refrains, is a type of self-consciousness. It puts on display not just that it *is* a difficult form, but that it *knows* that it is. Not just that its writer is writing in a difficult form but that they *know* they are. In fact, it is no coincidence that the first villanelle quoted in the present chapter is a villanelle *about* the writing of villanelles. Combined with the artificiality an accumulation of rhymes tends to produce in English poetry, all of this means that villanelles present writer and reader alike with a ludic experience: a game of strictures, of anticipation and (perceived) participation. Given these remarks, it is unsurprising that the villanelle used to be defined in these or similar terms, and that – for all the craftsmanship necessary to compose a villanelle – criticism of the late nineteenth and early twentieth century tended to regard the form as facile, a playful thing for playful occasions. To illustrate, in 1926, Louis Untermeyer offered this description of the villanelle:

> The villanelle ... is not usually employed for serious effects ... . The great majority of villanelles are content to rely on a lightness of execution and the bright ripple of rhyme. The form lends itself to a combination of quaintness and flippancy ... . (95)

The remainder of this chapter is concerned with the way in which the villanelle outgrew this definition in the mid-twentieth century, but also how its current image has come full circle, returning to something comparable to what it was in the early twentieth century.

II

Perhaps the most famous, and in all likelihood the most highly regarded villanelle in the English language, was written by Welsh poet Dylan Thomas. "Do not go gentle into that good night" (written in 1947, first published in 1951) is written as an address to the speaker's father during the latter's old age and life-threatening illness. Alternating the incipit[4] with the exhortation "Rage, rage against the dying of the light", Thomas spins a complex comparison between others who fight hopeless causes with all their might, such as intellectuals, who cannot change the course of events or nature (ll. 4–5); the benevolent, who realise their efforts are in vain (ll. 7–8); impulsive people following their instincts to the last (ll. 10–11); and his father, whose capitulation the speaker simply cannot accept.

The feeling of playful repetition and joyful participation is avoided by the seriousness of the subject matter, but also by the changing grammatical aspect of the refrain ("Do not go" used as an imperative elsewhere but used in the indicative form in "they / Do not go" in l. 5). Finally, the combination of the two refrains in the closing quatrain heightens the emotional stance of the poem by invoking a scene in which the grieving son begs for his father's blessing in the form of the latter's continued struggle with death.

That death is inevitable will be a familiar notion to most, but it is an utter truism where the poetry of Dylan Thomas is concerned (as you can also see in "A Refusal to Mourn", a poem discussed in the chapter on the ⟲ elegy). But it is the emotional impact of the demeanour of the dying on those left behind that is outlined here in the starkest of terms. Thirty years later Philip Larkin, who, as a young man, admired Thomas but later resisted his youthful enthusiasm, would write the line "Death is no different whined at than withstood" in his poem "Aubade" (l. 40). In Larkin's view, it seems selfish to expect the dying to pretend to put up a fight when it is only for the benefit of onlookers (ll. 37–39). Thomas' poem convinces us that at this moment in time, there is nothing more vital to the speaker than to see his father resist his inevitable demise, and the way he convinces us of this existential (though possibly selfish) need is by framing the entire struggle in a form that, twenty-one years before, someone had claimed, "lends itself to a combination of quaintness and flippancy" (Untermeyer 95). Thomas refused to have the poem published in Britain while his father was still alive, only agreeing to its publication in Italian literary magazine *Botteghe Oscure* during the latter's lifetime.

226   *Patrick Gill*

Another poet equally well-known on both sides of the Atlantic had her famous villanelle first published in a magazine as well, though in the case of Sylvia Plath's "Mad Girl's Love Song" (1953), it was young women's magazine *Mademoiselle*. If that place of publication suggests "quaintness and flippancy", the poem itself goes out of its way to dispel any such notion. Plath's villanelle may be concerned with the emotional life of a 'girl', but that is not to say those emotions do not run deep. In fact, what is most arresting about her poem is its interweaving of questions of epistemology and ontology: what and how can we *know*; and how does that affect the way we *are*? Mixed in with this is the meta-aspect of a productive imagination becoming less and less distinguishable from actual madness. Plath employs the double refrain "I shut my eyes and all the world drops dead" and "(I think I made you up inside my head)" to express her speaker's increasing frustration with her lover and growing uneasiness as to his elusive nature. At the same time, they express a deeply solipsistic worldview in which the outside world depends for its existence on the willingness of the speaker *not* to shut her eyes: she herself can no longer distinguish between cause and effect, between internal and external reality.

What this brief discussion of Thomas' and Plath's villanelles shows is that sometime in the mid-twentieth century the villanelle outgrew its reputation for "a bright ripple of rhyme" and instead was employed to approach very serious topics indeed. And it wasn't just Thomas and Plath who availed themselves of this particular form: from Auden's "If I Could Tell You" (1940) beginning "Time will say nothing but I told you so", to Elizabeth Bishop's "One Art" (1976), the mid-twentieth century seems to have produced an uncharacteristic accumulation of serious-minded villanelles. The first question that arises is how this form, so restrictive, so repetitive that its effects in English should be comical rather than touching, could have been used to serious effects by serious poets, and the simple answer is that the form was used where it was seen as commensurate with a given topic. What – besides their rigid verse form – do the villanelles by Auden, Thomas, Plath, Bishop have in common? A preoccupation with repetition, circularity, obsession, the ceaseless march of time, the inevitability of death. Where the topic is the insistence of something unavoidable intruding upon the speaker's life again and again, the villanelle's repetitiveness can provide an apt form of expression.

If this is the case, the next question is why this discovery is made in the mid-twentieth century of all times. If the villanelle carries within it the potential to express serious thoughts on serious topics – as long as those topics are characterised by ideas of repetition, insistence, and obsession – why was this potential not tapped into much sooner? Why does it take until the mid-twentieth century for the villanelle to become a fashionable form among introspective, contemplative poets? While there may be a myriad reasons incrementally contributing to the villanelle's popularity among poets from after the First World War to the end of the Vietnam

The Villanelle 227

War, there are two factors I would like to outline in the present chapter, as they will provide further examples of influential specimens of the villanelle form.

III

The first of these influences is poet and critic William Empson, "who almost single-handedly smuggled the villanelle into serious twentieth-century poetry" (French 28). What is perhaps most remarkable is that far from penning a runaway success in villanelle form himself,[5] Empson reintroduced the form into English poetry not so much by example but by way of his abstract interest in its meticulous precision. So while he did write three villanelles (the best-known of which is probably "Missing Dates"), it is his interest in form itself that stokes his fascination with the villanelle. A trained mathematician, Empson treats difficult forms like the villanelle as a challenge not just to his powers of expression but to his command of numbers and logic. Having published the highly influential critical study *Seven Types of Ambiguity* (1930) when he was just twenty-four, Empson was an influential voice in English literary criticism of the 1940s and 1950s.

The second influence in establishing the villanelle as a form in which to write serious poetry in the twentieth century takes a more circuitous route. James Joyce's novel *A Portrait of the Artist as a Young Man* (1916) features a protagonist, Stephen Dedalus, who writes a villanelle. Variously referred to as "Stephen Dedalus's Villanelle", "Villanelle from *Portrait of the Artist*", or "Villanelle of the Temptress",[6] the poem fuses the languages of religious worship ("seraphim", l. 2; "eucharistic hymn", l. 11; "chalice", l. 14) and sexual desire ("longing gaze", "languorous look", "lavish limb", ll. 16–17) to represent a developmental stage in the titular artist, where his sensibilities are all addressed in equal measure by sensual input from any domain: art, sex, and God all seem to provoke the same visceral reaction in young Stephen as he sets out to discover the world and his role in it.

While *A Portrait of the Artist as a Young Man* is of course a famous novel that poets writing in the mid-twentieth century would have been aware of, its influence on Thomas in particular is illustrated by the fact that the latter gave his collection of autobiographical short stories the title *Portrait of the Artist as a Young Dog* when it was published in 1940. But whatever influence Joyce's villanelle had on Thomas, Plath, and other writers of the mid-twentieth century, it represents a curious enough case to merit further consideration, as this will also further our understanding of the villanelle form in the eyes of Joyce. "Villanelle of the Temptress" is included in *Portrait of the Artist* to represent a certain stage in Stephen Dedalus' artistic development, and given the poem itself but also the context of the surrounding chapters, it is safe to say that that developmental stage is not seen by Joyce as one of full maturity (see French 22). The whole point of the inclusion of "Villanelle of the Temptress" in the novel is to mark a

228   *Patrick Gill*

stage at which young Stephen has achieved the level of technical mastery required to fill the lines of a villanelle in accordance with the rules governing that form – but without any actual artistry, any originality or vivacity. In Stephen's hands, the villanelle form becomes a connect-the-dots exercise that he can complete proficiently if rather soullessly. Critics who see in Stephen's villanelle proof of the young artist's genius are in danger of failing to see the wood for the trees: the real work of genius is not Stephen's use of an old restrictive form that produces a staid and unoriginal use of regular metre and rhyme. The truly artistic text is Joyce's prose in which the villanelle is framed: the stylistic experiment that is *Portrait of the Artist* itself. It is in his prose narratives that Joyce finds the desired scope for originality. While it may have helped to popularise the form of the villanelle, Joyce's poem was in fact included in his novel as a foil, a means of comparison, an indication of what old art (rules-based, formal, regular) *used* to do as opposed to what modernist art (innovative, original) *could* do. Ironically, then, a poem included to exemplify the death of a certain kind of writing helped revive exactly that kind of writing among later poets.

IV

As has been shown, the villanelle is hard work. Its repetitiveness tends to draw attention to itself as a construct, a verbal trick, to such a degree that it becomes difficult writing villanelles on serious topics. Here or there you will come across a poet capable of employing the villanelle form in the serious contemplation of phenomena related to repetitiveness, insistence, unavoidability, and in Plath and Thomas we have discussed two famous examples. So we could perhaps ask ourselves how widespread the villanelle is in English poetry, and there are two very different answers to that question. The first way of answering the question of how widespread the villanelle is in English poetry is to point out that while there are plenty of sonneteers in English literary history, there certainly are no 'villanelleers', i.e. no poets specialising in the writing of villanelles. Empson wrote three, and that would appear to be a relatively high number already. The fact of the matter is that, in contrast to the sonnet, the villanelle form offers a very particular tool that poets may wish to avail themselves of once or twice, but that – given the stringency and repetitiveness of its own internal strictures – itself becomes repetitive quite quickly. In that sense then, the villanelle is not a particularly widespread form in English poetry.

A different answer awaits us if we ask how widespread the villanelle is in English poetry when contrasted with other traditions. As we have seen, the English language does not furnish the villanelle with the most useful phonemic inventory to work with since English words rarely end in vowels, which makes finding rhymes more difficult. Romance languages provide a much more reliable source of rhymes, and in the case of the ⟁ sonnet we saw that this led to the introduction of a more varied rhyme scheme when the form crossed the Channel during the Renaissance. Based on this familiar phenomenon in the case of the sonnet, the basic idea would be to argue that the villanelle is *not* particularly widespread in English poetry when compared to other linguistic traditions. After all, conditions in France or Italy might be thought of as much more favourable for the dissemination of the villanelle form. Surprisingly, though, that is not the case. While the villanelle enjoys a rarefied status as a special form for special circumstances in English literature, it has virtually gone extinct in Italy and has barely been heard of in France since the beginning of the twentieth century. It thus seems that while it disappeared from the traditions of Romance literatures as just another form holding no particular interest, it survives in the anglophone world for the very reasons that make it such an unlikely form to be written in English: its difficulty, artificiality, and repetitiveness. As a going concern, we could justifiably claim that the villanelle has become an English form.

Having established itself not *in spite* of its difficulty but *because* of it, doubling down on its strictures and celebrating its ostentatious use of rhyme and repetition, the villanelle can never be a mass phenomenon, a poem for everyday use. But as the poetic form of "quaintness and flippancy" that may occasionally be hijacked to express profound ideas and emotions related to the themes of iteration, insistence, and obsession, the villanelle's place in English literature is secure. In contemporary poetry, the direction of travel vis-à-vis use of the villanelle seems to lead away from the mid-twentieth-century earnestness of Empson, Auden, Thomas, and Plath. In their use of the villanelle form as a means of discussing the villanelle form (see Billy Collins' "Villanelle") or for humorous purposes more generally (see Anita Gallers' "One Fart"), contemporary poets seem to have taken the form full circle, back to Untermeyer's verdict, in 1926, of the villanelle as light, quaint, and flippant.

NOW READ ON...

- In contrast to the villanelle, the ⟐ sonnet is a form whose rhyme scheme adapted to the English language.
- To encounter a form structured as stringently as the villanelle, turn to the chapter on the ⟐ sestina.
- Make sure to seek out additional villanelles such as "The Waking" by Theodore Roethke; "Villanelle for an Anniversary" by Seamus Heaney; "Lonely Hearts" by Wendy Cope; "Keep Them All" by Suzanne Allen; or "The Caged Thrush Freed and Home Again" by Thomas Hardy.

Notes

1 For a more detailed discussion of the origins of the form and its name, *see* French 10–14.
2 While you will have no difficulty finding the poems referenced here in editions of the respective poets' works, I am citing all my examples from the book *Villanelles*, hoping that if you happen to get hold of it, it will encourage you to read many more of these poems and think more deeply about them.
3 The distinction I am making here is between art and ritual. In art, we appreciate the aspect of variation: we valorise originality over repetition. Rituals, by contrast, are fundamentally dependent on their predictability: if you do not know what to respond to the priest in a Catholic mass, say, there is little point in taking part, and sheer originality on either your part or the priest's would not be appreciated. The villanelle, I suggest, combines both these elements.
4 An incipit is the use of a poem's first line in lieu of a title. Incipits – even though functioning as titles – are given as printed in the respective poem's first line, and are thus not subject to the rules of capitalisation that apply to titles. For instance, the chapter on ⌀ concrete poetry refers to Wordsworth's "The Daffodils". That is a title, and thus the word 'Daffodils' is spelled with a capital initial letter. In fact, the poem has no title, and should technically be referred to by the incipit "I wandered lonely as a cloud". Since this is not a title proper but simply the first line used instead of a title (or in the absence of same), words are not capitalised but given as in the original spelling of the first line.
5 Empson will in all likelihood be remembered as a critic long after he is remembered as a poet, but while his poetry never gained much popularity with a broader audience, he remains something of a poet's poet: a writer other poets read for his technical mastery and almost obsessive use of difficult forms.
6 In the anthology of villanelles on which this chapter is based, the poem is, confusingly, called "A Portrait of the Artist as a Young Man" and is cited as such in the list of references at the end of this chapter, even if that is not the title by which it is referred to in the text. It is noteworthy that, like Henley's poem but in contrast to Thomas's and Plath's, Joyce's villanelle is written in tetramer, the shorter line making the repetition of rhymes even more conspicuous.

References

Auden, Wystan Hugh. "If I Could Tell You". *Villanelles*, eds. Annie Finch and Marie-Elizabeth Mali. Knopf, 2012, p. 44.
French, Amanda. *Refrain, Again: The Return of the Villanelle*. Diss. U of Virginia, 2004. https://villanelle.amandafrench.net/.
Henley, W.E. "Villanelle". *Villanelles*, ed. Annie Finch and Marie-Elizabeth Mali. Knopf, 2012, p. 32.
Joyce, James. "A Portrait of the Artist as a Young Man". *Villanelles*, eds. Annie Finch and Marie-Elizabeth Mali. Knopf, 2012, p. 41.
Kane, Julie. "The Myth of the Fixed-form Villanelle". *Modern Language Quarterly* 64.4 (December 2003), pp. 427–443.
Larkin, Philip. "Aubade". *Collected Poems*, ed. Anthony Thwaite. Farrar, Straus and Giroux, 2004, pp. 190–191.

Plath, Sylvia. "Mad Girl's Love Song". *Villanelles*, eds. Annie Finch and Marie-Elizabeth Mali. Knopf, 2012, p. 50.

Preminger, Alex, Frank J. Warnke, and Osborne Bennett Hardison, ed. *Princeton Encyclopedia of Poetry and Poetics*. Princeton UP, 1974.

Thomas, Dylan. "Do Not Go Gentle into That Good Night". *Villanelles*, eds. Annie Finch and Marie-Elizabeth Mali. Knopf, 2012, p. 47.

Untermeyer, Louis. *The Forms of Poetry: A Pocket Dictionary of Verse*. Harcourt and Brace, 1926.

Index

Note: Page numbers followed by "n" denote endnotes.

9/11 137

Abrams, Meyer Howard 51, 190
activation 4, 11–12, 15–16, 18, 20, 106, 112
address 41, 47, 52–53, 58, 66–70, 88, 96, 98, 114, 120, 160, 185–186, 190–191, 220, 225; *see also* apostrophe
adynaton 136, 140n3
aestheticism 125, 127–128
agency 97, 126, 129, 148, 163, 210, 215–220
allegory 162, 189, 198
alliteration 10–11, 18, 23, 43, 45, 48, 82, 142, 145
ambiguity 31, 105–106, 136–137, 170, 179–180, 195
anapaest 26, 28, 31–35
Apollinaire, Guillaume 106
apostrophe 38, 43, 47, 70, 184, 190; *see also* address
Aristotle 124, 176
Armitage, Simon 191; "Ode to a Clothes Peg" 191; "The Shout" 138
Arnold, Matthew 33
Ashbery, John 204
Assmann, Jan 2
assonance 18, 38, 82
aubade 52, 56, 225
Auden, Wystan Hugh 198–199; "If I Could Tell You" 226, 229; "In Praise of Limestone" 198
Augustan Age 29, 159, 162, 175–177, 181–182

ballad 5, 18, 23, 35, 47, 68, 75–83, 99
BBC (British Broadcasting Corporation) 63–64

Beowulf 142–144
Bishop, Elizabeth; "One Art" 226; "Sestina" 207–208
Black identity 89–91, 148, 160–161, 164n6, 164n7, 209–210, 219–220
blank verse 23, 35–36, 85–93, 168
blazon 4, 94–101
Bloom, Harold 2
Boileau, Nicolas 176
Booth, Wayne C. 51
broadside ballad 77–78
Brooks, Gwendolyn 163; "In the Mecca" 89–92; "the mother" 162; "The Sundays of Satin-Legs Smith" 161–162
Browning, Elizabeth Barrett 43
Browning, Robert 43, 54, 56, 115–117, 119, 127; "Andrea del Sarto" 115; "The Bishop Orders His Tomb" 115; "Caliban upon Setebos" 54–55; *Dramatic Idyls* 115; *Dramatic Lyrics* 115; "How They Brought the Good News from Ghent to Aix" 41; "Johannes Agricola in Meditation" 115; "My Last Duchess" 54, 114, 116–119; *The Ring and the Book* 119; *Sordello* 54
Burns, Robert 116
Byron, George Gordon 54; "The Destruction of Sennacherib" 33–34; *Don Juan* 168, 182

caesura 15, 20, 27–28, 32, 38–50, 78, 86–87, 92, 158
Cage, John 106
Campion, Thomas 97
Campos, Augusto de 106
Carpenter, J.R. 112

234 Index

Castiglione, Baldassare 119
catalexis 23, 34
catalogue 41, 46, 94, 96, 101, 151; *see
  also* list poem
Chaucer, Geoffrey 25–26, 38
Child, Francis James 77
Cibber, Colley 181
Coleridge, Samuel Taylor 78;
  "Dejection: An Ode" 190; "Frost at
  Midnight" 85, 88; *Lyrical Ballads* 78;
  "The Pains of Sleep" 26
Collins, Billy 229
Collins, William 189
common metre 79
conceit 119, 213–215
concrete poetry 103–113
consonants 10, 44
content word 30–31
contreblazon 95
Cope, Wendy 77–78
Cotton, Charles 175
counterfactual 20, 87
couplet 4, 16, 19, 28, 95–96, 119,
  158–165, 178, 213–216, 224
COVID-19 2
Cowley, Abraham 185, 188
Cowper, William 181–182
Cullen, Countee 161, 163
Culler, Jonathan 40
cultural memory 3, 81, 121
culture 2–5, 61, 75–76, 81–82,
  90, 108, 133, 139, 142–144, 146,
  166–167, 169–170, 172, 207,
  218, 220
Cummings, Edward Estlin 105
cycle 167–168

dactyl 26, 28, 31, 34–35, 186
Dadaism 103, 106
Daniel, Arnaut 205
Daniel, Samuel 15, 17, 18
Dante Alighieri 117, 119, 205
Darwin, Charles 9
decorum 92, 119, 135, 138, 159,
  161–162, 183
Denham, John 197–200
Dennis, John 158, 164n2
Dickinson, Emily 47; "The Only News
  I Know" 25
dimeter 25, 186
Donne, John 52–53, 56–57
Doolittle, Hilda (H.D.) 56–57
drama 25, 29, 35, 51, 64, 67, 85–87, 92,
  114–115, 118, 128, 147, 218–219

dramatic monologue 47, 54, 100,
  114–122, 128, 167–168
dramatis personae 51, 53, 115–116
Drayton, Michael 94
Dryden, John 123, 176–177;
  "Alexander's Feast" 188–189, 191;
  Mac Flecknoe 175, 177, 181
Duffy, Carol Ann 117, 120; "Mrs
  Lazarus" 121; *The World's Wife*
  120–121
Dunbar-Nelson, Alice Moore 44
Duplan, Anaïs 191–192

early modern period 39, 86, 94, 98–100,
  106; *see also* Renaissance
ekphrasis 123–131
elegy 4–5, 36, 47, 132–141, 151, 162,
  184, 186, 208, 225
Eliot, Thomas Stearns 153–154; "The
  Love Song of J. Alfred Prufrock"
  114, 119–120, 154; *The Waste Land*
  169–171, 182
elision 34
Elizabethan Age 26, 43, 94
empire 41, 45, 98, 175
Empson, William 227–229, 230n5
end rhyme 12, 16, 18–20; *see also* rhyme
envoi 203–204, 208–210
epic 27, 29, 35–36, 41, 45, 47, 54, 63,
  81, 85, 92, 120, 128, 142–149, 151,
  159–160, 166–169, 173n1, 175–176,
  178, 180–182
euphonic 9, 17, 18
Euripides 150
expectation (readerly) 4, 15–16, 18,
  20–21, 29, 34, 36, 43–45, 47–48, 79,
  82, 103, 144, 147, 161, 214, 216

Feeney, Elaine 62, 64–70
feminist criticism 68, 96, 99–100, 112,
  121
Fielding, Henry 181
film 4, 97; *see also* movie
Finlay, Ian Hamilton 108–111
Flecknoe, Richard 177
foot (metrical unit) 25–28, 31–32, 34,
  41–43, 45, 79, 87, 91–92
fragmentation 89, 100–101, 125,
  166–167, 169–171, 173
free verse 46, 78–79, 89–91, 120,
  150–157, 169
Fresnoy, Charles Alphonse du 123
Frost, Robert 89, 150; "The Need of
  Being Versed in Country Things"

28–29; "Neither Out Far nor In Deep" 32
function words 30–31
Fussell, Paul 92
Futurism 103, 106

Gallers, Anita 229
Garth, Samuel 175–176
Gautier, Theophile 123
Gay, John 180
gender 27, 42, 48, 99, 101, 112, 191
gestalt 17
Gilgamesh 142
Ginsberg, Allen 152–153
Goldsmith, Oliver 196
Gomringer, Eugene 106
Gosse, Edmund 80, 207
Gramont, Ferdinand de 204, 207
Gray, Thomas 189
grotesque 101, 179
Grundtvig, Sven 77
Gunn, Thom 81; "Considering the Snail" 40; "Lament" 163

Haiku 157n2
Hardy, Thomas 80–81, 83n2, 132; "In Time of 'The Breaking of Nations'" 79–80; *Under the Greenwood Tree* 80; "The Voice" 82
Hayden, Robert 155–156
Hayley, William 181
Heaney, Seamus 40; "Digging" 49n2; "Feeling into Words" 49n2; "Follower" 40; "Glanmore Sonnets" 49n2
Henley, William Ernest 224
heptameter 25
heraldry 94
Herbert, George 106
heroic couplet 4, 119, 158–165, 178
Herrick, Robert 26–27
hexameter 26, 33–34, 63, 186
Hill, Geoffrey 136
Homer 117, 120, 142, 145, 150, 160, 175–176
Hopkins, Gerard Manley 34, 40, 43–44
Horace 123, 185–187, 190, 191
Housman, Alfred Edward 186–187, 191
Howard, Henry, Early of Surrey 85
Hughes, Ted 58
hyperbole 63, 95, 124, 140n3, 186, 188–189, 206

iamb 5, 15, 23, 25–36, 44–45, 75, 77–79, 85–86, 88–91, 117, 145, 158, 178, 187
imagism 56
implied author 51
incantation 62–63, 67, 81, 125
incipit 104
incrementality 12, 15
Ingarden, Roman 14
inversion 20, 27–28, 101
irony 44, 55, 58, 90–91, 107, 119, 121, 156, 160–162, 171, 175, 177, 179
irregularity 31, 121, 152, 185, 188–189, 199–200

Jago, Richard 198
Johnson, Samuel 184–185; *The Vanity of Human Wishes* 161
Jonson, Ben 85, 187, 192n1
Joyce, James; *Portrait of the Artist as a Young Man* 227–228, 230n6; *Ulysses* 148

Keats, John 130, 132, 191; "Bright star, would I were steadfast as thou art" 218–219; "Hyperion" 168; "Ode on a Grecian Urn" 124–126; "Ode to a Nightingale" 190–191
Kipling, Rudyard 83n2
Kizer, Carolyn 41, 48

Larkin, Philip 225; "Aubade" 225; "Money" 162
Larsen, Nella 209–210
Leader, Mary 203
Lessing, Gotthold Ephraim 123–124
Levine, Caroline 3
limerick 3, 35
list poem 65, 67, 69, 70; *see also* catalogue
literacy 76, 82
long poem 87, 161, 166–174
Longfellow, Henry Wadsworth 35
Lorde, Audre 44
love poetry 94–96, 99, 101
Lowell, Robert 89
Loy, Mina 48

Mackenzie, Henry 181
MacNeice, Louis 41
Majmudar, Amit 92
male gaze 97–100
Mallarmé, Stéphane 106

236 Index

Marlowe, Christopher 85; "The Passionate Shepherd to His Love" 116

Marvell, Andrew; "The Garden" 24–25; "To His Coy Mistress" 28–29

McKay, Claude 219; "If we must die" 219–220

medieval 61, 94, 99–100, 127, 147, 168, 170

memory 2, 18–20, 64, 76, 80–81, 138–139, 142, 191, 196–197, 200, 206–207

mental lexicon 10–12

Merrill, James 92

Merwin, William Stanley 132

metaphor 36, 44, 58, 66, 69, 91, 95, 98, 105, 125–127, 142, 152, 154, 203, 208, 214

metre 12, 15–16, 18, 23–37, 38–39, 41, 43–44, 70, 75, 78–82, 85–86, 89, 92, 100, 140n1, 150, 153, 185, 190, 221n1, 228

Millay, Edna St.Vincent 64–65

Milton, John 41, 217; "Lycidas" 36, 133–134, 136–137, 138; "On the Late Massacre in Piedmont" 41–42; "On the Morning of Christ's Nativity" 187–189, 191; *Paradise Lost* 25, 27–28, 85–88, 142–148, 173n1, 175, 179, 182

mnemonic 9, 17–18, 66, 75, 81, 142

mock-heroic poetry 143, 148, 160, 175–183, 189

Modernism 56, 87–88, 103–104, 106, 108, 119, 128, 148, 153–154, 166–167, 169–170, 228

monometer 25

Morgan, Edwin 111–112

Morris, William 63

mortality 2, 129, 133, 139, 186–187, 216, 218

movie 14, 203; *see also* film

muse 133, 145, 164n6, 178, 180, 187, 217

music 4, 9, 17–18, 35, 70, 76, 83n1, 103, 106, 156, 162, 172, 184–185, 187–191

narrative 14, 35, 41, 51, 56–57, 75–76, 81, 87, 89, 91, 105, 119–120, 124, 126, 130n1, 142–144, 146, 148, 166–169, 173, 210, 228

Nash, Ogden 26

neoclassicism 108, 110, 123, 176, 188–190

Nicholson, Norman 194, 198–200

Niikuni, Seiichi 108

Noigandres 104, 106

novel 13, 14, 51, 80, 144, 148, 173, 181, 209–210, 219, 227–228

octameter 25

octave 94–95, 99, 213–215

ode 4–5, 41, 47, 184–193

Olds, Sharon 192

Olson, Charles 43

Ong, Walter 62

onset 10–11

orality 2–3, 17–18, 47, 61–62, 64–66, 70, 75–76, 80–82, 111–112, 142–143, 145

order 4, 12–14, 20, 38, 44, 47, 87, 97, 108, 110, 121, 143–144, 146, 148, 159, 162, 196–197, 204, 210

Ovid 169

Owen, Wilfred 41, 135

painting 2, 4, 54, 99, 104, 109, 115, 123, 125, 127, 129–130

parallelism 18, 65–66, 87, 172, 187, 198–199

parody 48, 95, 175, 189

pastoral 79, 133, 195, 200, 206, 223

Patmore, Coventry 101n2

pentameter 15, 23, 25–27, 30–32, 35–36, 43, 85, 87, 88–93, 145, 158–160, 162, 178, 187–188

Percy, Thomas 77–78

performance 47, 61–72, 76, 85–86, 103, 184–185, 188, 192n1

persona 51–60, 114–116, 121, 136–137, 167, 215, 218, 219

Personification 105, 208

Petrarch 94–95, 101n1, 204, 214–215, 221n1; "The burdened air and unrelenting cloud" 205–206, 209; *Il Canzoniere* 94

photography 137–138, 200

Pignatari, Décio 107

Pindar 185–186, 188–191

Plath, Sylvia 57–59; "Daddy" 57–59; "Mad Girl's Love Song" 226–227, 229

Plot 14, 89, 124, 173

Poet Laureate 114, 177, 181, 191

Pope, Alexander 17, 143, 160, 177, 180; *The Dunciad* 175, 177, 181; *An Essay on Criticism* 160; *An Essay on Man* 160; *The Iliad* 160–162, 164n6,

176, 178; *The Odyssey* 176; "On a Certain Lady at Court" 26; *The Rape of the Lock* 36, 160, 175, 177–180; "Windsor-Forest" 26, 194
postmodernism 52, 59, 166, 169
poststructuralism 52
Pound, Ezra 43, 78, 154–155
praise 95–96, 134–135, 176–177, 181, 184–185, 189
predictive coding 13
Pre-Raphaelites 99, 127
pre-rhyme 16–18, 20–21
prescriptive forms 5, 132
prospect poem 166, 194, 202
psychology 2, 9, 12, 14, 57, 81–82, 114, 116–117, 132, 181, 214
pyrrhic 26, 28–29, 31–34, 88

quatrain 19, 36, 63, 82, 95, 186, 213, 216, 218–220, 225
Quintilian 117

Reading, Peter 171–172
recording 12–13, 61–64, 69
Renaissance 54–55, 61, 103, 115, 119, 123, 147, 193, 207, 215–216, 223, 229; *see also* early modern period
repetition 1–4, 17, 42–43, 66–67, 70, 87, 125, 129, 153, 224–226, 229, 230n3, 230n6
Rhyme 9–22, 23, 27, 35–36, 75, 77–79, 81–82, 85, 87, 89, 117, 120, 145, 150–151, 153–156, 157n2, 158–162, 188, 213, 220, 221n1, 223–224, 228–229, 230n6; *see also* end rhyme
rhythm 10, 12, 15, 17, 19, 21, 23, 27–30, 34–35, 38–39, 42, 44, 46–48, 63, 70, 79, 82, 85–87, 91, 145, 150, 191
ritual 63, 124, 136, 138, 224, 230n3
Romanticism 41, 53–54, 56, 79, 87, 104–105, 115–116, 127, 130, 167–169, 172, 190–191, 194, 197–198, 218–219
Rossetti, Christina 99–100
Rossetti, Dante Gabriel 99–100
Rukeyser, Muriel 156

Sappho 56
Sassoon, Siegfried 135
satire 76, 95, 143, 161–163, 175, 181
scansion 3, 29–34, 88–89, 92
Scarron, Paul 175
sculpture 4, 108–110, 123
secularisation 127, 135, 138–139, 191
self-referentiality 57, 105, 218

sequence (of poems) 44, 94, 99, 101n1, 167; *see also* cycle
sestet 45, 94–95, 99, 213–215
sestina 203–212
Shadwell, Thomas 177
Shakespeare, William 25, 85, 94, 121, 169, 182, 217; *Hamlet* 29; *King Lear* 42; *Macbeth* 35; "Sonnet 12" 29; "Sonnet 20" 27; "Sonnet 130" 95–96; *The Tempest* 54–55
Shelley, Mary 219
Shelley, Percy Bysshe 53–54; "Adonais" 132; "Mont Blanc" 30; "Ode to the West Wind" 190; *Prometheus Unbound* 219; "To a Skylark" 53–54, 56
Shockley, Evie 208–210
Siddal, Elizabeth 99
Sidney, Philip 94; *The Countess of Pembroke's Arcadia* 206; *Defense of Poesy* 43, 46; "I might, unhappie word, ô me, I might" 216–217; "Since wailing is a bud of causeful sorrow" 206–209
simile 94, 97, 105, 133, 210
sitcoms 1, 159
slavery 91, 151, 159–160, 164n4
Smart, Christopher 181
Smith, Charlotte 217–218
Smith, Stephen James 62, 70
Smith, Stevie 162
Solt, Mary Ellen 104, 112
sonnet 3–4, 23, 25, 35, 41, 43, 45, 47, 89–90, 94–96, 98–99, 106, 151, 156, 161, 166–167, 190, 194–197, 213–222, 223, 228–229
speaker 3, 41, 47, 51–53, 56–59, 63–67, 69–70, 86, 88–89, 96–98, 104–105, 114–121, 124–128, 133–138, 152–155, 167–173, 184, 186–187, 190–191, 203, 205–206, 208, 215–218, 220, 225–226; *see also* persona
Spenser, Edmund 94–95, 206; *Amoretti* 94, 101n1; "Amoretti 15: Ye tradefull merchants that with weary toyle" 94–96, 98–99; "Amoretti 75: One day I wrote her name vpon the strand" 216–217
spondee 26, 28–29, 31–34, 66, 86–88
stress 9–10, 15, 21, 23–34, 75, 79, 82, 86–90, 150
structuralism 52
sublime 53–54, 185, 188–189, 191, 196
substitution (prosody) 27–28, 31–32, 35, 88–89, 91–92

238 *Index*

Swinburne, Algernon Charles 43, 207;
  "Before the Mirror" 125–130; "The
  Leper" 100–101
syllables 9–10, 12, 15, 19, 21, 23–34,
  38–39, 41, 43–44, 46, 79–80, 85–92,
  150, 158, 188, 199
Szymborska, Wisława 137–138

teleuton 204–206, 208–210
Tennyson, Alfred 43, 83n2, 115, 117,
  127–128; *In Memoriam A.H.H.*
  36, 132; "The Lotos Eaters" 115;
  "Ode on the Death of the Duke of
  Wellington" 191; "Tithonus" 115;
  "Ulysses" 114–115, 117–118
tercet 224
tetrameter 5, 23, 25, 27–28,
  33–36, 75, 77
text comprehension 9, 11–14
Thatcher, Margaret 172
Thomas, Dylan 106, 225, 227; "Do
  not go gentle into that good night"
  225–226, 228; "A Refusal to Mourn
  the Death, by Fire, of a Child in
  London" 135–136, 225
Thomas, Edward 27
Thomson, James 194, 196
Thoreau, Henry David 152; *Walden* 64;
  *A Week on the Concord and Merrimack
  Rivers* 152
Thornbury, George W. 115
Tollet, Elizabeth 195
tornado *see* envoi
tragedy 36, 91, 184
trimeter 5, 23, 25, 32–33, 35,
  75, 79, 188
trochee 26–27, 31–32, 34–35, 41, 86,
  91–92
typography 34, 61–62, 64–65, 68–69,
  92, 103, 106, 108

variation 1–4, 19, 25–27, 29, 32–35,
  66–67, 81, 85, 89, 145, 224, 230n3
Victorian Age 43, 87, 99, 115–117, 119,
  151, 168
video 62, 70, 72n4

villanelle 3, 223–231
Virgil 117, 146, 175–176
volta 45–46, 95, 100, 214–216, 221n2
vowels 9–10, 17, 63, 223, 228

Walcott, Derek 142, 148
Webster, John 85
Wheatley, Phillis 161–163,
  164n6, 164n7
Whistler, James Abbott McNeill 125,
  127–129
Whitman, Walt 151–153, 156, 157n1;
  Leaves of Grass 151; "Pioneers! O
  Pioneers!" 151; "Song of Myself"
  151–152, 169, 173n2
Williams, William Carlos 69–70
Wimsatt, William K. 17
Wolcot, John 182
Wordsworth, Dorothy 196–197,
  201n1
Wordsworth, William 78–79, 81, 199,
  217–218; "Composed after a Journey
  across the Hamilton Hills, Yorkshire"
  194–198, 200, 201n1; "Composed
  upon Westminster Bridge" 195 "I
  wandered lonely as a cloud"
  104–105, 230n4; *Lyrical Ballads*
  78; "My heart leaps up" 168; *The
  Prelude* 25, 36, 168–169, 173n2, 196;
  "Ode: Intimations of Immortality"
  190, 196; "The Tables Turned" 79;
  "The Thorn" 79; "Tintern Abbey"
  194–195, 199–200
World Wars 43, 61, 79, 133, 135,
  169, 226
Wyatt, Thomas; "The Lover's Appeal"
  116; "Who so list to hounte"
  215–216, 218

Yeats, William Butler; "In Memory of
  Major Robert Gregory" 134–135,
  138; "The Lake Isle of Innisfree"
  62–64, 70; "Leda and the Swan"
  45, 48

Zizek, Slavoj 99

Printed in the United States
by Baker & Taylor Publisher Services